D0435821

THE
BILLIONAIRE
BOONDOGGLE

THE
BILLIONAIRE
BOONDOGGLE

How Our Politicians
Let Corporations and Bigwigs
Steal Our Money and Jobs

PAT GAROFALO

THOMAS DUNNE BOOKS   ST. MARTIN'S PRESS ✠ NEW YORK

THOMAS DUNNE BOOKS.
An imprint of St. Martin's Press.

THE BILLIONAIRE BOONDOGGLE. Copyright © 2019 by Pat Garofalo. All rights reserved. Printed in the United States of America. For information, address St. Martin's Press, 175 Fifth Avenue, New York, N.Y. 10010.

www.thomasdunnebooks.com
www.stmartins.com

Designed by Steven Seighman

The Library of Congress Cataloging-in-Publication Data is available upon request

ISBN 978-1-250-16233-5 (hardcover)
ISBN 978-1-250-16234-2 (ebook)

Our books may be purchased in bulk for promotional, educational, or business use. Please contact your local bookseller or the Macmillan Corporate and Premium Sales Department at 1-800-221-7945, extension 5442, or by email at MacmillanSpecialMarkets@macmillan.com.

First Edition: March 2019

10 9 8 7 6 5 4 3 2 1

To Dina, for everything

CONTENTS

THE
BILLIONAIRE
BOONDOGGLE

INTRODUCTION:
THE BILLIONAIRE BOONDOGGLE

"ARE YOU NOT ENTERTAINED?"

So asks Russell Crowe's character, Maximus Decimus Meridius, in the 2000 movie *Gladiator*, a moment that lives on today in eternal internet GIF fame. The film is built around the concept of the Roman coliseum, and the spectacles that famously took place in those ancient arenas as a way to placate and distract citizens with what the Roman poet Juvenal derided as "bread and circuses."

Today's entertainment industry is quite a bit different. No one's being fed to any lions, and even mixed martial arts can't match gladiatorial combat when it comes to sheer bloodletting. More important, the government is generally not in the business of organizing violent displays to keep the plebeians from rioting in the streets.

But don't think that means the government is out of the entertainment business entirely. No, the biggest entertainment corporations in America today are very much entangled with lawmakers at every level, from federal on down to local. However, public money is spent not on keeping citizens happy to ensure they are pliant, but on keeping corporate leaders happy so they continue making campaign donations and don't threaten to move their businesses to some other jurisdiction. Your tax dollars bolster the entertainment industry's bottom line in an unholy convergence of private and public. And that's merely the tip of the iceberg when it comes to the many ways corporate America makes off with your money, while not creating the jobs it promises.

Consider these stories.

In the spring of 2018, if you had taken the Green Line in Washington, DC, to the Navy Yard stop on a Tuesday night, then followed the sea of red-and-blue hats up onto the street, you'd likely be headed to a Washington Nationals game (barring some oddly placed political protest that evening). The Nats, as they're known, have called America's capital home since 2005, when the Major League Baseball franchise left Montreal, depriving Canada of the Expos. They have played in Nationals Park, on the shores of the Anacostia River, since the 2008 season.

The area around Nats Park, the shorthand favored by DC residents for the rather nondescript stadium, is up-and-coming, with hip new apartment buildings, fancy restaurants, and chain coffee shops—as well as the constant presence of construction equipment. Both a brewery and a winery are within shouting distance. A lot of people, from city council members to DC sportswriters, think all that development is thanks to the stadium—and they make their case, constantly, since the city paid to have Nats Park built.

The sticker price of the stadium was about $700 million, but once interest and other costs are factored in, Washington will have coughed up about $1 billion for the privilege of having an MLB facility within its borders. To convince taxpayers in the city to pay up, especially since DC has its fair share of nonbaseball problems and advocates clamoring for money to solve them, the story told by the stadium's boosters was that it would revitalize a part of DC that desperately needed some economic activity, juicing development thanks to an influx of fans and their money. And new stuff is cropping up in that part of town every day, so mission accomplished, right?

Not so fast.

Disney's *The Avengers* made well more than $1 billion at the box office. That's not a bad return on a $220 million budget. Actor Robert Downey Jr. alone was paid some $50 million for reprising his role as Iron Man in the film, and the multiple sequels that followed made billions more.

Those are big numbers, but another one nowhere near as large should be just as eye-popping: $22 million. That's how much New Mexico provided to *The Avengers* in film subsidies—tax breaks, essentially—even as the state was dealing with budget woes that required it to cut a plethora of government services, including funding for both pre-K and higher ed.

Those in favor of the subsidies argued that giving public money to blockbuster film productions would turn New Mexico into a "second Hollywood," as former governor Gary Johnson put it, providing jobs to New Mexicans who wouldn't have them otherwise and creating an entire industry where there had previously been nothing at all. Scores of folks who would have had to move elsewhere for work could instead stay in New Mexico, as an industry sprang up from the ground; people who previously had no interest in the state would flock in, fleeing the high taxes in places such as California and New York. It would be a win-win for taxpayers, workers, and industry alike, and all for the relatively low cost of a few tax incentives.

The case against? "We could have spent that twenty-two million dollars on all kinds of things, like education for our children. We could have spent it on roads," lamented one New Mexico state representative at the time.

So was this actually a heroic move on the part of New Mexico's lawmakers or not?

As of January 2018, the state of Georgia has been providing tax breaks to concert tours that begin in the Peach State, as well as to recording or scoring sessions that take place there. Pinched by industry concentration in Nashville to the west and New York to the north, the state that was home to Ray Charles, the Allman Brothers Band, and R.E.M. wanted to prevent the biggest acts in the country from passing it by and preserve the recording industry's foothold, so Georgia wouldn't become another casualty of the ever-more-transportable nature of twenty-first-century capital. To qualify for one provision, bands needed to rehearse and begin tours right in Georgia. "Music made by Georgians, whether it's the names you know or one of the thousands of unknown creatives behind the scenes, is one of Georgia's biggest international exports," said one of the proponents of the tax measures.

Other states had tried unsuccessfully to pass similar laws before. When New York Governor Andrew Cuomo vetoed an effort to spend $50 million on music-related tax incentives in the Empire State, advocates claimed he was shooting down a measure that would have helped some one hundred thousand New Yorkers find and keep jobs. In Georgia, meanwhile, small-government advocates and lefty policy wonks alike complained that the state was wasting money on yet another targeted tax break in a state already addicted to them, mirroring the debates that happened in state legislatures from California to Maine.

So who was hitting the right notes?

All of these stories and questions—which perhaps seem disconnected, since they're about a stadium in DC, a movie made in New Mexico, and concerts in Georgia—have something important in common. They're all part of the big lie propagated by the entertainment industry, in all its various iterations, and by the rest of corporate America, as well as by the lawmakers who do its bidding: that entertainment drives economic development and your tax dollars are needed to grease the skids.

From coast to coast, Maine to Hawaii and Washington to Florida, public money is being used to support the most high-profile cultural icons America has to offer, all based on a broken economic theory, one that says publicly supporting hugely profitable corporations or billionaire sports team owners will redound to the public's benefit. That entertainment drives an economy is a myth, but it has permeated every facet of policymaking despite the overwhelming evidence that it results in a raw deal for the taxpaying public and windfalls for the already well-off; almost no one is immune from the effects, even if most don't know it.

How did this happen? There's no one moment to highlight, no inception-style instant to point to, no back room where shady corporate bigwigs smoked cigars, ate steak, and decided with their bought-and-paid-for members of the statehouse that it was time to start subsidizing some of the country's most profitable entertainment entities. Instead, over the last several decades, America's antitax fervor, penchant for crony capitalism, and genuine desire for economic growth and job creation have all combined into a toxic public-policy stew that benefits America's corporate bigwigs. Subsidizing the entertainment industry up the wazoo is one of the results. What should be extraordinary—a hugely profitable TV show, massively popular sporting event, or grand luxury hotel receiving dollars from the public dole—has become commonplace, something that executives expect and public officials deliver as a matter of course. Whenever either conscientious citizens or concerned lawmakers make a fuss—suggesting that maybe, just maybe, companies run by billionaires that make huge profits year after year don't need to be publicly subsidized—the policy blackmail begins: Threats of job losses, dooming a place to an eternity of economic malaise, are the currency of choice for the titans of industry.

This sounds like a lot of doom and gloom, and from a policy standpoint it is. But the way it's portrayed in real time is precisely the opposite: Netflix, the NFL, Hilton, or Bass Pro Shops comes riding into town pledging to ignite an economic renaissance for the cost of a few tax incentives; executives make big promises about gleaming new facilities and the jobs they'll create, putting out press releases touting economic development that will make other towns envious; politicians say that the deal is a slam dunk and that nothing but good times will follow the ribbon cutting; local reporters get caught up in the euphoria and uncritically regurgitate whatever positive numbers the company in question is throwing around; and a grand opening gets held at which everything seems hunky-dory.

Yet the downside gets hidden from public view. It remains invisible to those who don't take a closer look or who understandably don't have the time to delve into the ins and outs of their city or state budget: the revenue for the local school that goes uncollected, the health care program that gets underfunded to cover the cost of tax breaks, the library that gets closed so debt service on a stadium can be paid. The opportunities that cities and states miss when they decide to subsidize the entertainment industry often don't garner headlines, but they can be far more important to the people who go without public services than an arena or sporting goods store is to the patrons who visit them.

It's not only the entertainment industry, in all its iterations, that takes advantage of economically dunderheaded tax breaks and giveaways. Amazon's high-profile search for a location for its second headquarters—which had cities and states tripping over themselves to give away tax breaks, land, and other public infrastructure, with some even saying they'd let Amazon decide how the town spent tax revenue going forward—shows just how pervasive the pro-corporate mind-set can be when it comes to American policymaking. The idea that we should all be okay with politicians effectively bribing corporate leaders to expand, build, and create new jobs is so commonplace that's it's often hardly remarked upon.

But the way in which TV, movies, sports, and other fun and games have taken hold of the public purse strings is, perhaps, the most egregious, because it plays off not only the legitimate desire for jobs and development but our cultural heartstrings and celebrity longings, too. We can have new jobs and famous athletes plying their trade in our town? We can support local businesses and see movie stars congregating on Main Street? Where do we sign up?

However, the promises made regarding the benefits of such policies rarely come true, while the negatives are all too real. The development doesn't materialize, while the costs pile up, forcing impossible choices onto lawmakers and making residents of a place choose between their entertainment and their health or education.

Spoiler alert: Nats Park isn't what caused an economic boom on DC's waterfront, nor did *The Avengers* do heroic things for New Mexico's economy. Subsidizing the next Rihanna tour isn't going to give Georgia a leg up over its neighbors on the next Bureau of Labor Statistics jobs report. Upon closer inspection, as I hope you'll learn from flipping through these pages, the economic theory for publicly supporting entertainment behemoths is built on a myth, one that persists despite the evidence against it that piles up every day.

The corporate leaders, sports team owners, international committees, hoteliers, or the lawmakers who help them out are not all bad people or corrupt, intentionally hosing the public in a cynical bid for money, power, and reelection. (Though that does happen!) No, a lot of what I'm going to describe can be explained by the simple fact that too many people have, because it is good for them personally and politically, bought into a theory of economic development that doesn't make any sense, while the case against that theory doesn't get enough attention. Those fighting for more public dollars to be blown on entertainment goodies are a cohesive, concentrated lobby, while opponents are often a mishmash of good-governance types, economists, and random members of the public, a group too diffuse to do much good and always underfunded compared to their opponents.

The good news is that the latter group have the facts on their side. Delving into these deals, it's easy to see why: They're the epitome of boondoggles, the sort of things that liberals and conservatives alike can join up and hate, if for different reasons. When enough people find out what's going on and prove themselves determined not to throw public money down a rat hole—as Boston

1

THE BLOCKBUSTER SCAM: HOW HOLLYWOOD IS RIPPING YOU OFF

IT WASN'T AS BAD as shoving a reporter in front of an oncoming subway train, but it was still a move worthy of Frank Underwood, the unscrupulous, conniving pol at the center of Netflix's *House of Cards* (who, spoiler alert, offs a journalist in just such a manner during the show's second season). The move was calculated, cold, and ultimately bad for the people whom government is supposed to serve, much like nearly everything Underwood does in his unstoppable quest for Oval Office power—except it occurred in real life, to actual lawmakers and a real, live taxpaying public.

House of Cards had been filmed for its first two seasons in parts of Maryland, including downtown Baltimore, thanks in part to a generous subsidy program provided by the Maryland legislature. For season three, though, state lawmakers were threatening to yell "cut" on the flow of money, questioning whether the use of public dollars was worthwhile to subsidize a popular, successful TV show that aired on a premier website and seemed as if it could support itself in the absence of public funds. "It seems to me that *House of*

Cards isn't doing so badly that it needs taxpayer help," said state delegate Kathy Szeliga.[1]

And so the arm-twisting began.

In a letter sent to Maryland's governor, Martin O'Malley, Charlie Goldstein, a senior vice president of Media Rights Capital, the show's production company, wrote, "While we had planned to begin filming in early spring, we have decided to push back the start date for filming until June to ensure there has been a positive outcome of the legislation. In the event sufficient incentives do not become available, we will have to break down our stage, sets and offices and set up in another state."[2] A similar letter was sent to the speaker of Maryland's House of Delegates.

The threat was anything but subtle: Provide us enough "incentives"—i.e., taxpayer money—to stay, or we'll take our show and all its Maryland jobs elsewhere. Underwood himself—or at least Kevin Spacey, the now-infamous actor who portrayed him—even personally lobbied Maryland lawmakers at an Annapolis wine bar in an effort to seal the deal. "We are enormously honored to be in this state," he told the gathered representatives. "I can only tell you that every single day I go to work, there's no doubt in my mind that the faces I look at of Marylanders are incredibly happy that we're here."[3]

That happiness was, perhaps, not as universal as Spacey might like to think. As one Maryland state delegate correctly noted, "We're almost being held for ransom."[4] Indeed, as Szeliga, a consistent opponent of the film subsidies, said later, *House of Cards'* ultimatum was the moment the downside of providing the show with subsidies should have been clear-cut to everyone. "Threatening to leave if you don't get your money?" she said. "If everybody doesn't see it in black and white today, they never will."[5]

But even if it wasn't the most sympathy-earning move, the

show's team had good reason to use this tactic: If there's anything local lawmakers hate, it's being blamed for job losses and accused of not doing enough to keep local people employed. Having Spacey deliver the message ensured that it gained media coverage, putting the potential departure of jobs directly in front of the public. TV stars from one of Netflix's hottest shows were saying how much they loved working in and around the community and saying what a shame it would be if politics forced them to go somewhere else. Politicians, on the other hand, were trying to explain why what those stars were saying perhaps wasn't true. A fair fight, this was not.

The ending of the episode wasn't hard to predict: Resistance among the legislators crumbled and Maryland paid $11.5 million in film production tax credits and another $7.5 million in grants authorized by the state's assembly, which the *House of Cards* crew graciously accepted. "We're going to keep the thirty-seven hundred jobs and more than one hundred million dollars of economic activity and investment that *House of Cards* generates right here in Maryland," O'Malley bragged.[6]

It's no surprise the legislators ultimately caved, as Hollywood has gotten very, very good at wringing public dollars out of governments via these sorts of threats, and their attendant media campaigns, lobbying efforts, and even biased economic-impact studies. It's all part of the blockbuster scam, the many and various ways in which taxpayers are being ripped off by the film and TV industry.

As of this writing, about three dozen states subsidize movie and TV production in some way via tax dollars. This largesse comes in several forms, but the most popular is simply a credit toward production costs: Prove you spent X dollars in this place, and you will receive a percentage of it back via what is essentially a check. Some states provide rebates as high as 40 percent. Various exemptions from other forms of taxation, including breaks on sales taxes or corporate income taxes, are also provided. As I'll explain later, these credits can provide a windfall to companies that have no tax liability at all or even be sold off to third parties so that the buyers can reduce *their* taxes. The fancy language used to describe these credits shouldn't obscure that we're talking about cash that once belonged to the public and no longer does.

The theory behind providing film subsidies is simple and seductive: Give production companies and filmmakers money, and then jobs that would have gone elsewhere will instead be in your state or city, and they'll be high-paying film industry jobs, too, with all the glitz and glamour that entails. These very visible jobs in the community—such as security guards, camera workers, or in construction—are usually accompanied by lots of newspaper articles about Hollywood A-listers coming to town, so it's easy to see why politicians have tripped over themselves for the last several decades to provide the biggest and the best subsidy programs. As one budget analyst put it, "There's an allure to policymakers, who get irrationally starstruck and like the idea of being at a production shoot with Ben Affleck or whoever."[7]

Production companies, of course, love this. One director explained it like so in 2006: "Hey, you know what? Studio executives? They'd shoot a movie on Mars if they could get a twenty-five percent tax break."[8] The advent of digital filmmaking, which can make anywhere look like anywhere else, has helped the cause; shooting a movie about New York City doesn't mean one has to be anywhere near the Big Apple. (A lot of movies set in American cities are shot in Vancouver or Toronto, thanks to Canada's lucrative movie subsidies.) Studios have chased tax breaks around the country and beyond, leading to a massive proliferation of schemes in state after state after state, as nearly all of them have attempted to get in on the action.

The first explicit tax break for movie production was created in Louisiana in 1992, and a few other states started up small programs in the years after. But the golden age of the US film credit began in 2002, when the Bayou State initiated the Louisiana Motion Picture Investor Tax Credit program; after the number of productions in the state clearly increased, it set off a great race among the others to subsidize silver screen activity. By 2009, forty-four states and the District of Columbia had some sort of film incentive program on the books, as did the federal government. Only Delaware, Nebraska, New Hampshire, Nevada, North Dakota, and Vermont held out.[9] The total cost of these programs in fiscal year 2010 was $1.5 billion.[10]

These dollars aren't going to boosting independent films made by locals or to giving smaller production companies a leg up against Hollywood behemoths, which would perhaps have been defensible as an effort to build an industry from the ground up. Instead, it's money going to Twentieth Century–Fox, Warner Bros., Disney, and DreamWorks, a veritable who's who of the moviemaking elite, the corporate giants of the industry. In 2015, nearly every Academy Award Best Picture nominee, including the eventual winner, *Birdman*, received some public funding.[11] Ditto in 2014, when *American Sniper* led the way in public largesse. "The name of the game, all over the country, is tax incentives," said Lee Shapira, who works on sets and lighting in Maryland.[12]

But these programs don't work as advertised. They often don't come anywhere close to justifying their cost when it comes to economic activity, jobs, or sustainable development. States and cities have been buying precious little but some short-term glam and a long-term hole in their budgets.

Louisiana is an instructive place to start in trying to explain why these subsidies are almost always a waste but create the illusion that they do some tangible good. Undeniably, Louisiana's tax credit program has convinced production companies to look at the state seriously when previously few did. In 2002, before Louisiana started doling out serious money to entice silver screen moguls, just one motion picture was filmed there. Five years later, the number had jumped to 54.[13] In 2013, 107 projects qualified for public help, 49 of which were feature films, more than in any other state in the nation.[14] Some of the biggest film franchises of the day—the likes of *Terminator* and *Jurassic Park*—called Louisiana home, as did some of TV's biggest names, including *NCIS: New Orleans* and *Duck Dynasty*. Hollywood had moved, in a major way, from L.A. to LA.

The total cost of all this to Louisiana taxpayers was nearly $1.5 billion over the last decade. About $1 of every $6 spent subsidizing film production in the United States was spent by the Bayou State, as of 2015. And that's where the trouble begins.

To start, it's worth remembering that nearly every state in the United States—unlike the federal government—has a balanced-budget requirement; the states are constitutionally required to have outlays not exceed revenue. They can't run a deficit or add debt via the annual or biennial budget. That requirement means every dollar dedicated to one thing is one less dollar for all the other responsibilities state governments have. Whereas the feds can argue that borrowing money to invest in a program is worthwhile, states often can't, constrained as they are by legislative budget fiat. Thus, trade-offs are inherent in everything a state does, every fiscal decision it makes, every cent it decides to spend on one thing versus another, more so than they are on Capitol Hill in Washington.

So the first measure of whether a subsidy program is working is how much of a return it's generating. And study after study, analysis after analysis, report after report, year after year after year, has shown how little money states recoup when they dole out funds for film production.

In Louisiana, one analysis found that the state received about $44.3 million in revenue—state and local taxes combined—in 2010 thanks to its film program, which cost nearly $200 million that year.[15] A 2012 analysis found similar numbers: more than $200 million in outlays, about $50 million in revenue.[16]

The most oft-cited analysis of the state's film program took place in 2005, conducted by its chief economist, Greg Albrecht. He found that the state only recouped about 16 percent to 18 percent of the cost of its film subsidies through tax revenue.[17] He wrote that those numbers should be considered "generous," as "a number of aspects of this particular analysis work to overestimate the likely true impact of the program."

That's not a great return, to put it mildly. And the same result has held across the country, consistently.

Maryland found that its film subsidy program recouped just six cents in revenue for every dollar spent. For Massachusetts, it was thirteen cents, New Mexico fourteen, and South Carolina nineteen. Few independent analyses have found a return that cracks thirty cents per dollar spent. Just two that I've seen—a study from New Jersey and an analysis from California—found the revenue even getting back half of what was initially spent.[18] The dollars that went out the door were not coming back; in the strictest sense, these programs do not come close to "paying for themselves" in the popular governmental parlance.

So if that is the case, the next question is "What are these states paying for?" After all, it's not necessarily bad for states to spend money on things that are worthwhile, even if the return on investment is less than 100 percent. Governments do that all the time, filling gaps that the private sector won't or fulfilling other responsibilities that are unprofitable or prohibitively complicated for private entities but necessary for the public good. There's not much profit in Medicaid or building roads, for instance, but few say we shouldn't do such things. However, what film production programs are buying isn't worth having most of the time.

The top-line justification is jobs. "This is a crown-jewel industry that provides jobs and opportunity for middle-class families in every region of our Golden State," said one California state senator in support of upping such spending. "We're sending a powerful signal today that we are one hundred percent committed to keeping the cameras rolling and bright lights shining in our state for years to come."[19] The same rhetoric is used everywhere else: Subsidize movies and get good jobs. It's a simple equation on paper and one that makes for a nice sound bite. University of Southern California professor Michael Thom has found that rising unemployment is one of the most reliable predictors of whether a state will create a film tax credit.[20] "Rising unemployment increased enactment likelihood, and falling unemployment increased termination likelihood," he wrote.[21]

The simple "subsidies equals jobs" equation suffers from a few problems, however. First, by their very nature, these are temporary jobs. Even television shows that run for years aren't filming all the time, while movie productions clearly have a limited time frame, even in an age in which it can feel as if every other film is part of some "franchise." A Massachusetts study noted that "since all film productions are short-term," employees on those projects end up "working from a few days to at most a few months."[22] A study by the Center for Economic Analysis at Michigan State University found that the "typical 2008 production filmed for 23 days" in that state, so it took 2,763 short-term positions to create the equivalent of just 250 full-time, yearlong jobs.[23] This isn't creating jobs so much as renting them for a few weeks at a time.

That dynamic is fairly evident at the anecdotal level. I lived in Baltimore when the early seasons of *House of Cards* were being filmed there. The production would come in, do its thing, and leave. Trailers and lights would proliferate for a few days, then vanish. By its very nature film work is not the sort of gig that local politicians should dream of building their economies around. (Yes, *House of Cards* did have a permanent set in the area, but that opened and closed with the production schedule, too.)

Szeliga, the state lawmaker, described a neighbor who works in trucking. He did get some work hauling materials to and from the movie sites, but inconsistently. "That's not the same as a permanent Maryland job," she said.[24] This effect was even more apparent when it looked as if *House of Cards* might get canceled in the wake of Kevin Spacey's sexual-assault scandal; positions associated with the show looked for all the world as if they would just disappear into the black hole that had become Spacey's career. Headlines blared about the economic effect a cancellation would have on Baltimore, making the city yet another casualty of the Hollywood sexual-assault scourge. (Those same jobs will presumably also vanish when the show ends as planned after its sixth season, but everyone seemed less worried about that.) Film jobs come and go with popular sentiments of the TV-viewing public and the whims of financiers; structurally, no one can do a whole lot to change that.

The line of thinking at work here also assumes that the jobs created by film subsidies go to locals, helping people in the show's filming location who wouldn't have found employment otherwise. But that is often not the case. As economist Robert Tannenwald, who has done some of the most in-depth and critical work on film tax credits in the United States, explained in a 2010 paper, "Most locations in the United States (other than Los Angeles and New York City) lack 'crew depth'—an ample supply of workers possessing the skills needed to make a feature-length movie. However, movie-making is so mobile that producers import their own scarce talent, such as principal actors, directors, cinematographers, and screen writers. . . . These non-resident 'top personnel' enjoy the best jobs and a large chunk of the income created by feature film production."

Tannenwald said he became interested in film tax credits because "my boss asked me to look into it. It impressed me as just the sort of nightmarish subsidy that in the long run hurts the state more than it helps." He found that "existing writing didn't get to the heart of the problem" since the focus was on the benefits of film tax credits in the aggregate, without accounting for the downside. "People were not focusing on the full range of costs," he said. "Those other measures [such as the film's effect on GDP] capture benefits that redound to nonresidents, and those don't really matter."[25]

Benefits redounding to nonresidents is a recurring feature of film tax credits. In Massachusetts, for example, the state Department of Revenue found that while its film production credit created nearly two thousand jobs in 2012, only seven hundred went to residents of the state. In Georgia, producers of the Fox TV drama *Red Band Society* flew their own construction workers into Atlanta after not being able to find any.[26] One worker I spoke to—Michael Davis, who worked on set construction for both *House of Cards* and *Veep*, another show that called Maryland home for a time—explained that he went to Michigan for temporary work after that state began its tax incentive program and started poaching productions, and that such moves were not out of the ordinary.[27]

Even if major movie studios pick up extras from the local population, they aren't exactly putting local, struggling actors into their blockbuster films, so some portion of the public money inevitably goes to fund perks and pay for the actual millionaires who get cast by big studios. For instance, Missouri taxpayers helped subsidize the installation of satellite TV in Ben Affleck's hotel room during the filming of 2014's *Gone Girl*, as the Show-Me Institute's Jessica Stearns found.[28] Louisiana taxpayers covered actor Matt Dillon's massages and local gym membership that same year during the making of *Bad Country*.[29] According to an Associated Press review, in 2009 about a quarter of the money spent by Massachusetts on its tax credit program went to pay the salaries of nonresident actors who made more than $1 million—so that year, $82 million in Massachusetts money was spent subsidizing nonlocal millionaires, while film companies spent just $42 million paying wages to local workers.[30]

This is a consistent problem with subsidies of all sorts and will come up again and again in this book: A nontrivial portion of the money leaks out to nonlocal workers, nonlocal companies, and even other countries, missing its target—and therefore the justification for it being spent in the first place—entirely. Local tax money, raised from the local tax base, gets spent to line pockets or generate economic activity somewhere else. Giant movie productions take their largesse and move it back to corporate headquarters, or offshore, or into the bank account of one of Hollywood's biggest names, none of which does any good for the local worker trying to catch a break. By using a bank shot instead of directing payments straight into the communities they serve, lawmakers lose control over whether the funds benefit their constituents or instead go to foreign multinationals, foreign governments, or the richest of the global elite. A dollar paid out to a production company via a film tax credit may end up in an executive's Swiss bank account or funneled through the Cayman Islands as part of some multinational's tax evasion scheme. Control of local money simply goes "poof," magicked away like something out of a *Harry Potter* film.

So that's two problems already with the job-creation story boosters of these tax breaks tell: First, the jobs are temporary, and second, many of the best ones go to people not from the local area anyway, meaning the money leaks out of the community. Then there's the simple cost per job: When talking film subsidies, it often gets outrageous. Michigan's state Senate Fiscal Agency pegged the cost of that state's film subsidy program at as high as $193,000 per directly created job.[31] It would have been simpler to just hire four workers at $45,000 for a year and pocket the extra $13,000, instead of spending that all on just one job. While that's the high end, it's not an outlier. Massachusetts found that it was paying $108,000 per film production job.[32] Other states have seen costs in the $60,000 range.

But even the statistics I've cited give movie subsidies more credit than they're due. One of the main problems in assessing the effectiveness of not just film production subsidies, but most government-subsidy or job-creation schemes, is treating them as if they exist in a vacuum, as if all the people who benefit would have been sitting around doing nothing otherwise, twiddling their thumbs just waiting for some enterprising lawmaker to create a tax credit that would save them from the unemployment line. That's not how it works. Some of the people who pick up jobs with various productions had other work before, so their new employment was not a job created; it was merely a job shifted. The tens of thousands, or even hundreds of thousands, of dollars that it cost to "create" that job were totally wasted.

William Luther, an adjunct scholar at the right-leaning Tax Foundation, explained it well: "A hairstylist might go from serving the public to crimping and curling on film sets. Earnings might be higher on the film set, and that's a plus, but it's one job shifted, not one just created," he said. "If tax incentives merely allow those already employed to upgrade to a better job, the real gains from job creation are much lower than boosters suggest."[33] Indeed, that's inefficiency at its finest. Missouri touted the success of its film program after the hiring of a few off-duty police officers to provide security on the set of *Gone Girl*.[34] Couldn't it have spent money on, well, hiring more cops or increasing the pay of the cops it currently had on the payroll, or hiring other public sector workers, rather than funding their extra pay through a movie subsidy that also spent money on a host of other non-security related things?

Let's expand the critique out a little bit because jobs are not the be-all, end-all measure of the effectiveness of government spending if that spending boosts economic growth in some other fashion. Film subsidy boosters bank on the "ripple effect": It's not just that the money creates jobs, but it helps other people who already have jobs—think the bars and restaurants patronized by the cast and crew, the local shops where set supplies are purchased, or the local drivers hired to ferry people around. Even if workers aren't directly finding jobs with the production, all of that other stuff is helpful to the overall economy, right? "Whatever sacrifice we make in revenue on the tax credit, we more than make up for through the multiplier effect of economic development," Georgia Governor Nathan Deal said in 2013.[35]

So do movies cause this "multiplier effect," a critical idea in economic development that I'll examine more later in the book? In the short term, maybe. In the long term, nope.

The temporary nature of film productions makes it unlikely that any lasting ripple effects occur. If any boost happens, it's more akin to a sugar rush than anything sustainable. And that sugar rush comes at the expense of long-term investments that would build something with a more lasting impact or an industry that can eventually stand on its own without subsidization. The Maryland Department of Legislative Services in 2015 said that the state is worse off over the long run due to its film production credit than if it had none at all, because the investment is so short-term and the benefits so fleeting.

"The state essentially continues to pay for the credit after the production activity has ceased," the department found, adding that several years out the state's economy would actually be smaller—yes, smaller—because of the credit. In a backfire of epic proportions, the state's film credit shrank the state's GDP by millions of dollars; personal incomes over the long run were lower than they would otherwise have been, too.[36] The state could instead have spent the money it plowed into film production on an investment in something that was self-sustaining or at least had benefits that didn't disappear so quickly. But no.

That brings us to one of the great ironies of film production credits—and, again, to a larger problem with subsidy schemes writ large: The money often goes to subsidize activity that would have happened anyway.

As Darcy Rollins Saas, a policy analyst with the New England Public Policy Center at the Federal Reserve Bank of Boston, has pointed out, New England had plenty of film activity prior to the advent of its film subsidies, and "producers already filming in New

England and planning to continue to do so will be able to avail themselves of film tax credits without having to expand their activity." Sure, in places, such as Louisiana, that had next to no film industry before the subsidies kicked in, this argument doesn't hold. But plenty of locales with other inherent advantages throw money at movies anyway to keep up with the Joneses or because they are afraid of losing what they have and bearing the subsequent bad press.

Saas calls these "tax windfalls" for movie firms and said that states need to be asking whether their tax credits are "inducing the economic activity desired or granting benefits for activity that would have happened anyway." Oftentimes, it's the latter.[37]

Perhaps nothing illustrates this more perfectly than the fact that California—California!—decided it needed to spend big on film subsidies despite its tons of advantages in attracting film production that other states can't hope to match. In 2014, the Golden State concluded that the $100 million annually it was spending on film tax credits wasn't enough, so it decided to more than triple its program. That's $330 million to entice movies to the state that's the home of Hollywood.

"This is a great day for Hollywood, for California," said Governor Jerry Brown at the bill signing. "We will create thousands and tens of thousands of jobs."[38] Los Angeles Mayor Eric Garcetti agreed, "This legislation targets the heart and soul of this industry and our middle-class people who swing hammers, run cable, and serve food on set so they can pay the bills and spend money in our economy."[39]

Productions have indeed fled California for other locales, which local lawmakers find distressing—the worst-case scenario for a politician is for jobs to depart on his or her watch, especially those in a core industry with a history such as moviemaking has in the

Golden State. These jobs were not only moving overseas from California, but to places such as Louisiana and New Mexico. Elected officials understandably wanted to be seen as doing something about it; a politician who is seen as losing jobs for his constituents often loses his job himself.

But California is still California, and it's always going to have advantages for filming that other states won't, including a steady stream of talent that lives and moves there and a concentration of existing facilities. Subsidizing film production there is akin to New York City paying Wall Street banks to create jobs or Houston handing out tax rebates to oil companies for office expansions. The industry is already there. Paying for it is just a windfall for the companies involved.

Every dollar spent paying a company to do something film related is one less dollar to spend on everything else a state does. At least California's budget was in okay shape when it tripled film subsidies. But that's not always the case. Take, once again, Louisiana. Thanks in large part to the bungling and presidential ambitions of its then-Governor Bobby Jindal, by 2015 the state was facing a budget mess of epic proportions. Just about everything was on the table to be sliced and diced—except for film credits. Jindal initially claimed that changing the film subsidy program would amount to a tax increase, rendering it unacceptable. He was eventually persuaded to cap the program, limiting the amount doled out in any one year.[40]

But here's the trade-off Louisiana was facing, as noted by Bloomberg News: "The state approves enough incentives each year to make up at least $200 million in proposed cuts that led Louisiana State University to say that it may plan for insolvency."[41] At the time, *Duck Dynasty*, the A&E reality show about bearded, ultraconservative makers of duck calls, was receiving $415,000 per episode from Louisiana.

Even the subsidy cap didn't do all that much good. In 2016, Louisiana paid out its largest-ever subsidy to a single film: $38 million to the producer of *Deepwater Horizon,* a movie about the massive and tragic 2010 Gulf of Mexico oil spill. As Louisiana's *Advocate* noted, that's more money than the state spent on the University of New Orleans and the Southern University at New Orleans combined; it equals $8 for every single person in the state.[42]

These priorities matter for reasons other than efficacy. It'd be one thing if film subsidies were just a well-intentioned economic development idea that backfired. But in addition to being ineffective, they also hand precious state dollars—that could go to something such as education—to already well-off people and businesses. Adding insult to injury, the businesses benefiting may not even be the film companies that originally receive the subsidies, but other large, profitable corporations that don't need help from the government.

Here's how that happens: To start, to be eligible for subsidies film companies usually have to certify that they've spent money in a particular state. But they, crucially, do not need to have paid any amount in taxes, because film subsidies are almost always crafted as "refundable" tax credits, meaning the recipient can benefit from them even if he, she, or it owes nothing in tax payments. (The earned income tax credit—one of the federal government's most effective and important antipoverty efforts—is refundable, meaning recipients can claim it even if they don't have any federal income tax liability.)

This means that these subsidies are more akin to checks cut to the film production company by the government, rather than "tax breaks"—you can't give a break on taxes that aren't owed—though they are frequently portrayed as the latter when being debated by lawmakers. That framing also, as in the case of Jindal above, can prove advantageous when states reevaluate their programs. If the subsidies are a "tax break," then eliminating them is a "tax increase" and thereby a tougher sell. And everyone falls into this rhetorical trap; I certainly haven't gone out of my way to not call these subsidies "tax breaks" myself, even if it is a somewhat inaccurate characterization of what's happening.

Not only are these credits often refundable, but many states also make them "transferable," which is where more trouble starts. Rendering the credits transferable means they can be sold to other companies in the not-all-that-rare instance in which the company receiving them actually has no tax liability to be offset. More than a dozen states, to date, allow film companies to sell their tax credits in this manner, meaning an already-ineffective program then reduces the tax liability of a random smattering of other companies it was never meant to aid.

An entire industry has cropped up around helping the holders of film tax credits off-load them to other companies.[43] In Massachusetts, to use one example, insurance companies and financial institutions have been the main beneficiaries of this transferability, not only reducing the tax liability of firms the legislature presumably had no interest in helping when it set out to subsidize film production, but also creating a bookkeeping nightmare for the state's accountants, as these companies were holding on to their credits and cashing them in at a later date.[44] Back in 2011, *The Economist* even noted that film credits have "become an industry unto themselves" thanks to their tradability, with their getting sliced and diced into tranches as if they were subprime mortgages before the 2008 financial crisis.[45] Compounding this problem is that many movie productions are incorporated as individual limited liability corporations, not attached to their parent company in the legal sense, so they are able to drive down their tax rates to next to nothing, even if the parent company itself still has significant tax liabilities. The production then sells on its tax credits, banking the cash and sending it on to the parent company before the production corporation dissolves.

Other nations are not immune to the seduction of the blockbuster scam, either. Take *Star Wars: The Force Awakens,* one of the most successful box office draws of all time, with global earnings eclipsing $1 billion in 2016. A tiny detail of the film you'd be forgiven for overlooking is that George Osborne, then the United Kingdom's chancellor of the exchequer, receives a line in the credits, as does Ed Vaizey, then minister of culture.[46] But why would a British cabinet member—one who is celebrated or reviled depending on which side of the debate over fiscal austerity you're on—be receiving that sort of thank-you? Because of his unwavering support of the United Kingdom's film tax subsidy scheme, a tax break for movies and television shows produced in the country.

"These tax credits that support both film and TV production create around two billion pounds' worth of business for Britain," Osborne claims. "That's many thousands of jobs and lots of different industries, not just acting but filmmaking and costume design and set design. All of those things are really brilliant jobs supported by this brilliant industry. It's also a great advert for the country."[47]

All told, Disney, the studio behind *Star Wars* after creator George Lucas sold the rights, received a bit more than 31 million pounds for *The Force Awakens*. (Films in the United Kingdom are eligible for up to a 25 percent rebate on their production costs once they're officially categorized as a British production ex post facto.)[48] Since 2007, when the United Kingdom's current tax break was created, Disney has received some 170 million pounds ($250 million) from the country's public pot, out of a program that dishes out nearly $240 million annually.[49] As of this writing, the British film subsidy program has cost more than 1.5 billion pounds ($2.2 billion).[50]

Osborne and many in the British film industry may say this is money well spent, but the same dynamic that exists in the United States doesn't get magically reengineered by a transatlantic voyage. Consider these numbers: Proponents of the UK credit claim that eliminating it would cause the country's GDP to drop by 1.4 billion pounds ($2.2 billion) a year, which, taken at face value, sounds like a lot.[51] But the United Kingdom has a nearly 2 trillion pound economy, so it's a drop in the bucket.[52] And nothing keeps that money on the Queen's shores. As British director Matthew Vaughn has said, "We're subsidizing Hollywood. We're service providers. We're not an industry."[53] Another director added, "While the tax break is good for Hollywood films shooting here, it's probably not that great for British films shooting in the UK. Some middle-to-low-budget films are going to find themselves without crew because all the American films are shooting here."[54]

For all my US bashing up to this point, it was Canada—and particularly British Columbia, its westernmost province—that made a big leap into subsidizing film production in the late 1990s, poaching thousands of US productions and bringing them north. At its apex, thanks to documents dumped as part of the 2014 hack of Sony Pictures, filmmakers in BC were having nearly 60 percent of their labor costs covered by the state.[55] As Jordan Bateman, former British Columbia director of the Canadian Taxpayers Federation, said, "All told, the BC government cut checks for a billion and a half dollars in film subsidies over the past five years. That's more than taxpayers spent on the ministries of aboriginal relations, agriculture, and environment—combined."[56] And as the Canadian dollar weakened, the cost of the subsidies increased.

Other countries around the world have joined the party, too. Australia provides film tax rebates of up to 40 percent, as does Colombia. It's around 30 percent in Ireland, the United Arab Emirates, and Malaysia. France, South Africa, and the Czech Republic only offer 20 percent, by comparison.[57]

This brings up perhaps the biggest reason film subsidies don't work: the opportunity for economic hostage taking. It's not that hard for productions to cross borders to get a better deal, so companies and projects can easily play nations and US states off against one another.

At the top of this chapter, Netflix's *House of Cards* used a threat to abandon Maryland as leverage to ensure that its flow of public dollars wouldn't be stopped by the state legislature. Another show, though—HBO's *Veep*, starring Julia Louis-Dreyfus as bumbling, incompetent, and extremely politically fortunate Vice President Selina Meyer—best illustrates the problem and consequences of subsidizing film production.

Over its first three seasons, *Veep* received nearly $14 million from Maryland to film there—evidently today's networks regard the state as a good fill-in for Washington, DC. But then California came calling, offering more than $6.5 million if the show would relocate.[58] And relocate it did, leaving Maryland high and dry. That $14 million left nothing permanent behind.

As Robert Travis Scott, president of the Public Affairs Research Council, a Louisiana-based good-governance organization, said, "The only way the movie tax credit program works is you have to keep paying them that incentive every year. . . . I think one of the movie promoters gave the best argument against this program when he said, 'If you change or eliminate this program, we'll all go to Georgia tomorrow.' That, to me, speaks volumes."[59]

Tannenwald has called the dynamic of states constantly needing to up their subsidies just to maintain the same level of economic activity "perpetual competitive purgatory." "If they try to backpedal a little bit, even if the subsidies are generous, the companies say, 'We're out of here,'" said Tannenwald. "The states that are really serious about the competition can't get out of it."[60]

The *Veep* episode perfectly illustrates the problem with subsidizing such a transitory industry: Unless lawmakers agree to pay for it in perpetuity, and usually in ever-growing amounts, the state or city can be left with nothing. A severe case of diminishing returns is at work. In the case of *Veep*, Maryland paid for jobs for several years and wound up with no jobs; with *House of Cards*, the state paid more and more money each year for the same amount of jobs, under threat that the production would leave and the state would be stuck holding the bag.

This leverage works in other ways as well: For instance, the 2014 hack of Sony Pictures, likely undertaken by the North Korean government, revealed emails in which filmmakers agreed to a host of changes to *Spectre*—a James Bond film released in 2015—demanded by Mexican authorities in exchange for tax incentives, including casting decisions and changing the ethnicity of characters. "You have done a great job in getting us the Mexican incentive," wrote Jonathan Glickman, one of the executives involved. "By all accounts we can still get the extra $6M by continuing to showcase the modern aspects of [Mexico City], and it sounds like we are well on our way based on your last scout. Let's continue to pursue whatever avenues we have available to maximize this incentive."[61] The incentive money was so important that wholesale changes were made to the script to ensure it came in. And such requirements aren't uncommon: While *Spectre* was an outlier in the scale of changes demanded, many locales require positive portrayals as a prerequisite to paying out their incentives.

But diminishing returns and a loss of artistic control aren't even where the problems end. The later adopters of film subsidies also wound up paying a premium—and getting far less out of their money—than did the states or nations that piled in early. Consider Michigan: A later entrant into the film subsidy game, which it barreled into at the behest of then-Governor Jennifer Granholm, it didn't create its tax credit until 2008, several years after other states had entered the business. So it had to play catch-up, doling out more generous credits than did earlier states to entice filmmakers from places in which they were already receiving a lucrative payoff—thus, as noted earlier, Michigan paid up to an astronomical $193,000 per direct job created.[62] But as the Mackinac Center, a conservative think tank based in Michigan, has noted, between the film subsidy program's inception in 2008 and 2014, the state actually lost film jobs. In 2013, zero full-time jobs were created in the film industry there. Not a one. Oops.

It's worth noting at this point the odd politics at play when it comes to movie subsidies. They've been a decidedly bipartisan boondoggle, with both major political parties piling on at times in support. The subsidies are also scorned by economists on both sides of the aisle, for different reasons: Conservatives don't want the state to pick winners and losers, preferring that money funneled to specific industries instead be used to lower taxes across the board. Liberals, meanwhile, don't want the government spending money to subsidize already well-off corporate giants and note that the dollars spent on film subsidies could be used for a plethora of other public goods. The dynamic creates some strange bedfellows both in the analytical realm, where economists who agree on little else are in lockstep, and in the advocacy world, where right-wing antitax organizations work with left-wing social justice outfits toward dumping what they both view as wasteful, unfair, and ineffective programs.

Thus far, it might seem that no paperwork makes the case that film subsidies work as intended. But a healthy body of industry-funded literature actually claims large economic impacts, loads of job creation, and tons of ancillary effects for states and cities willing to pay up to have movies come in. A quick Google search turns up lots of this stuff. In just about every state where such a program exists, local economic development offices trumpet the findings of this genre of work, significantly muddying the waters regarding how effective film subsidies can be. The Motion Picture Association of America (MPAA)—the main lobbying arm of the film industry in the United States—has its fingerprints on a lot of this paperwork, whether it's producing its own studies or funding others.

According to economists, studies finding a bonanza of benefits from film subsidies suffer from several flaws. First, they use a much bigger multiplier effect than do independent researchers, resulting in inflated benefits. One Maryland study claimed an economic impact of nearly $4 per $1 spent on movie production, the same amount Georgia boosters claimed. Economists say these estimates are way, way too high, and that the effect should be closer to $1.50 or $1.80 at the highest end. Those aren't even the most absurd examples of huge effects being bandied about—one study in North Carolina claims that every dollar spent on film subsidies there results in economic benefits of $9, a number with which most economists would take real issue.[63]

Boosters also likely vastly overestimate the effect of "movie tourism" on state budgets. For instance, one study of New Mexico's film subsidy found huge tourism effects in the state, based on a few surveys that most visitors there didn't even bother to fill out.[64] The tourism argument also falls apart once you remember that many of the locales are explicitly filling in as other, more expensive locations. Are those who watch *House of Cards* or *Veep* going to want to visit Baltimore, where the shows received their subsidy money, or Washington, DC, where they supposedly take place? How about when various locales are simply made to look like New York City? This argument assumes that the effects of movie productions happen in a vacuum, as if no tourists would visit these places in the absence of their being on the silver screen, an absurd notion when talking about, say, California, Louisiana (hi, New Orleans), or North Carolina. (Tannenwald does say that other locales need to study this more, as there may be a tourism effect that current studies haven't picked up on.)[65]

At their low point, industry-funded studies resort to simple hand waving. One MPAA-funded study produced in 2012 by the accounting firm Ernst & Young didn't even bother using a concrete example to bolster its cause in its "case study," instead relying on calculations regarding a hypothetical $10 million production that produced more than double that amount in various economic benefits. "It's as if the MPAA hired E&Y but then didn't let them see any industry numbers," snarked the liberal tax-policy organization Citizens for Tax Justice.[66]

As Joseph Henchman at the Tax Foundation wrote, "The MPAA is correct that subsidizing film production results in more film production, but they stop the analysis there. Good public policy means going further to determine whether those benefits are worth the costs, including a discussion of opportunity costs (alternative uses of resources)." It's not enough to say that a movie production did some good. The argument has to be made that a dollar spent on film production is the best use of a state's limited resources, outweighing all the other public goods that the money could have provided, including all of its other job-creation or economic-development efforts. Lawmakers should not be plowing dollars into inefficient economic efforts, even if they do have some benefits, given the myriad other options available.

There is some good news, though. In recent years a handful of states have decided that their film subsidies aren't worth the cost. In 2015, New Jersey's film credit program expired, and Governor Chris Christie vetoed an attempt to extend it the next year, arguing that it "offers a dubious return for the state in the form of jobs and economic impact."[67] (In 2011, New Jersey lawmakers were embarrassed to learn that MTV's *Jersey Shore*, which was not the most flattering portrait of the Garden State ever committed to film, was receiving hundreds of thousands of dollars in taxpayer money.) As if to prove the point of those who said New Jersey would still be an attractive place for films even in the absence of a big tax break, other films, including *Sully* and *Red Oaks*, were still made in the state.[68] Alas, Christie's successor, Democrat Phil Murphy, signed a new $425 million film credit into law in 2018.

Other states have ended their programs and stuck to it, though, including Alaska and Michigan. "Michigan has much to offer the movie industry, including top-notch talent and beautiful backdrops that will continue to draw filmmakers to Michigan, even without taxpayer-funded incentives," said Governor Rick Snyder when he signed a bill ending his state's giveaway.

Still, some three dozen states maintain their film subsidies, and some large ones—such as California—are still boosting the totals they spend. In 2015, overall spending on movie subsidies reached $1.8 billion nationally.[69]

The ultimate insult to taxpayers is buried in a report issued in

2011 by the Congressional Research Service, the nonpartisan research arm of Congress. In an analysis requested by Oregon senator Ron Wyden, analysts found that in 1995, before film credits took off in the United States, the film industry made up about .4 percent of US gross domestic product. In 2010, when more than forty states were serving up money to entice filming within their borders, the film industry made up .4 percent of US gross domestic product. The service also pulled data from the US Bureau of Economic Analysis showing that film industry employment actually declined by about 18,000 between 1998 and 2010, falling from 392,000 to 374,000. So after billions plowed into subsidies in the name of job creation and economic development, the industry was employing fewer people than it had more than a decade earlier. Corporate profits in the film industry, though, were up.[70] Jobs and economic activity may have shifted all over the country, but actual growth was nowhere to be found, while executives increased their payday.

The theory behind using the government to encourage economic development is that, eventually, the supports can be removed and an industry worth having can stand on its own. If the growth of film subsidies has shown anything, it's that this doesn't often happen. Instead, the industry in question gets subsidized in perpetuity, forcing the public to pay ever higher costs simply to maintain the level of economic activity it had before.

This gives producers all the leverage over lawmakers. And honestly, one can hardly blame production companies for chasing dollars, considering how eager governments are to throw money at them. The funds are there for the taking, so the companies would be irresponsible to not shop their wares looking for the best deal. At the end of the day, it's not the responsibility of corporate America to ensure legislators are good stewards of public money, even if the companies' tactics in pursuit of these funds are less than savory.

"It's classic game theory, playing states against each other," said Tannenwald. "If all the states just stopped giving tax credits, the film industry would film where it's most economically efficient."[71]

But this leaves state lawmakers stuck in a sort of prisoner's dilemma: If they all held together against providing the film industry any more subsidies, everyone would be better off in the long run. But if only one state breaks ranks, providing some money, it reaps the short-term benefits at some other state's expense and starts the cycle all over again. By the time the bill comes due, it's going to be some other elected official's problem.

To be clear, I don't discount that cutting these programs will hurt some people. "Being employed is wonderful. Because of the programs, I've been steadily employed," said Tiffany Zappulla, a Baltimore set decorator. She's certainly not alone; she tells the tale of a colleague who half jokes that *House of Cards* put his kids through college.[72] Change in public policy will almost inevitably produce winners and losers, and the losers in cutting film subsidy programs that already exist may not have a ton of options short of moving to more established film hubs.

But workers in the industry understand that a policy game is being played. "I wish the Canadians had never started this whole thing," said Michael Davis, the set constructor. "What should we do? Unilaterally disarm? That just means a whole lot of people are out of work and have to move."[73]

It'd certainly be nice if a simple solution were at hand, but unless Congress comes in with a national moratorium, there's no magic-wand fix for the blockbuster scam. State legislators need to be made aware of what they're buying when they toss money at film productions and not be swayed by short-term job creation, red carpets, industry-funded studies, or A-list actors descending on their cities singing the praises of spending public dollars on private movie-making.

In *House of Cards*, Frank Underwood said, "There's no better way to overpower a trickle of doubt than with a flood of naked truth." In this case, it's more like attempting to overpower a flood of nonsense and bad incentives with a separate flood of truth that often gets reduced to a trickle. That makes it difficult to prevent the Underwoods of the world—or whatever actor, producer, or company comes along next—from building the next *House of Cards* on the backs of the public.

"Look, if you believe the alternative is the government is going to turn around and throw the money in the river, then the film tax credit is better," said Tannenwald. "I'm not that cynical."[74]

2

HAVE A GOOD NIGHT'S SLEEP ON US

THE PROTESTERS SLOWLY MOVED AWAY from the White House, where the bleachers from the inauguration still stood outside the back gates, blocking the view of the president's residence from the adjacent Lafayette Square Park. The gathered crowd—many of whom were holding signs with slogans such as FIGHT IGNORANCE, NOT IMMIGRANTS; FIRST THEY CAME FOR THE MUSLIMS AND WE SAID NOPE; and DEPORT MELANIA—hung a right around the Treasury Department's main building, hooking past Old Ebbitt Grill, a Washington power-lunch mainstay, then swung left down Pennsylvania Avenue.

Eventually, many of them paused for a few moments to shout "Shame!" at DC's Old Post Office building and its iconic clock tower before moving on to the Capitol, the culmination of yet another protest in a January that was chock-full of them.

Just days before, newly inaugurated President Donald Trump had announced the first version of what became known as his Muslim ban, an executive order aimed at restricting immigration from certain, mostly Middle Eastern, countries. (The ban was struck down by the courts shortly thereafter; a second version was deemed to have run afoul of the law in March, and then the Supreme Court rescued it from judicial purgatory in late June 2018.) Washington's Old Post Office building—which was completed in 1899 and used as the capital city's main mail-sorting site until World War I— earned the ire of the gathered crowd because, as of 2016, it is DC's very own Trump International Hotel.

Opened in October, just weeks before Trump won one of the most surprising upsets in electoral history, the hotel added some gold-plated glam to an area of Washington best known for Smithsonian museums and national monuments. As *The Washington Post*'s Jonathan O'Connell detailed, when Trump's organization was first granted the rights to redevelop the Old Post Office building by the federal General Services Administration—in a surprising upset all its own—the hope was that the project would "help restart the revitalization of Pennsylvania Avenue east of the White House toward the Capitol."[1] "The hotel may spark a revival for a tired area of the city that's prime real estate, but somehow still forlorn," added *Post* metro columnist Petula Dvorak.[2]

Trump's organization was chosen to redevelop the site over the bids of other major hoteliers such as Hilton, as well as groups who wanted to use the building for different tourist attractions, including a museum of Jewish history.[3] Donald not only brought the Trump aesthetic to the more staid DC downtown, layering the hotel's lobby with gold, but brought Trump prices, too. Want a $29 hummus plate instead of patronizing one of DC's food trucks or hot-dog stands? The Trump hotel has you covered.

Because the goal of the project was economic revitalization— and in a building that is on the National Register of Historic Places—Trump received some public money for undertaking it. Specifically, he benefited from the National Park Service's historic-rehabilitation tax credit, which provides developers with 20 percent of the cost of redoing buildings that are "certified as a historic structure."[4] Even before Trump became president, Oklahoma senator James Lankford was dinging the break as a waste.

"Eliminating the tax credit would also not lead to the collapse of iconic historic structures that have long been protected and preserved by the federal government," Lankford wrote in a report he titled "Federal Fumbles." "Instead its elimination will prevent the federal government from doling out hundreds of millions of dollars to luxury vacation destinations, Major League Baseball teams, and practically any other renovation project in a building that is included in the not-so-selective list of more than one million buildings on the National Register of Historic Places."[5]

Lankford is a conservative ideologue, but in this instance he hit upon something important and often wasteful: tax breaks for hotel properties. While the moneys Trump benefited from in DC—which will total more than $30 million when the project is all said and done—weren't intended as a boost for hotel projects specifically, he has been helped by many other pools of public largesse that were.

According to an investigation by *The New York Times,* Trump's properties in New York City alone have been on the receiving end of $885 million in tax breaks.[6] That includes $37.5 million for Trump Tower, $13 million for Trump Plaza, and $8 million for the Trump Palace Condominiums. "Donald Trump is probably worse than any other developer in his relentless pursuit of every single dime of taxpayer subsidies he can get his paws on," one city official said. As is his wont, he sued the city of DC over the Trump International's property tax bill.

But to find the granddaddy giveaway of them all, one has to go back to the very beginning of Trump's career, when he was the recipient of a forty-year break on property taxes to refashion New York's Grand Hyatt hotel, his first major development in the Big Apple. To date, it has cost the city $360 million. Even after Trump sold his interest in the Hyatt in the 1990s, the tax break lived on, zombielike, sucking away revenue from New York City. It doesn't expire until 2020. The justification for it—that no one wanted to take on that sort of project in that part of New York at the time Trump was willing to dive in—was also bunk. By the time Trump started work on the site, other major developments in the neighborhood were under way, which worked out without receiving decades' worth of tax breaks. Like purchasers of Trump Steaks, Trump Vodka, or a degree from Trump University, New York city taxpayers found themselves on the wrong end of a bad deal.

While Trump may be more aggressive than most in searching out every dime of tax relief he can unearth or sweet-talk his way into, he's not at all alone in the hotel development world in taking advantage of public funds. According to the Subsidy Tracker database at Good Jobs First, just about every major US hotelier is receiving public moneys somewhere in the country: Marriott, Hyatt, Hilton, Wyndham, you name it. They're all there. Many receive property tax abatements, just as Trump did on his Grand Hyatt, which means they are either exempt from paying the normal property tax on the hotel, or they receive some percentage of their property tax bill back as a payment. Others receive a percentage of hotel occupancy taxes as a lump sum, a convenient way for politicians to claim it's not really the local population paying for the hotel, but only out-of-town visitors. Or cities and states simply contribute to the construction costs of a particular hotel by floating bonds, putting the money raised toward the hotel project, then servicing the debt, instead of letting private developers cover the whole cost.

Plenty of big cities that one thinks of as major American tourist destinations, including DC, New York, and Los Angeles, subsidize hotel construction, but so do smaller cities and towns all across the country, such as Enid, Oklahoma (population fifty thousand) or Owensboro, Kentucky (just shy of sixty thousand). "There wouldn't have been any way that someone would speculate on building this size and quality of hotel without the public support," developer Malcolm Bryant said of his Owensboro Hampton Inn project.[7] In a 2014 survey, researchers Robert Nelson (who makes more of an appearance later in this chapter), Jan deRoos, and Russell Lloyd identified more than a hundred hotels in the United States that had received public funding, to the tune of $8 billion.[8]

How did America become so enamored with providing hotel beds on the public dime? Heywood Sanders, a political scientist at the University of Texas, San Antonio, and an expert in the politics of urban development, traces the trend in hotel projects back to the era of President Jimmy Carter, when the politics of urban renewal came into vogue.

"We begin to see large-scale subsidized hotel development in the 1970s," Sanders said. "This country blossomed with UDAG-financed hotels."[9] UDAG stands for Urban Development Action Grants; in just over a decade, the program dispensed about $4.5 billion to support three thousand projects in twelve hundred cities across the United States, including hotels, with the goal of revitalizing urban areas. The program eventually fizzled out, with Congress failing to fund it beginning in the late 1980s, but it did, as one researcher noted in 1989, create "a new model for private sector and public sector collaboration in economic development," in which public funds were plowed into private properties in an attempt to engineer benefits to neighborhoods that weren't materializing on their own.[10]

But the thinking that caused first the federal government and then, as is most often the case today, city governments to barrel into hotel projects can lead to some hefty bills for taxpayers. In the current political climate, the goal often morphs from urban development into claims that the local economy needs a boost of tourism or more big, organized business meetings, which can only increase if visitors have enough places to rest their heads. Or the hotels are simply the result of big corporate players throwing their weight around, much as Trump did, convincing a city that a hotel is the amenity needed to take whatever tourism or development goals it has to the next, yuuuuge level, as the man himself might say.

Consider the case of Anaheim, the sunny Southern California city perhaps best known as the location of Disneyland. In 2016, its city council decided to give two hotel developers, including Disney, more than half a million dollars in tax breaks to build three luxury hotels. Under Anaheim's program, which was first approved in 2015, new luxury hotels would get back 70 percent of what guests spend on the city's hotel occupancy tax; renovated hotels would get 50 percent.

"These hotels aren't just for the visitors, they are for the residents," Anaheim city council member Lucille Kring argued at the time. "We get back what they produce."[11]

But is that actually true? I corresponded with Robert Nelson, a professor at the University of Delaware who studies the tourism industry and the role of the public in supporting it, to find out.

"There are considerable benefits that come from large hotels that accrue to the community rather than the developers. It is these benefits that justify public subsidies to encourage projects that might not otherwise be built," Nelson told me via email, sharing part of a draft paper he was working on. "To the extent that these benefits to the community exceed the costs of the subsidies, a justification can be made for government to invest in the subsidies."[12]

Disney sold Anaheim on the hotels as a new revenue stream, telling the city council its hotels would "help pay for essential city services for its residents for decades to come."[13] Without some new luxury hotels, Disney argued, wealthy visitors to Disneyland wouldn't stay near the park, but instead at nicer digs in nearby cities, thereby depriving Anaheim of its just rewards for hosting the self-styled "most magical place on Earth." It's a tale as old as time, one might say.

Money isn't the only benefit. In addition to revenues to spend on whatever else government needs to do, hotels supposedly bring with them another crucial upside: jobs that can't be outsourced, moved, or automated, unlike so many occupations in twenty-first-century America.

"Most of these jobs have the added advantage of being connected to place," Nelson said. "In this age of mobile capital there are countless examples of manufacturing, banking services, insurance, pharmaceuticals, telemarketing, and other industries that pick up and move to another region. While these activities can be done just about anywhere, the bellman's job cannot be done remotely. It is forever tied to place."[14]

So that's the plus side, on paper. On the flip side, the logic of hotel building with public subsidies is a bit circular. After all, if enough tourist demand exists in a particular area to make a hotel worthwhile, the private sector should be able to handle construction all on its own and then reap the benefits, while paying the normal taxes any other corporation would pay. If there's insufficient demand for a private sector hotel, or lackluster tourist demand for rooms in a location in general, then a hotel all on its own isn't going to create that demand out of thin air.

Anaheim's mayor, Tom Tait, made that exact argument as he dissented from his council's decision to grant the giant hotel tax breaks. "This is a thriving hotel market, probably the best in decades," Tait said. "Why would a hotelier not want to build now?"[15] Indeed, Disney had made significant investments in both its amusement park and its accommodations in the years preceding the debate over its luxury hotels, giving the distinct impression that it didn't need financial incentives to undertake a new project. And other companies had also jumped into the game. "More than a thousand hotel rooms have been built in Anaheim in the last two years and none required a subsidy," the *Los Angeles Times* editorial board pointed out in a piece questioning Anaheim's decision to subsidize yet more construction. "Would Disney or the other luxury hotel developers have eventually built these projects anyway? If a tax break goes to a hotel—or a film production, or a company expansion—that would have happened without a subsidy, then taxpayers trade away money that could have been spent on streets, parks and other public services."[16]

To be sure, the jobs created by a hotel are nice, but cities have other ways to engage in job creation that don't require giving developers money to build a hotel. As with so many public efforts to boost the economy through private endeavors, the lack of imagination regarding how to create jobs results in throwing dollars at companies to build things they would probably have built anyway or for which there was insufficient demand to make the project worthwhile to private interests in the long run. In the case of

Disney and Anaheim, it seems that the company suckered the city council into paying it to do something that it would have done anyway, for good old business reasons, while letting other hotel companies draft off it to receive big payouts, too.

Disney is no stranger to giant tax subsidies from the public. Since the 1990s, the company of Mickey Mouse and Donald Duck has garnered some $788 million in public funds. About $487 million of that has come from California alone, with Anaheim tossing in the biggest contribution.[17] All told, the city's tax break for Disney's luxury hotels will top $200 million, for a company that makes huge profits already and for a project that benefits its own resort and amusement park. At the time of the debate, Tait said that nearly one-third of Anaheim's $300 million annual budget went to support Disney and other resorts.[18]

For the voters of Anaheim, though, enough was quickly enough. The 2016 elections there ushered in a new "people's council," the members of which said they were going to stand up to Disney and its streams of public largesse. Disney spent nearly $1 million on contributions in an unsuccessful bid to keep the anti-Disney faction from prevailing at the ballot box. In December of that year, the council did indeed cancel the program that granted tax breaks to luxury hotels—after grandfathering in the hotels that were already in the pipeline.[19]

That Disney went so hard for a tax break to build a hotel on such flimsy evidence is ironic since a case can be made that an amusement park, for two reasons, is a much more constructive thing to subsidize than many of the other boondoggles discussed in this book. The first is that, unlike, say, a sports stadium, it will actually bring in new visitors who wouldn't have come anyway, instead of just shuffling around money that would have been spent on entertainment no matter what. Also, its self-contained nature—often outside city limits—means leakages are much lower. People come, spend their money at the park, and don't prevent other tourists from doing whatever it is they wanted to do downtown. So the case for decades-long breaks on ticket taxes—which Anaheim also doles out to Disney like a genie granting wishes—is much stronger than a plan to help it build hotels.

Most cities, though, don't attempt to subsidize a hotel so explicitly beneficial to a single corporate patron engaged in other business. Instead, lawmakers in these locales convince themselves that a hotel is a necessary part of their downtown tourism and urban revitalization goals, in concert with other development strategies, especially if it's connected to a convention center. Not only will such facilities bring outside spenders to town, lawmakers tell themselves and the public, but all that money will help beautify downtowns. This was a particularly alluring strategy for cities in the mid-to-late twentieth century, and into the twenty-first, as the effects of white flight and then millennial-led reurbanization dramatically changed urban landscapes.

"Tourism strategies have become central to the larger strategy of urban renewal as communities throughout the country realize that residents as well as tourists are attracted to cultural activities, shopping, dining, and entertainment options," Nelson wrote me. "These amenities, which tend to emerge when a critical mass of tourists makes them possible, also appeal to a range of residents from baby boomers to millennials who are increasingly opting for urban living."[20]

This strategy has become particularly appealing for local lawmakers when they're looking to boost convention centers—which have also typically been heavily subsidized by public money themselves, a point that I'll revisit later. Los Angeles, for instance, spent more than half a billion dollars subsidizing hotel construction around its convention center in the early 2000s.[21] In fact, LA has joined its Southern California counterparts in Anaheim by helping one corporation, the Anschutz Entertainment Group (AEG), build quite a bit in one part of the city, creating an entire entertainment district.

Owned by Philip Anschutz, who has a net worth of more than $12 billion, AEG oversees a large entertainment district in Los Angeles called L.A. Live.[22] Located next to the Staples Center—home of the Los Angeles Lakers and the Los Angeles Kings—and the Los Angeles Convention Center, both of which are also managed by AEG, L.A. Live is a complex of bars, restaurants, and concert venues, all of which was meant to revitalize a then-moribund section of the city. Included in that fiesta of stuff is a JW Marriott that cost the city $270 million in refunded bed taxes over twenty-five years.

"For all practical purposes, that whole section of the city is AEG's turf," said Heywood Sanders.[23] In 2016, AEG even had the gall to get upset about the city's attempt to subsidize other hotel construction in the area, warning of the "severe operational and economic consequences" should it happen.[24]

Still, several other hotel deals followed, including for a Wilshire Grand and more Marriotts, each worth tens of millions of dollars in lost revenue to the city. With downtown booming, Los Angeles simply continued to dole out tax breaks for hotel construction, unable to pull the plug even though the justification for the deals, many argued, had already been accomplished.

My hometown of Washington, DC, got in on the action, too, in a much smaller way, when it spent some $200 million on the Marriott Marquis abutting its Walter E. Washington Convention Center downtown (just a few blocks from the apartment where I wrote some of this book), covering about 40 percent of the overall cost of construction. In addition to receiving a new downtown hotel for their tax money—the efficacy of which as a revitalization tool has been questionable at best—DC residents also received a Marriott-run whiskey bar called The Dignitary that uses an unorthodox Manhattan recipe.

The DC council partly justified its hotel investment by claiming that the taxes raised to cover the cost—levied on hotel rooms themselves, rental cars, and restaurant tabs—will come from convention business, as the hotel would lure new meetings into the convention center. Thus, the argument went, it doesn't cost the city as much as the price tag would imply. Mayor Adrian Fenty's office promoted the deal with Marriott by saying, "The District-sponsored portion of the financing for the project will be repaid over time using tax revenue generated by the hotel."[25]

That may sound like a free lunch, but don't be fooled. For one thing, since analysts consistently overestimate how much business a convention center will bring to a city, guesstimating how much tax revenue will be generated thanks to incoming visitors can leave a city short on the funds it needs. Banking on revenue generated by a center is never, ever a sure thing. But more important, not everyone who eats a meal or rents a car—or even books a hotel room—across the breadth and width of the city is doing so because of a convention. Only about 6 percent of the city's hotel visitors are conventioneers, perhaps not surprising given the vast array of other tourism opportunities in the nation's capital.[26] But everyone gets dinged by the same taxes. Now when my mom comes to town to visit, she gets to chip in via the hotel occupancy tax for her share of the Marriott, as do my wife and I anytime we eat out on the town. So the city's residents do cover the cost of the hotel, despite the sunny spin from the mayor's office.

For some cities, such as Baltimore, St. Louis, Phoenix, and Myrtle Beach, even subsidizing a hotel isn't enough, so they've opted for public ownership: hotels that don't just receive some support but that are owned outright by the city and leased to a management company. The first such arrangement was in Chicago, which opened a hotel in 1998 in an attempt to bolster the fortunes of its convention center after developers evinced little interest in putting a private hotel on the spot, even though it is the largest such center in North America. After a years-long fruitless search for a developer, the Windy City eventually decided to build the thing itself. Thus was the Hyatt Regency McCormick Place born.

This puts the city in an even more precarious financial situation than does just subsidizing hotel construction. With a publicly owned hotel, not just the cost of some construction bonds but the annual gains or losses from the facility become the public's problem for as long as the city owns the property.

Take the Hilton Baltimore, opened in 2008 after Mayor Martin O'Malley (who, you may remember, also made an appearance in chapter one promoting movie subsidies, after he had moved up to become governor of Maryland) and the Baltimore city council approved its construction for more than $300 million. The hotel was projected to be pumping $7 million annually into city coffers within a few years.[27]

It's easy to see, when you step into the Hilton Baltimore through its giant revolving door advertising the hotel's in-house tavern, both why the city thought it would be a moneymaker and why it will never actually be. The building—sided in a silvery metallic substance, with a foundation of bricks, and EAT LIKE A LOCAL, DRINK

LIKE A LOCAL written in the windows—is across the street from Camden Yards, home of Major League Baseball's Baltimore Orioles, and is connected to the Baltimore Convention Center. On the second floor, where the hotel has a slew of meeting rooms and some truly ugly orange-and-blue carpet, you can look straight into the stadium and even see home plate from the right angle. Downtown Baltimore's iconic Seltzer Tower is just a block away.

However, even in years during which convention business was up and the Orioles were making play-off runs, the hotel was losing millions of dollars. As of this writing, a $2.9 million loss in 2013 was the hotel's best financial performance.[28] It lost nearly $5.5 million in 2016.[29] But city officials still hope it will start making a profit by the 2020s.

The proximity to the stadium, the convention center, and Baltimore's tourist-happy Inner Harbor and aquarium, which are just a few blocks away, could certainly, on paper, make the case that the hotel should be a moneymaker. But the other very noticeable thing once you start to look around is that three other hotels are right nearby, too: a Marriott, a Hampton Inn, and a Holiday Inn. So the city hotel is competing with three other major hotels within throwing distance, never mind those in the rest of the city. That area lacks enough business for all of them to be full all the time, no matter how many conventions come through or how good a season the Orioles are having. And the presence of those other hotels shows that Baltimore had little reason to run one publicly anyway. Other chains seemed happy to be there, all on their own. The city is undermining itself by having its own hotel lose business to those other hotels, and it's undermining the other hotels by having them compete with a publicly subsidized hotel that will likely be bailed out by the city if it gets into truly dire financial straits. The whole thing is clearly a mess.

And Baltimore is not even the worst example of a city's experiment in hotel management going utterly awry. "Oh, there are lots of them," Robert Nelson, the University of Delaware professor, wrote me. "Perhaps the most convincing case for thorough economic review is the Trenton Marriott at Lafayette Yard. This $46 million conference hotel, that was developed and owned by the City of Trenton, opened in 2002 only to be sold under bankruptcy for pennies on the dollar." Indeed, the sale price for the hotel at its bankruptcy auction was just $6 million, and the city was left servicing millions of dollars in debt even after the hotel itself was off the books.

The saga didn't end there for what is, remarkably, the only hotel in the capital city of New Jersey. After it was bought by Edison Broadcasting in 2013 and renamed as a Wyndham property, the hotel continued to struggle; Wyndham cut bait and ran in the spring of 2017. After that, rebranded as Lafayette Park Hotel and Suites, it was shuttered for safety violations by the state, including one citation for use of panini makers that were not cleared for commercial properties.[30] Through it all, the people of Trenton were paying off the debt incurred by the original, disastrous decision by the city to get into the hotel business.

"We've embarked on a great experiment in hotel socialism in this country," said Heywood Sanders, the Texas political scientist. "Even places that you would expect wouldn't do it, do it in a big way."

It's not that this scheme can't work, though examples of really successful ventures are few and far between, even to those who are far less skeptical of them than I am. But cities too often barrel into them headlong without stopping to consider the logic of what they're asking city taxpayers to do: pay for an amenity that supports tourism without actually drawing many, if any, tourists by itself.

If the hotel business lacks logic for a city, the convention center business can, on paper, make more sense. It's worth dwelling on that for a moment because, as noted before, supporting the local convention center, which was also often built with public moneys, is often the reason cities wind up subsidizing hotels. Without a hotel, they say, how can we attract conventions and conventioneers who will spend money? The convention center and hotel are supposed to work in tandem to bring big meetings and their scores of lanyard-wearing, drink-desiring attendees to town.

So does that strategy have anything to it? Sanders, who wrote the book *Convention Center Follies: Politics, Power, and Public Investment in American Cities*, gives it generally a big thumbs-down, detailing a "build it and they will convention" strategy that is based much more on local politics than economic imperative. In what sounds a lot like the subprime-mortgage crisis that nearly pushed the US economy off a cliff in 2008, cities barreled into building convention centers with the belief that the business of big meetings would expand forever. Turns out, it didn't.

Between 1989 and 2011, American cities nearly doubled the total exhibition space available in their convention centers, going from 36.5 million square feet to a bit more than 70 million.[31] Much of this new construction—in St. Louis, DC, Phoenix, Atlanta, Chicago, and city after city—was financed in one way or another by the public. However, there simply wasn't enough convention business to go around: There are only so many large meetings, after all, and building more convention centers doesn't cause more trade associations or consumer-facing groups to suddenly want to hold large events. First the post-9/11 economic slump and then the 2008 Great Recession put a serious dent in the convention business: For many cities, the number of conventioneers was underperforming expectations even years later. For instance, in the case of DC, the opening of a new convention center in 2003 was supposed to herald a new age in the city's meeting business. Instead, for years it underwhelmed: By 2010, when the convention center was supposed to be generating some 750,000 room-nights a year—convention center parlance for the number of nights conventioneers stay in hotels—the total was less than 275,000. Back in the 1990s, when the new convention center was merely an idea, the city council told Congress that it would generate direct spending of some $618 million in its first year alone; by 2003, with the center set to open, the estimate was already revised down to $328 million.[32]

The solution from local lawmakers and business interests was almost always to simply keep expanding the convention center, as if there were a magic size at which big conventions would suddenly materialize out of thin air.

"The pattern is pretty clear that you don't wash your hands of this business," Sanders said. "You say, 'Let's do it a little bit more.'"[33]

Not that this was a new phenomenon. In 1900, Kansas City opened a new convention center to host that year's Democratic National Convention, but by the 1920s, the city's business leaders were already clamoring for something better. "We are gradually being eliminated from consideration through the lack of two important civic facilities now possessed by virtually all of the larger cities in the country," said the local Chamber of Commerce in 1929. "One is dining and meeting space in hotels . . . and the other is of course the lack of a convention hall with which to care for larger gatherings."[34]

But this leads cities down a dangerous path of one-upmanship. If convention business isn't growing or simply isn't growing fast enough, bringing more meetings to town means poaching them from other cities, a beggar-thy-neighbor strategy that means plowing more money into a convention space in the hopes of enticing organizers to abandon their current digs. Even if it results in one city receiving a boost—which oftentimes doesn't happen—it will be at the expense of other cities.

Case in point, the high-water mark for Washington's convention center between 2003 and 2010 was 2005, when big meetings had to relocate out of New Orleans after Hurricane Katrina; one city's tragedy was another's revenue boost. If the requirement, then, is to force meetings to move around from one city to the next to make each one's investment worth it, in the long run everyone loses.

Plus, this is all money that could have been spent on productive uses, instead of convincing convention organizers to ditch one city for another. As the *Washington Post*'s Steven Pearlstein explained, "Another way to think about convention subsidies is the way most economists would—in terms of the opportunity cost." For instance, the city "could have used the proceeds from those taxes for other purposes, such as reducing income or property tax rates or giving more services to residents. Because of those forgone opportunities, it is Washington's taxpayers who are really paying for the convention subsidies."[35]

This all holds true even with perhaps the most watched and well-known conventions of them all: the quadrennial Republican and Democratic National Conventions.

Every four years, major cities across the United States go toe-to-toe to bring home the presidential nominating conventions, convinced that landing either one will bring hundreds of millions of dollars in spending to town by the tens of thousands of delegates, journalists, and other assorted politicos, as well as providing four days of essentially free television advertising. Before the 2016 Democratic National Convention in Philadelphia, for instance, city and convention officials said the City of Brotherly Love stood to gain an economic boost worth $250 million to $350 million from hosting the event. "There's no question, I would anticipate during that week virtually every, any kind of serious restaurant or other business to pretty much be sold out," Mayor Michael Nutter bragged.[36]

However, according to economists Robert Baade, Robert Baumann, and Victor Matheson—who looked at the effect of every national political convention between 1970 and 2005—such events "have a negligible impact on local economies." They found that "neither the presence of the Republican nor the Democratic National Convention has a discernable impact on employment, personal income, or personal income per capita in the cities where the events were held."

There's no sugarcoating it. The three researchers conclude, "People should view promises of economic windfalls from hosting national political conventions in the same way they should view the campaign promises of the candidates at these very conventions—with skepticism."

They found less of a boost than the boosters expected because giant political conventions are a huge hassle. They crowd out lots of other economic activity in the host city. Estimates claiming hundreds of millions of dollars in new impact generally fail to account for spenders who get chased away by the increased security, crowds, traffic, and general all-around annoyance that accompanies an event the size of the DNC or the RNC.

A good example of this effect took place in 2004, when New York City hosted the Republican National Convention to renominate President George W. Bush. During that week, Broadway ticket sales fell precipitously; one account has total ticket sales down 20 percent, while the TKTS half-price ticket booth, a good proxy for tourist-related foot traffic, recorded drop-offs of 50 percent.[37] So the benefit of some of the increased spending at the convention was simply shifted from the theaters to events and venues around the RNC, with no net boost for the city. Another study even found that net taxable sales fell by $19 million in Houston when that city hosted the Republican National Convention in 1992.[38]

Lauren Heller, an economist at Berry College in Georgia, along with Matheson and E. Frank Stephenson, looked at daily hotel data to see if some of the "heroic," to use Heller's word, assumptions about convention spending at these mega-political-events actually occurs. By drilling down on what is the largest expenditure for most conventioneers, she hoped to find what sort of economic impact the assorted politicos were really bringing to their four-day speechifying and party-building soiree. They found an economic impact to be sure, but nowhere near what boosters claim.[39]

"What we found was, yes, there is some economic impact from these conventions, but it's much, much smaller than most estimates," Heller told me.[40] Whereas cities like to say that a convention will bring hundreds of millions of dollars of benefits, Heller and company found that hotels were only reaping tens of millions of dollars: $12 million in Charlotte for the 2012 DNC, for instance, or just shy of $15 million for the Republicans' 2012 effort in St. Paul. For there to be hundreds of millions of dollars more than that, then conventioneers would have to be going bananas in the restaurants and bars every night, spending orders of magnitude more than what they spent on their hotel rooms. And there's no evidence that actually happens. "Basically, people would have to spend a ton of money in addition to their hotel bill locally in order for those numbers to add up," Heller said.

Also, that many hotels are owned by big national chains blunts the effect of conventions, since that money leaks out of the community to corporate headquarters, just as movie subsidies leak out to the big Hollywood corporations. Sure, the usually jacked-up prices around conventions are good for hotel owners, but that extra money likely does nothing for the local population, instead just going to line the pockets of shareholders elsewhere.

"Hotel owners are smart. If they know a convention is coming to town, they're going to raise prices," Heller said. "If we're selling this to taxpayers as if the local area is going to get the gains, if a big part of that hotel revenue is in average daily rate, and if it's for national chains, which most of them are, that's going to end up in the pockets of the shareholders of those corporations."

One final reason locals might want to filibuster against their city hosting a political convention is that doing so brings a whole host of (completely understandable) security measures, which also help to minimize the economic impact of the event—first by driving away other tourists or locals who would normally spend money, and second by limiting the ability of conventioneers to move around to different venues.

"I have family and friends that still live in Cleveland," said Heller, a native of that town, which hosted the 2016 Republican convention, "and around the Cleveland convention people were saying, 'Let's get out of Dodge, we're not going downtown, everybody's there.'"

I had the good fortune to attend the Democratic convention in Philadelphia that year, which nicely illustrated why so many preconvention estimates look so out of whack. While the smaller daily events were held in the Pennsylvania Convention Center in the heart of downtown, and people were indeed patronizing the close-by eating and drinking establishments, the main evening speeches were held at the Wells Fargo Center, which was surrounded by not much of anything other than a huge security perimeter and acres of parking. Once the gathered delegates, journalists, and politicos were in for the evening, they wouldn't leave due to the struggle to get through security, with nowhere to go but the arena concourse to procure food and drinks. Any local eating establishments hoping for a boost were left literally outside the gates looking in.

The upside, then, may only be that a presidential nominating convention gives a city a several-night, prime-time infomercial. "We can't measure this, but one discussion that I've had with folks is, 'Well, everybody rags on Cleveland,' for example, or 'Everybody rags on Minnesota,' or whatever. Maybe just the reputational effects of having a convention, having it go well, having people not hate the city while they're there, can bring some good PR to the city," Heller said. "I don't think that's probably worth the millions of dollars spent, but I think that's a nontrivial thing as well." Like the Olympics, though, which you'll read much more about in a later chapter, that effect is probably more beneficial for cities that weren't on the radar as tourist attractions initially, as opposed to helping out a place such as New York City. Minneapolis may be able to play the part of Barcelona, that oft-cited Olympic hero of a city, but Boston or Los Angeles won't.

It's not that there's no benefit, then, to cities looking for the most politically salient reason that a national party would want to bring its convention to town. It's that there's a downside that often doesn't even make it onto the preconvention ledger, while the upside gets blown all out of proportion.

"I'm not an economist who thinks spending for spending sake is good. It really matters what we spend it on," Heller said. "You could look at our work and say, 'Hey, they found a benefit, right?' Because we do find an increase in the number of rooms. And that's fine, but you also have to look at all of the costs."

"Hey, they found a benefit, right?" is perhaps the perfect summation of not just the politics and economics of political conventions, but of public spending on hotel and convention centers in general. Lawmakers take one little bit of logic—"tourists spend money, but only if they have somewhere to sleep"—and use it to justify often unjustifiable public expenditures on building hotels or hosting presidential nominating conventions, failing to account for all the costs associated with doing so. That attitude then spirals into outright ownership of often flailing hotels by the cities themselves, or constant doubling, tripling, and then quadrupling down on bigger convention centers or newer hotels to keep pace with every other city in the country, while the number of tourists or conventioneers simply doesn't increase by an amount large enough to make all those investments possibly pan out.

"This has been fun, this whole political convention thing, because us economists aren't used to people, I don't know, caring what we have to say," Heller told me. If a few more people cared, it would save taxpayers quite a bit on having to pay to put up tourists for the night. Instead, cities are stuck in the same old dreamland, thinking they're just one good hotel away from a downtown boom.

As I wrote the first draft of this chapter, the Trump Organization announced it intends to build a second hotel in Washington. I hope our city council has the good sense to put to bed any inkling that we DC taxpayers will be pitching in to help build it.

3

"ALEXA, CAN I HAVE A JOB, PLEASE?"

AMAZON WANTED A BIDDING WAR, and a bidding war it received.

When the internet retail giant decided in the summer of 2017 that its continued growth could not be confined to its headquarters in Seattle, Washington—a city where Amazon already occupied some 19 percent of the prime office space, more than the next forty employers combined[1]—it began to search for a city in which to situate a second North American headquarters. In early September 2017, it released a request for proposals, laying out the conditions that would entice it to come to town.

Of course, bringing in Amazon would be considered quite a coup for any city: It was promising tens of thousands of new jobs and some $5 billion in investments. Major metropolitan centers began tripping over themselves to catch Amazon's eye. More than fifty initially said they intended to make a pitch.[2] Tucson, Arizona, even sent Amazon chief Jeff Bezos a twenty-one-foot cactus in an attempt to stand out.[3]

Among the criteria Amazon said it would use to determine

where its second headquarters would land was everything you'd expect: a large enough population, good schools, solid public transportation, an absurd amount of office space, and proximity to an international airport.

Oh, and tax breaks. Lots and lots of tax breaks.

"Incentives offered by the state/province and local communities to offset initial capital outlay and ongoing operational costs will be significant factors in the decision-making process," said Amazon's official request for proposals. "The initial cost and ongoing cost of doing business are critical decision drivers."[4]

The info Amazon desired on the how, when, and why of the "incentives" it would receive was a thing to behold. The company wanted to know the amount of money, the timeline for disbursing it, and what the specific requirements to receive it would be. It wanted to know whether the tax credits offered would be "refundable, transferable, or may be carried forward for a specific period of time." And it wanted a political game plan for getting the whole thing approved: "We acknowledge a Project of this magnitude may require special incentive legislation in order for the state/province to achieve a competitive incentive proposal. As such, please indicate if any incentives or programs will require legislation or other approval methods."

Of the nine specific requests for information Amazon made of the prospective cities, three of them were solely about the incentive package.[5]

It makes sense that Amazon wanted this level of information; it didn't achieve its market dominance by being lax regarding its financials. But that the company was so explicitly auctioning off its new headquarters to the highest bidder—and that so many cities piled into the competition headfirst, with nary a day's contemplation of whether it made any sense to join the fray or whether the company might bring some negatives that would outweigh its promises of jobs and an income bonanza—says nothing good about the way American states and cities use their tax systems to dole out goodies to the country's biggest, richest, and most profitable corporations.

Back up a few years and you'll find Tesla pulling the same trick, pitting states against one another to gin up tax breaks for its vaunted "gigafactory," where it would build batteries for its sought-after electric cars.[6] Several states jumped in, tossing big numbers and promises Tesla's way, with Nevada emerging as the eventual winner.[7] The incentives that state will provide to the electric-car maker could eventually reach $1.3 billion.[8]

However, it's not only New Agey tech companies that inspire this sort of behavior. In fact, the biggest corporate tax subsidy of them all was dished out to a good old-fashioned megamanufac-turer, Boeing, which wrung $8.7 billion out of Washington State. The justification for that heap of tax breaks in 2013—which don't even kick in until 2024—was that it would ensure Boeing would build a new jet, the 777X, there, as opposed to taking its produc-tion somewhere else. Boeing said it would "pursue other options" if the state legislature didn't play ball, a thinly veiled threat to take its airplanes, and therefore a slew of manufacturing jobs, else-where.[9]

"I don't feel like we're being blackmailed at all," said one Wash-ington lawmaker in response to the episode. But that *blackmail* was the word of the hour made it clear what was going on. Boeing essentially proclaimed, "Nice jobs you have there. Shame if any-thing were to happen to them." And Washington lawmakers paid up, afraid of what would result if they didn't.

This is how big corporations operate in modern-day America: They pit cities and states against one another in a battle to see who can dish out the most tax breaks, incentives, land grants, and other giveaways to an already-mammoth moneymaking organization. They initiate a race to the bottom, with the "winner" being the government that forgoes the most revenue for the longest time in return for, usually, nothing but promises. Companies hold their workforces for ransom and threaten to effectively kill them off by moving elsewhere, and lawmakers cave and pay up. And it happens because those lawmakers are unable to see past the immediate promise of jobs and income to the long-term costs of allowing corporate America to erode their area's tax base.

Meanwhile, the local media are often too understaffed, unequipped, or simply befuddled to explain what is going on, so they take corporate claims regarding job creation and economic superboosters at face value. The headlines and ribbon cuttings are the immediate payoff for those in power; the long-term costs are foisted onto the rest of us in the form of fewer services and more economic inequality. And almost no one follows up in subsequent years to see if anyone's promises have been kept, perpetuating the cycle.

Though the entertainment industry is one of the worst players in this cynical game, it's worth wrapping our arms around just how widespread the problem is, across a whole host of important American business sectors.

Estimates for how much state and local governments spend annually on corporate tax incentives vary. Timothy Bartik of the W. E. Upjohn Institute for Employment Research pegs the amount at $45 billion.[10] University of Missouri–St. Louis political scientist Kenneth Thomas put it at $65 billion in 2005.[11] In a 2012 investigation, Louise Story of *The New York Times* came up with a figure of $90 billion.[12] Since 1990, the amount of these incentives has roughly tripled.[13] Per Bartik, some 70 percent of what is doled out is property tax breaks—which usually directly undermine the education system—and job-creation tax credits.[14] That's, at a minimum, tens of billions of dollars dished out every single year that goes straight into corporate coffers.

None of these numbers likely capture the whole story, because navigating subsidies requires keeping tabs on thousands upon thousands of government agencies, offices, and officials, many of whom don't do an adequate job of tracking what they're handing out. That we have any sense of the scale at all is a testament to the yeoman's work of the academics and good-government types who wade into a swirl of documents, Web pages, and media reports to sort out what's what and which dollars are going where. But no matter which figure you go with, that's real money that could be spent on providing tons of other stuff for the taxpaying public.

Deals for Amazon, Tesla, and Boeing are the sort of high-profile examples that earn headlines and national media attention, that wind up penetrating cable news and Twitter. Every year, though, many smaller deals go through, in big cities and tiny towns alike, for new tech companies, old manufacturers, retailers, data centers, and more, as a grand competition to be more "business friendly" takes place in town halls, city council meetings, and economic development offices all across America, with an alphabet soup of agencies and programs dishing out money.

The process is usually pretty simple: A company professes a desire to move a plant, headquarters, or regional office from one place to another, promising to bring new jobs and other benefits. Politicians in the potential new locales who like the sound of those supposed benefits start wooing the company, while those in the company's current location who don't want to see headlines with the words *closes* or *job loss* in them panic and throw themselves into the fray to convince the company to stay. The companies hire lobbyists and site-relocation experts to ferret out the best deal and to talk up the benefits their clients will bring. And politicians can do a lot to not only throw fuel on the fire, but to light it in the first place.

Former Texas governor Rick Perry, for instance, famously launched job raids in other states, going on tour in places such as California to convince Golden State businesses to uproot themselves and move South. He would even cut radio ads to run in the state he was targeting, claiming that doing business anywhere but in Texas was akin to throwing your money down the sewer. "Building a business is tough, but I hear building a business in California is next to impossible. This is Texas Governor Rick Perry, and I have a message for California businesses. Come check out Texas," he said in one.[15]

When other states understandably took exception to what Perry was up to, he downplayed the tactic as "not a serious story." He said, "It's not a burp, it's barely a fart."[16] But it wasn't a burp or a fart; it was a deliberate strategy to get companies to move, and Perry had a big pot of incentive money he used to get them to do it. And he was often successful.

President Donald Trump, too, encouraged states to fight among themselves in this way. Post–2016 election but pre–Inauguration Day, Trump with much fanfare announced a package of incentives totaling $7 million that would supposedly keep the manufacturer Carrier from sending a bunch of Indiana jobs to Mexico. In remarks congratulating himself on the deal, he proclaimed that while international competition for jobs is bad, interstate competition is perfectly fine: "They can leave from state to state, and they can negotiate good deals with the different states and all of that."[17] (For the record, Carrier ended up sending a bunch of jobs to Mexico anyway.) "Today's announcement is possible because the incoming Trump-Pence administration has emphasized to us its commitment to support the business community and create an improved, more competitive U.S. business climate," said a statement from Carrier as the deal was announced. "The incentives offered by the state were an important consideration."[18]

I bet they were.

These are extreme examples from high-profile politicians. But Perry and Trump only took to eleven what just about every other official does: try to hoover up jobs from other places and deposit them in front of his or her voters. The competition is so intense that it is often dubbed "the second war between the states."

War metaphors, in fact, abound when it comes to this job poaching. To get a sense for just how absurd this game can get, consider what came to be known as the "Border War" in Kansas City. Since the city's metropolitan area straddles the state line between Missouri and Kansas, it gave companies the perfect opportunity to play the two states against each other.

So they did.

Within just a few years, AMC, J.P. Morgan Retirement Plan Services, and KeyBank Real Estate Capital moved from the Missouri side to the Kansas side of the border. Going the other way were the headquarters of Applebee's, North American Savings Bank, and the tech company Velociti.[19] One insurance firm—CBIZ—even moved from Missouri to Kansas and then back to Missouri. When asked whether the company could switch again, an executive predictably replied, "We would evaluate whatever makes the most sense for our employee base. We can say that you would never say no to anything."[20]

In just one five-year span, the Hall Family Foundation, a Kansas

City philanthropic organization, found that the two states had lost $217 million collectively in tax revenue thanks to the border-battle shenanigans.[21] Between 2010 and 2015, 5,702 jobs moved from Missouri to Kansas. And 3,998 went in the other direction.[22] In many instances, the same workers wound up keeping those jobs; they just had to change their commute to the office, crossing a border where before they had stayed on their own side of the state line.

In 2014, Missouri finally proposed a truce via legislation that would have prohibited subsidies to companies that were simply jumping the border. Kansas didn't respond with its own action for two years. Now the two states are not only fighting over jobs, they're fighting over how to stop fighting over jobs.

The border war is an extreme example, but this hopscotching of companies happens all over, all the time. New Hampshire poaches jobs from the Boston area. New Jersey and Connecticut poach them from New York City. Mississippi does it to Memphis. And on and on and on. It's the great jobs shuffle, the mixing and matching of jobs, places, and money that benefits no one but the companies that get to stick their metaphorical hand into the public trough and extract dollars, and the politicians who get to look good for doing nothing real.

Plenty of research has been done on the efficacy of corporate tax incentives, and the consensus is that they don't cause much economic effect. For CityLab, journalist Richard Florida worked with the Martin Prosperity Institute to examine the relationship between corporate incentives and state economic performance. Their finding: "There is virtually no association between economic development incentives and any measure of economic performance. We found no statistically significant association between economic development incentives per capita and average wages or incomes; none between incentives and college grads or knowledge workers;

and none between incentives and the state unemployment rate."[23] Timothy Bartik's research found the same thing, as he noted in a 2017 preliminary analysis: "Incentives do not have a large correlation with a state's current or past unemployment or income levels or with future economic growth."[24] As he put it in an earlier paper, "Most studies conclude that incentives are not cost-effective, either having no statistically significant effects or large costs per job created."[25]

Sure, there's some wiggle room here, as the data used to put together this research is often incomplete, but considering the amount of money we're talking about, real, tangible benefits should be a prerequisite for continuing down the same road. So far, not many have been found.

One study even finds that corporate tax incentives can backfire hard. In a 2002 paper, two Ohio researchers looked at the use of tax incentives in their state and found that "the average effect of incentives for establishments that received incentives is a decrease of 10.5 in the number of (actual) jobs created as compared to the number of (actual) jobs the establishment would have created without the incentive. The average establishment that received an incentive would have employed 457 workers two years after receiving the incentive compared to 467 workers if it had not received an incentive."[26]

That's right: Incentives were actually linked to fewer jobs in the establishments that received them than would have been created had those firms just been left to their own devices. However, the researchers also found that those firms receiving incentives announced more job creation than did the ones that received no money, even if those jobs never materialized in the real world. As the authors wrote, "These findings imply that establishments misrepresent their hiring plans to receive larger incentives from the government."[27] So publicity trumped reality. Fake job numbers thrown around in press releases received more attention and resources than actual positions with living, breathing workers.

Yes, this is just one study of one state from nearly two decades ago. But since then, there's been no slam-dunk refutation of the findings that corporate incentives don't do much of anything for the state in which they're used. Again, since we're talking about billions of dollars, the burden of proof should be on those who want to keep spending money that it's buying anything worth having. Thus far, there's precious little evidence that it has, and plenty of data to show that for all their dollars, cities and states are getting nothing but empty promises.

Incentives are so ineffective for two big reasons. The first is that taxes, for all the outsize attention paid to them by policymakers and business types, are still just a small part of the overall economic picture in any particular place. A host of other factors go into determining the business climate for an individual firm and whether it will expand or contract—regulations, the state of the local, national, and international economy, the state of that business's particular sector, what its competitors are doing, interest rates, other local, state, and federal policies, etc. Focusing only on taxes misses a whole lot. Oftentimes, conservative pundits and lawmakers act as if taxes are the be-all, end-all determinant of everybody's economic decision making, with a simple through line from "lower taxes" to "more economic growth and jobs." But it's nowhere near that easy.

So if taxes are only a small part of the equation for what a particular business does, then it stands to reason that focusing solely on taxes will result in lots of tax breaks being given for activity that a business would have undertaken even in their absence. And that's exactly what ends up happening: Tax incentives wind up "incentivizing" moves that companies would have made even if they hadn't received a dime, with companies creating or destroying jobs based on the same considerations that fostered the move, not any particular tax break.

Take the case of Toyota, one of the jewels in the crown of Rick Perry's Texas company-shopping effort. The carmaker received $40 million from the Lone Star State to consolidate three offices from around the country into one headquarters in the Dallas suburbs in 2013. It was the largest corporate tax break Texas had dealt out in a decade. And Toyota said afterward that the move would have made sense for the company even if those public dollars weren't on the table.

"That wasn't one of the major reasons [in] deciding to go to Texas," Toyota spokesperson Amanda Rice told the *Houston Chronicle* in the spring of 2014, referring to the subsidies. Instead, per the *Chronicle*, "company representatives referenced a host of other factors, including geography, time zone and quality of life."[28] Other executives echoed those comments. "It doesn't make sense to have oversight of manufacturing two thousand miles away from where the cars were made," one said. "Geography is the reason not to have our headquarters in California."[29]

Texas, in short, was an attractive place for Toyota to land for reasons that had nothing to do with taxes. Yet the company received a $40 million windfall anyway.

"I never made an investment decision based on the tax code," said former Alcoa CEO Paul O'Neill during his 2001 confirmation hearing to be US treasury secretary. "If you're giving money away, I'll take it. If you want to give me inducements for something I'm going to do anyway, I'll take it. But good businesspeople don't do things because of inducements."[30]

Amazon's search for its second headquarters is almost certainly going to end up the same way. The company has clearly outgrown Seattle and needs to land somewhere, and it will make that decision for a host of reasons, most of them having nothing to do with taxes. Economic and business necessity is driving the decision; tax breaks will just be some cherries on top.

Even if tax breaks were the deciding factor when it comes to corporate job creation, paying for them in the way that governments do is ridiculously inefficient. Lots of attempts have been made over the years to assess the cost per job created of the incentives used across the country, even though that number is often an imperfect way to consider such things (because the opportunity costs of what doesn't get paid for and the effects those investments might have had are often even more important). The results vary from a few thousand per job on the low end to as much as hundreds of thousands of dollars per position.[31] (Remember those film subsidies that were costing some $100,000 per job?)

Considering all of the above information, which is perfectly available to any official who wants to fire up a quick Google search, why are incentives still so ubiquitous? Are lawmakers falling for some Jedi mind trick pulled by savvy business executives? Are they simply desperate or overawed by the moment? Is Donald Trump's belief in the inability of public officials to make a good deal for the taxpayer true? Or is something more insidious at work, a too-cozy relationship between the stewards of public dollars and the titans of business?

For starters, these incentives persist partly because of the simple lack of transparency. It's often nigh impossible to track who is spending what on whom because government bodies either don't keep a comprehensive data set or do so somewhere that renders it inaccessible to all but the most dogged searchers. This allows politicians to cut sweetheart deals for corporate interests without letting the public in on the bad details.

One organization that has done its damnedest to change that is Good Jobs First, a DC-based team dedicated to tracking and highlighting how bad a deal corporate subsidies are, and pushing states to do a better job compiling and publicizing information regarding how much they're spending on whom.

Good Jobs First is housed in one of those nondescript office buildings that dot DC, just east of Dupont Circle and across from a little park and basketball court. You'd walk right by it if you weren't looking for it. When I visited, no one was in the office except for Greg LeRoy, the director, who has spent some thirty years working on subsidies and their ill effects. I awkwardly wandered down a hallway past some empty desks before finding him in the corner office, tapping away on his computer.

"I used to be a plant-closing activist. I backed into the issue of incentive abuse quite accidentally by trying to stop factory shutdowns in the Midwest," Leroy said. "We did lots of things to try to stop plant closings. We'd try to do worker buyouts, we'd try to do pressure campaigns to change companies' minds, and one thing we became known for was finding the public money—discovering whether or not the plant had gotten revenue bonds or tax abatements or whatever in the past." Because of previous jobs, "I sort of knew some of the alphabet soup and the concepts for the way things worked and where the information resided. I wasn't intimidated by the documents."[32]

One of the plants that LeRoy fought to keep open was the Diamond Tool and Horseshoe Company, in Duluth, Minnesota. The parent company for Diamond Tool—Connecticut's Triangle Tool Company—wanted to pick up shop and move to Spartanburg,

South Carolina, taking with it some equipment that had been financed by publicly backed bonds. The city sued, arguing that the company couldn't take its equipment out of the state under the terms of the funding it had received. And the city won.

"The reason we have the picture up there is we actually stopped the shutdown," LeRoy said, pointing to a framed photo flanked by a wrench and a horseshoe in his second-floor office. The wall on the other end of the office is covered in name tags and lanyards from his decades of speaking gigs. A T-shirt that says ECONOMIC DEVELOPMENT SUPER HERO, with ED within the Superman logo, is hanging nearby. "[Diamond] was at the time, in 1988, the biggest factory in Duluth, Minnesota. It employed more than three hundred people and the lawsuit stopped the shutdown, stopped it for six years until the bonds expired."

LeRoy wrote a book in 1994, *No More Candy Store*, detailing that and other fights relating to public subsidies. "I tried to say, 'Take my issue, please.' The whole point was 'I'm tired of copying the same files. Let me just put it all together in one place,'" LeRoy said. He thought that would be the end of it.

"I had lived all my adult life in Chicago at that point, and I moved back here to DC—I actually grew up near Tysons [Corner, Virginia]—and did some other things, went to work for a union, and thought I was going to do something else, but it kind of backfired because people would say, 'Well, you wrote the book. Why can't you take a day off to do this workshop? I have a bill I'd like you to look at,'" LeRoy said.

So Good Jobs First was born. Since it first got off the ground, the organization has been naming and shaming both states—into crafting better disclosures—and companies—for the shoddy job they do keeping the promises they make. In the last few decades, transparency has certainly improved, even if disclosures still leave a lot to be desired.

While lack of transparency aids lawmakers in doling out business incentives—because few know how bad the terms of the deals are except those happy few who benefit—it isn't the whole story. But the relative dearth of it helps on this next point: simple politics.

Politicians continue to dish out incentives, year after year, bad deal after bad deal, because the appearance of doing something to bring in jobs makes for good headlines for someone who is in elected office, and the cost can always be punted to the next person. What sounds good gets trumpeted while the downsides are buried.

"Politicians really do need to get reelected, so there really is a political value to issuing press releases and cutting ribbons and passing along the cost to your next three successors," LeRoy said when I asked him whether the root of bad business subsidies was as simple as lawmakers wanting a good headline and a photo op.

When it comes to politics, economists refer to what's known as the shortsightedness effect, the idea that political actors—politicians and voters alike—don't focus on the long term and therefore opt for policies that provide short-term benefits, but long-term costs. This principle is often cited to describe why governments don't balance budgets: It's too easy to put crowd-pleasing stuff on the credit card and leave the bill for someone else. (Let's leave for another time that the American polity—voters, lawmakers, and journalists alike—has an unhealthy rhetorical obsession with low deficits and debt, whether or not economic conditions actually warrant them.) There's also a collective action problem when it comes to specific subsidies: The company in pursuit of them has every interest in doing whatever it takes to secure its bounty, while opponents have diffuse interests and may not be particularly harmed by any one deal in a way that necessitates mass resistance. Since the subsidies are bad for the public at large in the aggregate, but beneficial for one interest group specifically, organizing to fight back is difficult.

Political scientist Nathan Jensen, currently at the University of Texas–Austin, has looked at corporate tax incentives and found that their use has an explicit political benefit. "A governor reaps more reward for new investment in his or her state if his or her administration offered tax incentives," he and three colleagues wrote in a 2013 study that looked at governors and whether their support was bolstered by the use of tax incentives to bring in new businesses. "In fact, a governor will be rewarded for offering tax incentives even if it does not succeed in luring the intended investment." The bonus with voters is even higher when the wooing fails. "Thus, whether or not the policy was effective, the incumbent gets credit (and votes) for trying. Few other policy actions by a governor can play so immediate a role," Jensen and company wrote.[33] Governors won politically just by playing the subsidy game, even if they didn't bring in the companies they wanted to bring in. Merely engaging was enough to convince voters that the governor in question was serious about job creation and economic opportunity.

This is true not only at the state level. "In a study of local governments, we learned more about official use of business incentives for electoral gain. We found that directly elected mayors, as opposed to appointed city managers, offered larger incentives and engaged in much weaker oversight of business incentive programs. Elected mayors offered more money and conducted fewer and less rigorous cost-benefit analyses to investigate whether the incentives were economically useful," Jensen wrote in 2016.[34] Electoral accountability really wasn't anything of the sort.

Another factor playing into the politics of incentives is that Americans are starting fewer businesses than they used to. In the 2010s, business start-ups hit rock bottom as the country emerged from the Great Recession, but that was only the culmination of a trend that has been occurring since the 1970s.[35] This decline in America's entrepreneurial spirit has inspired a lot of theories regarding its cause—some peg it to the decrease in robust antitrust enforcement, while others blame the regulatory state—but it's certainly happening. Fewer new businesses means fewer ribbon-cutting opportunities for lawmakers, so they're all fighting viciously over what's left and are willing to pay up for each opportunity.

"The supply of deals available for ribbon cuttings is permanently depressed. At the same time, obviously, that means you've got more politicians anxious to look aggressive on jobs, so you put those two things together and you've got a propensity to overspend. It makes it easier for Amazon and everybody else to do what they're doing," Greg LeRoy said.[36] The number of deals gets smaller, but the dollars thrown at them get bigger, so desperate are officials to show that they've captured some of what is becoming a more and more precious commodity.

Companies have also gotten more sophisticated in their pursuit, recognizing the dynamic at play. "Obviously, shrewd companies, ones that really come in for the big bucks, are not so dumb as to just go for the one cheap hit. They're now going to join the Chamber and sponsor a softball team and adopt a school and do the charitable stuff that big employers do sometimes, so the politicians, even when they're running for the next reelection, can point to that company and say, 'We're so proud to have 'em,'" LeRoy said.

Another example of the growing sophistication of companies is their ever-more extravagant claims for how the money they receive will help the wider community. It's as if they anticipated, well, books like this one and are doing what they can to make the opposite case. For instance, in the press materials for its second headquarters search, Amazon cited the work of the federal Bureau of Economic Analysis to bolster its claim that the company's investments have ripple effects in the economy.

"They are so ready to claim every fucking little ripple effect they can about this product. They're clearly ready to just run a total, full-court press messaging about everything they can claim," said Le-Roy.[37] Because local journalists are often too strapped for time or are ill-informed or are simply not willing to step on what sounds like a good story for the community, they often swallow whatever stats companies throw at them, simply regurgitating them onto the page devoid of context or analysis, even if they're utterly outlandish.

A lot of the companies I've brought up are very much symbols of modern America's business landscape: the internet giant, the jet manufacturer, the electric-car maker, the Japanese automaker. But corporate incentives are not a new invention in the United States. Their first use, most scholars say, was the 1791 offering of a property tax break in New Jersey to none other than founding father Alexander Hamilton, who was then US treasury secretary. His "Society for establishing useful Manufactures" was granted a ten-year tax exemption in what would become Paterson, New Jersey, because, per the legislature, "the granting [of] such Aid will be conducive to the Public Interest." To make it perfectly clear what was happening, the legislature proclaimed "that all Lands, Tenements, hereditaments, Goods and Chattels, to the said Society belonging, shall be and they are hereby declared to be free and exempt from all Taxes, Charges, and Impositions whatsoever under the Authority of this State, whether for State or County uses, or for any other Use whatsoever."[38] At the time, critics said that the law was "unjust," "arbitrary," and "injurious . . . to other states."[39]

The plan was mostly a flop, with the scale of factory activity Hamilton envisioned for Paterson never materializing.

So the more things change, the more they are the same. You might even say that, when it comes to corporate incentives, Hamilton was in the room where it happened.

By the 1800s, though, those other states that complained about Hamilton's unique break were themselves in on the act, with many of them directly subsidizing railroad companies as the country pushed the frontier westward. Pennsylvania, in particular, went gangbusters for corporate goodies, having spent some $100 million on private corporations by 1844. Both the Keystone State and Michigan made constitutional changes in the nineteenth century to try to cut off such cozy business-government arrangements.[40]

But the first real boom time for business incentives was the 1930s and their aftermath, as the nation tried to claw its way out of the depths of the Great Depression. Mississippi, at the time the poorest and most economically underdeveloped state in the nation, wanted to kick-start its moribund and largely agriculture-based economy. To that end, Columbia, Mississippi, Mayor Hugh White successfully ran for governor in 1935 on the pledge to "balance agriculture with industry." As mayor, he had lured the Reliance Manufacturing Company to town with a promise to help build its plant, and he applied that template to the whole state.

In 1936, Mississippi passed the Mississippi Industrial Act, which allowed its cities and the state to use bonds to bring new plants south, supported by a commission that vetted projects and presented them to the public for voter approval. These bonds were exempt from both federal income tax and property taxes and resulted in a parade of northern plants moving away.[41] Tennessee, Kentucky, and Alabama quickly emulated the program, and by the 1960s most of the South was using forms of the same strategy.[42]

This captured the ire of northern lawmakers, of course, who didn't like seeing their manufacturing base decamping for southern climes. Senator John F. Kennedy of Massachusetts decried the "raiding" of northern industry by the South. "Instead of utilizing their municipal bonding privileges for public works and the protection of the people from disaster and disease," said Kennedy, "the southerners put up streamlined mills which various cities and towns rented for almost unbelievably small amounts to bargain-hunting individuals up north. This naturally enabled the fugitives to pare down their tax bills and to slash their operating costs so drastically that they could undersell their northern competitors in the domestic and foreign markets."[43] Congress took a whack at regulating the mess in the late sixties, but by the 1980s, corporate subsidies were again out of control, followed by a threefold boom in their amount between the 1990s and today, when we're still discussing whether the Texas governor's raiding California for jobs is kosher.

The practice of governments in the United States trying to steal jobs from one another, then, is as old as America itself.

But all this shifting, moving, uprooting, and shifting again isn't creating anything new. It just shuffles jobs from one place to another. Moving a job from Texas to California hasn't created a new job; it's just taken one away from a Californian and given it to a Texan or forced a Californian to move to Texas to keep her position. They're still all Americans, working in America. Poaching from another place may make one politician look good, but it's a zero-sum game for the country as a whole. One locale's gain is another's explicit loss. In the aggregate, the nation and the wider economy haven't gained a thing. When he went shopping for jobs in other states, Rick Perry wasn't creating anything new or promoting economic activity that would be self-sustaining; he was just expending resources to move economic activity from other states to his own.

Maybe you want to argue that that's a healthy way for an economy to operate, but I see nothing noble in beggaring one place to boost another considering we're all living in one country. All the money expended in pursuit of jobs from somewhere else could be spent on providing services such as education that actually add to the economic pot.

Plus, whatever promises companies receive can have side effects that hurt the wider community, above and beyond the money that it loses when politicians give it away to corporate concerns. For instance, Perry and other Texas lawmakers attempted to woo Huy Fong Foods, Inc., the makers of sriracha sauce, that red stuff in the clear plastic bottles. One of the company's facilities in California was criticized for its fumes, which residents alleged were making them sick. Sensing opportunity, the Texans rode in and portrayed the whole affair as an unfair burden upon American businesses, promising that the company would face no such adversity down South. Said one, "When you start to overburden the creators of jobs, ultimately the creators of jobs have to consider alternatives."[44]

The city eventually dropped its case against the factory. But if the fumes from the Irwindale sriracha factory had been making residents sick, the town had not only the right but the responsibility to regulate. Texas, meanwhile, was sending the message that companies should move to the Lone Star State, suggesting there they'd be free to operate without consequences in the name of job creation. Jobs *über alles,* or something.

This sort of thing happens all the time when lawmakers pitch companies about coming to a new location: Not only do they promise money, but that environmental reviews will be waived or regulatory hurdles lowered. So residents lose several times over: Their tax money gets spent on things that don't support the entire community, and they may have to sacrifice their health or the environment, too, as companies are allowed to cut corners so long as they bring those precious jobs. Never mind that holding down a job is difficult if you're sick or your community is rendered impossible to live in.

One final ancillary problem with the jobs shuffle is that it breeds corruption. Again, using Texas as the example, a state audit in 2014 found that companies were often not even formally applying for the funds they received; the governor's office had sole discretion over the disbursement of tax breaks and simply handed them out to allies and business associates. Just a few years earlier, Iowa's film credit program was beset by a scandal that looked remarkably similar, leading to a slew of criminal charges.[45] The head of Louisiana's film credit program was even sentenced to two years of jail time for accepting bribes from film producers.[46] The American Dream mall, which you'll read about more in a coming chapter, also has all sorts of shady connections, raising questions about whether all those public goods that the public is purchasing are really quite so public after all.[47]

Per a study done by the Kansas City Federal Reserve, business tax incentives and corruption actually go hand in hand. "Cities and counties in states with troubled political cultures demonstrate the greatest willingness to offer business development incentives," researchers Alison Felix and James R. Hines Jr. wrote in 2011, "the evidence indicating that increasing the rate at which government officials are convicted of federal corruption crimes by 1 per 100,000 residents over a 13 year period is associated with a 2.9 percent greater chance that a community will offer business incentives."[48] More business incentives quite literally have a quantitative relationship with how many officials wind up getting nailed for corruption. As incentives goes up, so does the chance some official will end up doing some hard time.

It's easy to see why this would be: Business incentives are firm specific, so specific firms have a vested interest in obtaining them, making cozy arrangements with lawmakers all too easy. And the numbers thrown around in these deals are getting bigger and bigger and bigger.

So transparency and disclosure requirements have been getting better in recent years; it's not as if all the effort put into them by the advocates and academics out there has been totally for naught. Yet the political dynamic is leading to bigger, more destructive deals. Activists are playing whack-a-mole with the problems incentives create.

"Two things are true, and they're kind of hard for some people to keep in their head. We have a lot more transparency, clawbacks are a lot more common, job-quality standards are much more common," Greg LeRoy said. "Yet and but, we get this crazy megadeal trend and these crazy public auctions that make it sound like every mayor's a trained seal."

Why? "Because there is federalism. There is no leadership at the national level."

Indeed, national leaders have done nothing to end the economic war between the states. Some elected officials such as Trump even egg it on.

Back in the 1990s, the Minneapolis Fed senior vice president and director of research Arthur Rolnick, along with his colleague Melvin Burstein, wrote that the only way to end the corporate incentive scourge was for Congress to come in and bigfoot the whole thing, stopping the states from running amok; the national legislature needed to be the parent reining in its fifty annoying kids. "The powers granted to Congress under the Constitution enable it to fashion the legislative tools necessary to prevent the states from using subsidies and preferential taxes to attract and retain businesses," they wrote. "For example, Congress could tax the receiving business on the direct and imputed value of these benefits, it could deny tax-exempt status on debt of states that offer such subsidies, or it could deny federal funding that would otherwise be payable to such states, much as it denies highway funds to states that fail to meet federal pollution standards."[49]

In congressional testimony in 2007, some twelve years after his original piece appeared, Rolnick was still making the same case. "Only Congress, with its sweeping constitutional powers, particularly under the Commerce Clause, has the ability to end this economic war among the states," he said.[50] Because the Commerce Clause of the Constitution gives federal lawmakers the ability to regulate interstate business, Rolnick's argument went, they had the power to cut off the subsidy game at the knees.

Is there any reason to think this will actually happen, though? No; in the intervening years, no progress has been made on that front. Tax reform at the federal level is one of the hardest possible legislative tasks because of the many and varied interests all fighting to have the code favor them over their competitors. There's a reason the 1986 tax reform is still held up, more than three decades later, as the pinnacle of Washington deal making. The much-vaunted 2017 tax bill, which you'll read more about in a later chapter, didn't do anything to fix the problems of states whacking one another in doling out tax breaks to private businesses. The only positive effect you could say that bill had on the issues in this book is that, by cutting the federal corporate tax rate as low as it did, the new law made it slightly less important that companies minimize their state taxes, too, since they're paying so little already. Considering how rarely lawmakers at the national level delve into corporate taxation at all—and since most of the energy in the coming years will presumably be spent on battling over reversing or preserving the changes made in 2017—I wouldn't hold my breath on a concerted effort being made anytime soon at the federal level to rein in the warring states.

At the state and local level, things don't look too much better. Several times states have tried to form compacts pledging that they won't poach businesses from one another. But those deals have fallen apart every time as soon as one of the lawmakers involved sees an offer he or she feels can't be refused. As Rolnick explained when pitching a national solution, "As long as a single state engages in this practice, others will feel compelled to compete. New York, New Jersey, and Connecticut all recognized that they were losing from this competition, and in 1991 they informally agreed to stop competing with each other. It was not long, however, before New Jersey broke the deal." Just like it started the ball rolling with Hamilton, Jersey found a way to short-circuit a solution, as insufficient as it may have been.

It's a classic dilemma: The only way the game stops is if every lawmaker agrees to stop playing, and all it takes is one to break the pact for the whole thing to start all over again.

"I often thought, as governor, it would be sort of nice if all the governors just got together and said, 'Look, we're just not going to play this anymore,'" former Wisconsin governor Jim Doyle told NPR.[51] But that never happens. The political pull is too strong and the benefits too beneficial for an individual lawmaker to take a stand. And it's not as if many politicians have gotten credit for the things they didn't do while in office, even if those non-actions were the right thing. Just try to imagine the press release: "Re-elect me because I didn't blow your money on Company X when I had the chance."

Hope and change, that ain't, except to the wonks and budget analysts who study these things.

Eventually, Amazon is going to land its second headquarters somewhere. Lawmakers in Maryland offered it $8.5 billion in incentives and other goodies; New Jersey offered $7 billion. Others decided that they would let Amazon decide how local tax revenue would be spent, outsourcing one of the core government functions to a private corporation. Most cities that bid on HQ2 never even bothered to make their offers public, meaning that CEO Jeff Bezos and his crew knew more about how your money would be spent to woo the company than you did. Barring some big last-minute reversal, Amazon's corporate leadership is going to wind up with a sweet deal to pocket. After that, some other company is going to pull the same trick, launching a bidding war between cities, igniting the next battle in the economic battle between the states, the shot and countershot that, as in so many wars, has accomplished little. And it'll go on and on until every party involved finally feels as if they have nothing left to lose by surrendering.

4

DON'T GO FOR GOLD: IT'S A WASTE TO HOST THE OLYMPICS OR THE WORLD CUP

#NoBoston2024. That's how it started.

Boston, Massachusetts, seemed like a slam dunk to host the 2024 Summer Olympics. Symbolically, having the games in the city that had been victimized by the Boston Marathon bombing would prove the Olympics could still act as a symbol of unity and peace in the face of international turmoil. The United States hasn't hosted the summer games since 1996, a long stretch of time to keep them out of such a large, lucrative market. And Boston already had many of the facilities deemed necessary for pulling off such a huge, complex event, as well as a storied sports history and fanatical fans. There could scarcely be a better story for the US Olympic Committee to tell the International Olympic Committee, the body that would ultimately decide where the next games would reside.

But the city's residents had other ideas.

Led by a committed group of activists, Bostonians themselves scuttled the city's bid, claiming that the supposed benefits playing Olympic host would bring were not worth the money Boston would have to spend. An effective campaign, with the ubiquitous social media hashtag #NoBoston2024, bled support among those who live in Boston and would have had to deal with the game's effects. What had been a momentary majority in favor of hosting soon turned into a permanent minority; the city's leaders who had supported the bid were left flailing, trying to justify the necessary infrastructure investments, security, and other extraneous costs sure to crop up when the games came to town. Mayor Marty Walsh was forced to acknowledge that the concerns Bostonians had about the bid needed to be addressed before it could go forward, even as he was deriding those raising questions as "about ten people on Twitter and a couple people out there who are constantly beating the drumbeat."[1]

But it was clearly much more than that. "We always felt opposition was going to have to come from the grassroots level, from citizens," said Chris Dempsey, one of the cofounders of No Boston 2024, the organization whose name also topped the movement itself. And despite boosters outspending opponents $1,500 to $1, come it did.[2]

Finally, an embarrassed US Olympic Committee backpedaled and pushed a last-second bid from Los Angeles instead, citing a lack of support among Boston residents as their prime reason for the switch.

"Boston is a world-class city. We are a city with an important past and a bright future. We got that way by thinking big, but also thinking smart," said No Boston 2024 in a statement once the final curtain had come down on Boston's bid. "We need to move forward as a city, and Monday's decision [to revoke Boston's bid] allows us to do that on our own terms, not the terms of the USOC or the IOC. We're better off for having passed on Boston 2024."[3]

Here's the thing: The No Boston folks are absolutely right.

The modern Olympics have morphed into an orgy of waste, spending, and unfulfilled promises. For their investment, which is oftentimes astronomical, cities get few tangible benefits. They're sold the illusion of economic prosperity and urban rebirth and instead receive a large bill and a bunch of infrastructure projects that may not be worth the cost or ever used again.

For the World Cup, soccer's premier event and the only other international sporting competition comparable to the Olympics, it's the same story, with FIFA, the Fédération Internationale de Football Association, playing the role of the IOC: $3 billion was spent by South Africa to host the tournament in 2010, which grew to $15 billion in Brazil in 2014. The stadiums that these countries built stand as testaments not to their countries coming out on the world stage, but the folly of agreeing to host the World Cup in a place not yet having the necessary infrastructure.

Much of this cost is foisted onto the taxpaying public; while the International Olympic Committee and local governments like to make noise that they are paying for the games with private funds, costs inevitably spill onto the government's ledger; at the minimum, taxpayers wind up on the hook for infrastructure and security.[4] Those infrastructure projects run the gamut, from building the facilities needed to host, such as the Olympic stadium, pool, ski jump, or any of the other myriad things necessary to actually house the events, to transportation projects that even a major city requires to deal with a short-term influx of athletes, journalists, officials, and spectators. That's where costs inevitably explode. And per the Faustian bargain cities make with the IOC, they themselves are held responsible for any budget overruns. Toss in that corporations operating in and around the games receive a host of tax breaks—and are often exempt from taxation entirely—and taxpayers lose twice: They pay to host, then don't even receive the tax revenue that would have been raised from the event because the IOC insists on letting its corporate sponsors operate in a tax-free bubble.

When it comes to international sporting events, concerns over cost are not new. Pierre de Coubertin, the founder of the modern Olympic games, said back in 1911, "It would be very unfortunate if the often exaggerated expenses incurred for the most recent Olympiads were to deter countries from putting themselves forward to host the Olympic Games in the future."[5] Little did he know, presumably, how prescient those comments would be. Coubertin himself set a precedent by lowballing the costs of the first modern Olympics—the 1896 games in Athens, Greece—estimating that the entire spectacle would cost three times less than what was necessary to refurbish the Olympic stadium alone. The Greek prime minister, Charilaos Trikoupis, was also ahead of his time, balking at the public cost of hosting and forcing the organizers to scramble for private funds. If only his example had been followed more closely in the decades ahead.[6]

First, though, it should be noted that talking about the cost of an individual Olympics can be dangerous territory. Oftentimes budgets aren't published, costs are disputed, and it's difficult to untangle sports-related costs from other expenditures meant to improve transit, parks, or other public goods—and boosters would often prefer the latter not be counted toward the total. For many of the earliest editions of the games, budgets don't exist at all.[7] The task is further complicated by budget opacity in such places as Russia and China, as well as by currency fluctuations and inflation. I've gone with the best estimates for each location that I can find, but bear in mind that guesswork is going on even then, and that costs are not necessarily comparable on an apples-to-apples basis. I'd argue that most estimates of public spending on games in the

United States lowball the public expense, failing to factor in at least some of the ways taxpayers supported the effort. And that's how everyone involved wants it.

There's little doubt, though, that the pinnacle for Olympic spending has been reached in recent years. The Beijing 2008 summer games, at some $40 billion, shattered the on-paper record; but China wasn't on top of that dubious list for long, thanks to Russia, which reportedly spent more than $50 billion on the 2014 Sochi Winter Olympics as it turned a favorite location of President Vladimir Putin's that had little business hosting into an artificially bustling metropolis. These two are outliers—and we'll revisit why later in this chapter—but it's definitely the case that the costs of hosting have climbed dramatically in the last thirty years. Calgary spent less than $1 billion to host the 1988 winter games; the Moscow summer games eight years earlier, in US dollars, barely peaked above $1 billion. Prior to the 1980s, it was rare, though not unprecedented, to see costs climb into the billions for a host city.

Yet now, *billion* is a mainstay of the Olympic budget, even with the concurrent opacity: Sochi and Beijing aside, London spent nearly $15 billion in 2012, Vancouver eclipsed $6 billion in 2010, Athens blew through $9 billion in 2004, and Rio de Janeiro, Brazil, spent some $12 billion in 2016.

In the United States, the 1996 Atlanta summer games cost about $2.2 billion officially, though some analysts say that ignores another $2 billion in public costs, including $226 million in state funds and $857 million in local funds.[8] Other estimates put the combined state and local expenditures at as high as $1.58 billion.[9] The US Government Accountability Office (GAO)—the government's official bookkeeper and fiscal oversight body, which was then known as the General Accounting Office—in 2000 pegged the cost to just the federal government, not the state or local bodies, of the Atlanta games at $609 million in 1999 dollars. Of that, about $185 million was direct financial support for the staging of the games, including $96 million for security-related services, while the other $424 million was for infrastructure projects that may or may not have happened anyway. Some $56 million was spent directly on Olympic venues, including $22 million to build the Ocoee Whitewater slalom venue. Even federal money that would have been spent in Georgia anyway received priority funding and an accelerated schedule due to the games.[10]

For Salt Lake City in 2002, the GAO pegged the cost to the federal government before the games were even finished at about $1.3 billion, $342 million of which was spent on direct staging of the event. A healthy chunk of that was on security at these first post-9/11 games to take place in the States.[11] The state of Utah spent an estimated $150 million, while local governments spent $75 million.[12]

The US federal government picked up half the tab for the 1980 Winter Olympics in Lake Placid, New York—the games that provided us with the "Miracle on Ice," when the US ice hockey team defeated the heavily favored Soviet Union on its way to a gold medal—costing at the time an almost-reasonable-sounding $363 million. The state of New York kicked in another $63 million for venue construction.[13] And even unsuccessful bids have a cost: Chicago spent some $70 million on its effort to win the 2016 games, which left some egg on President Barack Obama's face when Rio de Janeiro emerged the winner instead.[14]

What did these cities and nations buy with this money? As with many *mega-events*—which is what economists call large, regularly scheduled events that cities, states, or nations undertake—the story told to the public is that they are purchasing economic development, increased tourism, and an infomercial on the world stage that will affect the host for years to come. The Olympics and the World Cup are hyped as a can't-miss opportunity that will have positive ripple effects throughout an economy.

Before the games, as cities are duking it out in the long, protracted bidding process, boosters toss around huge numbers as to the benefits the host city will accrue, one-upping each other every cycle in a sadly predictable spectacle. Boston was supposedly going to see a $5 billion economic boost from the games.[15] One estimate has Japan seeing a $250 billion benefit from the 2020 games in Tokyo.[16] The projected impact of the South Africa World Cup in 2010—at $6 billion—was more than 4 percent of the country's entire GDP. As the games get bigger and more extravagant, so do the promises regarding the upside to the hosts. The numbers are so large that they make passing on a hosting bid seem ludicrous, the equivalent of shooting oneself in the foot with a biathlon rifle.

But economist Jeffrey Owen said there's a problem here: Efforts to assess the impact of the Olympics after the event has happened "have consistently found no evidence of positive economic impacts from mega-sporting events even remotely approaching the estimates in economic impact studies." "The simple elegance of economic impact studies, injections of money circulating over and over in an economy to create a multiplier effect, has an alluring 'something-for-nothing' quality that is hard to refute," he said.[17] However, refuting them can be done.

The biggest issue when talking about the effect of the Olympics, World Cup, or any other large event, sporting or otherwise, is with what economists call the substitution effect. This stems from the theory that says consumers will replace buying apples that have gotten too expensive with pears, or some other similar product, which has effects for producers in traditional economic modeling.

When it comes to mega-events, accounting for the substitution effect means trying to figure out whether money spent on an event—in the form of tickets purchased, hotel rooms filled, restaurant tabs fought over, etc.—is new spending that wouldn't have occurred otherwise or spending that simply got shifted from something else to the mega-event, benefiting the latter while hurting the former.

As economist Victor Matheson put it, "The substitution effect occurs when consumers spend money at a mega-event rather than on other goods and services in the local economy."[18] For instance, if instead of going to the movies or a fancy dinner, someone decides to go to a sporting event, no new economic activity has been created. Consumer spending has simply gone from benefiting the movie theater or restaurateur to benefiting whoever profits from the sporting event. Not accounting for money that would have been spent in the local economy anyway—i.e., counting every cent spent at the Olympics or World Cup as a net benefit for the community as if it all occurred in a giant vacuum and without said sporting event the streets of a city would resemble something out of a postapocalyptic zombie flick—leads to some of the outlandish economic promises made in pregame analyses.

Problem number two coincides with problem number one. "Crowding out" is the failure to account for the spending or tourism that would have occurred but didn't due to the mega-event itself. Perhaps call it the hassle effect: People who would have visited a city or country don't because they would prefer not to deal with the crowds associated with the Olympics or a World Cup. Ever considered going to a particular bar or restaurant but then decided not to because "that place will probably be packed"? That's the effect we're talking about, on a grander scale.

In 2002, for instance, hotel occupancy rates and the number of passengers arriving in the airport didn't increase in Salt Lake City from previous years, despite its hosting of the Winter Olympics, indicating that perhaps as many tourists were scared away from the city as enticed to visit.[19] That same year, in South Korea, the number of European visitors coming in for the World Cup was directly offset by a decrease in the usual number of Japanese visitors.[20] The crowding-out effect is not limited to the few weeks during which a sporting event takes place. The European Tour Operators Association in a 2006 report found that hotel occupancy rates actually declined in Atlanta and Sydney when the Olympics came to town, compared to years in which they weren't playing host.

"During the Olympics, a destination effectively closes for normal business," the report said. "Both tourists and the tour operators that supply them are scared off immediately before and during the events. This 'absence' then creates its own effect, as the normal conveyor belt of contented customers begetting new arrivals has been broken."[21] In Atlanta, hotel occupancy rates fell from 72 percent in 1995 to 68 percent in 1996, the year it played host.[22] During the 2006 World Cup in Germany, the year-over-year utilization of available hotel accommodations fell from the year before by more than 10 percent in both Berlin and Munich.[23] Far from a mega-event-induced influx, these places wound up with tourism deficits.

This, again, is an issue that dates backs to the first modern games in Athens: *The New York Times* reported at the time that many Athens tourists "abstained from going . . . intentionally delaying their visit to Athens till after the termination of the games."[24]

Retailers often report a similar phenomenon. A spike in sales may occur during the games themselves, but an absence of tourists is seen before and after, because visitors who usually come to a place avoid the pregames hoopla and the postevent cleanup, saving their trip there for another year. Anecdotal evidence from London in 2012 backs up this idea: Retailers saw a boost around the time of the games, but it was more than offset by declines during the weeks surrounding the festivities, as the city's usual stream of shoppers declined to come out of a fear of a rather large hassle. "Go and interview a restaurateur in central London near Piccadilly or go and interview a theatre manager in central London about how their business was in central London in August 2012 [during the Summer Olympics] and they'll say, 'It was awful. It was like the Great Depression,'" said economist Andrew Zimbalist.[25]

Two other factors that complicate the story regarding an economic bonanza caused by big sporting events are worth mentioning. The first is what German economist Wolfgang Maennig has termed the couch-potato effect: people from a local population staying home to watch an event with friends or by themselves, thereby limiting their spending from its usual baseline. Adding a tourist but encouraging two locals to stay home, cook, and watch a World Cup game on television rather than going out to eat or watching their local soccer club's game from a nearby pub incurs both a benefit and a cost to the local economy, but most analyses don't attempt to grapple with the latter, treating the new tourist's money as a benefit with no cost.

That's not to imply it's necessarily a bad thing for the local population to have something worth staying home to watch. "The couch potato effect can be interpreted in a more optimistic, positive way. What better fun can you have as, let's say, a soccer fan, a football fan, than to invite friends who bring a six-pack and some potatoes and watching the game together," Maennig said. "It's much more fun than going out and having dinner, for example. . . . Indeed, the World Cup is positive, but it does not imply additional spending."[26]

The other factor is what's known as time switching, in which consumers merely alter their pattern of consumption to a different moment, instead of changing it entirely, but still adding no net benefit to the economy. This principle affects all sorts of questions regarding economic consumption patterns—usually having to deal with tax breaks and whether they induce new purchases or merely cause people to buy things they would have bought anyway, but at a different time, in order to take advantage of the break—and mega-events are no exception. Is that Olympic visitor to Paris really a new visitor who would have not come at all in the absence of the Olympics, or merely someone who would have come to the city anyway, but shifted her visit forward a month to see the event? If it's the latter, was their benefit to the local economy a result of the Olympics or not? Most boosters fail to acknowledge this effect, treating every visitor to a mega-event as if he or she would never have come if not for the event itself.

Finally, those leakages that plagued the movie and hotel chapters need to be taken into account. When talking about the effects of hosting the Olympics and the World Cup, this is of paramount concern, since many of the corporations responsible for organizing the events aren't locally based. For instance, does a Coca-Cola sold at the stadium hosting a World Cup game benefit the local economy or Coke's corporate bottom line in Atlanta, where it's based? Wouldn't it have been more beneficial for the economy for that Coke purchaser to buy a drink in a local pub instead?

So that's the theory behind why the numbers tossed around about mega-events should be taken with large grains of salt. And study after study backs up the theoretical. Researchers have futilely searched for some sort of ex post facto macroeconomic impact on a city or nation from either the World Cup or the Olympics, all in vain. As Jeffrey Owen wrote, "To date there has not been a study of an Olympics or other large-scale sporting event that has found empirical evidence of significant economic impacts."[27] He added that, when it comes to finding such an impact, "it is unlikely anyone ever will."

In 2012, researcher Samantha Edds took a look at three relatively recent Olympic games that were considered huge successes—those in Atlanta, Sydney, and Barcelona—and found that, compared to similar cities within each host city's country, the hosts themselves saw little to no impact in three sectors that would be considered ripe for mega-event benefits: construction, tourism, and financial services. In fact, the control cities—she used Charlotte, Melbourne, and Madrid, respectively—often saw greater GDP growth during the Olympics than did their hosting counterparts.[28] "It seems constituents, developers, hotels, and those who stand to make a profit (according to economic impact studies) should not take study numbers at face value that promise vast amounts of extra profit garnered by hosting the Games," she wrote. During the 1994 World Cup, cities in the United States that hosted games actually saw a net reduction in incomes, instead of the promised boost. Having World Cup games in town was the ultimate economic own goal, to use the soccer phrase.

This jibes with a host of other research finding that the Olympics and World Cup provide little to no benefits across a host of indicators: employment, incomes, GDP, you name it. At best, the games provide a sugar high for a few weeks. Victor Matheson and economist Robert Baade found that, in both the Los Angeles and Atlanta examples, a high percentage of the jobs created—and new jobs is one of the many benefits that boosters love to say will come to the host city—were simply temporary and transitory: They came and went, leaving no real economic development behind. Long term, the two economists believe it's possible that the games created job loss once the opportunity costs of spending on the games is factored in—i.e., what else the money dedicated to the Olympics could have been spent on.[29]

"The bottom line is, every time we've looked—dozens of scholars, dozens of times—we find no real change in economic activity," said economist Philip Porter.[30]

While the benefits of playing host are mostly a mirage, the costs are very, very real. According to research by Bent Flyvbjerg, Allison Stewart, and Alexander Budzier at the Saïd Business School at the University of Oxford, Olympics hosts overrun their budgets by an average of 156 percent.[31] Going over budget is pretty much a given. "The Games overrun with 100 percent consistency," the first two authors wrote in an earlier working paper. "No other type of mega-project is this consistent regarding cost overrun. Other project types are typically on budget from time to time, but not the Olympics."[32]

The poster child for the risks of playing host is Montreal, site of the 1976 Summer Olympics, which bested subsequent hosts Moscow and Los Angeles in the bidding to win Canada's first Olympics. Prior to hosting, Montreal Mayor Jean Drapeau said, "The Montreal Olympics can no more have a deficit than a man can have a baby." That turned out to be, well, not right.

According to Flyvbjerg and Stewart, Montreal overran its budget by 796 percent. What was supposed to be a cost in the hundreds of millions of dollars ballooned to $1.6 billion, then a record.[33] At the center of the boondoggle was the Olympic stadium, nicknamed the Big O due to its shape. Cost overruns and labor strife prompted the government of Quebec province to ultimately swoop in to help the overwhelmed city get it constructed.

The Big O wasn't even completed at the time of the 1976 opening ceremonies; when it was finally finished, the stadium was the second most expensive sporting venue in the world. But even worse were the long-term costs. The city didn't fully pay off the bonds for the Big O, which were covered via a special tax on tobacco, until 2006, three decades after the games had come and gone, prompting residents to give it the moniker the Big Owe instead.[34] Montreal's fiscal escapades left only Los Angeles to bid on the 1984 Olympics, which is considered perhaps the most economically successful and sensible games ever, for reasons I'll revisit later.

Montreal's cost debacle matters for two reasons. First, it highlights something that all host cities have experienced: the initial estimate for the cost of the games is too low, and often by a lot. In the United States, the percentage overruns for Lake Placid, Atlanta, and Salt Lake City were 321 percent, 147 percent, and 29 percent, respectively—and that's just for directly sports-related costs, not any ancillary stuff.[35] Those overruns can have budgetary impacts for cities for a long, long time. Second, every dollar that Montreal spent over three decades servicing the debt incurred from 1976 was one less dollar it could have spent on all the other things a city does. Money raised from taxing tobacco, which Montreal resorted to, could have, for instance, been put into smoking-cessation programs or health care. Instead, it went to pay for a stadium.

In Montreal's defense, at least that stadium was still used for a while. It was the home of Major League Baseball's Montreal Expos until they up and quit the city to move to Washington, DC, and become the Nationals in 2005, as noted earlier, picking on DC taxpayers for some $700 million. Other Olympic venues were reimagined as tourist attractions, including the velodrome, which was converted into what is now the Montreal Biodome. Other hosts, though, aren't so lucky in their ability to repurpose slightly used Olympic venues.

Take, for instance, Athens, host of the 2004 summer games. The Athens games cost some $11 billion, a figure that doesn't even include upgrades to the city's airport and metro system.[36] (Law-makers constantly highlight improvements in transportation infra-structure as a benefit of hosting the games, as if spending money on transit is impossible in the absence of spending even more on unrelated sporting facilities, which is obviously not the case. Just invest in transportation for the sake of making your own residents' commutes better!) Today, the sporting facilities in Athens sit empty and rotting as the country remains mired in the depths of a fiscal crisis to which, some analysts say, unfettered spending on the Olympics contributed.

Instead of using the money spent on the Athens games on more productive uses, it went toward white elephants—projects that were expensive and, while momentarily useful, have been rendered a burden by the passage of time. The term *white elephant* derives, supposedly, from stories that kings of Siam would give courtiers they disliked gifts of literal white elephants, so as to bury them with the expenses necessary for keeping the animal alive.

American cities are not immune to such things, either: Atlanta's $20 million tennis venue at Stone Mountain, used in 1996, has been abandoned and looted; efforts in recent years to rehabilitate it have gone nowhere.[37] In 2018, Pyeongchang, South Korea, which hosted that year's winter games, came up with a rather novel solu-tion to this particular problem: use its $109 million Olympic sta-dium four times and then simply tear it down.[38]

It's fairly obvious why the white elephant problem plagues the

Olympics: The sort of sports involved don't garner much attention in non-Olympic years. How often does a city need a world-class velodrome or ski jump? Hardly ever. Even cities in which much of the infrastructure to host the games already exists—a popular notion when it comes to bids from places such as Washington, DC, or New York City—still need to build facilities for more obscure sports that will have to be transformed into something else later or, like those in Athens, be left to rot.

Perhaps less obvious, though, is the trouble with the World Cup. After all, soccer is the most popular sport in the world. But the stain of its premier tournament has affected several countries, and two in particular: South Africa and Brazil.

For starters, just as with the Olympics, there's little evidence that the World Cup provides any lasting economic benefits to the host nation. (Remember, the World Cup takes place at sites throughout a country, unlike the Olympics, which all takes place in one city.) South Africa recouped only a fraction of its costs to host the 2010 World Cup, the first on the African continent.[39] And that's not an outlier. The 2006 tournament in Germany provided no boost to the country's economy, according to Wolfgang Maennig, the German economist.[40] Economists Matheson and Baade found that American cities hosting the 1994 World Cup actually "experienced cumulative losses of $5.5 to $9.3 billion as opposed to ex ante estimates of a $4 billion gain touted by event boosters." They added, "Potential hosts should consider with care whether the award of the World Cup is an honour or a burden."[41]

At least, though, in cases such as the United States and Germany, there is demand for the sort of stadiums required to host the event. In the United States, NFL stadiums work just fine. (The 1994 World Cup is still the most attended tournament in World Cup history.) European countries have no shortage of world-class soccer stadiums due to the huge demand for their domestic-league games—a place such as Germany or England can, in theory, host a World Cup on the cheap, without constructing new stadiums. That's one of the justifications for the successful joint 2026 US-Mexico-Canada bid, jokingly referred to as the NAFTA World Cup: All of the necessary stadiums are already in place, circumventing some of the white elephant concerns.

The same can't be said, though, of a place such as South Africa, where the stadiums used to such fanfare during the tournament now stand empty. South Africa built five new stadiums for the event, at a cost of nearly $2 billion. One of them, Cape Town Stadium, which cost $600 million, is losing an estimated $6 million to $10 million per year while hosting Ajax Cape Town, a team that draws about four thousand spectators per game into the fifty-five-thousand-seat facility. The same story repeats itself across the country, with local teams coming nowhere close to filling the soccer palaces they play in.[42]

Ditto Brazil. As a 2015 report by NPR's Lourdes Garcia-Navarro made clear, many of the stadiums built for the 2014 World Cup, even in a generally soccer-crazy country, are proving to be pretty much useless. One, which cost $550 million, has become a bus parking lot. Another "is trying to make money by hosting weddings and kids' parties—with little luck."[43] A stadium in Manaus, out in the rain forest of Brazil's vast and jungle-heavy Amazonas State, is being sold to a private company after being built with public money.[44]

Manaus nicely highlights the absurdity of using the World Cup as an economic development tool. Brazilian officials argued that the tournament and the stadium, in a place that many travel advisers explicitly warn against attempting to reach via road due to its remote location in the rain forest, would bring a long-term influx in tourism that would outlive the World Cup. But there was no reason to think that would be the case.

"There will be [another] World Cup four years from now, and everyone who is a World Cup tourist will have forgotten about Manaus and Brazil, and they'll be traveling off to Russia" for the 2018 edition of the tournament, explained Dennis Coates, an economics professor at the University of Maryland–Baltimore County, when I spoke to him ahead of Brazil's tournament. Plus, he said, Manaus is dealing with stiff competition from other sites within Brazil: "São Paulo, Rio—those areas are always going to be bigger tourist destinations, and there's not a lot Manaus can do, and there's not very much that a stadium can do, to change that effect."[45]

Meanwhile, domestic priorities almost always get the short end of the stick when governments are instead plowing money into international events. "People are going hungry and the government builds stadiums," Eleuntina Scuilgaro, an eighty-three-year-old Brazilian, told *The New York Times*, a sentiment shared by plenty of her fellow countrymen and -women who took to the streets to protest their country's hosting of not just the World Cup, which it spent $14 billion on, but the 2016 Summer Olympics.[46] Like Greece, Brazil plunged into economic crisis—this time post–World Cup but still pre–Olympics—bringing even more of a spotlight to bear on the out-of-control spending to play host. Brazil's Olympic effort was plagued by problems, from overbudget projects to uncompleted infrastructure to locations for water events that were, to put it bluntly, polluted beyond repair. Throw in the Zika virus, which was running rampant in the country in the months leading up to the games, and pretty much everything Brazil did looked like a mistake.

The USA didn't face costs like that from hosting the World Cup in 1994, but it still, as briefly mentioned before, didn't bring the economic benefits one might hope for. The $4 billion in promised benefits turned into billions of dollars in losses, after US cities spent some $370 million in infrastructure upgrades to host. American cities essentially paid good money to lower their own incomes.

Why, exactly, do costs spiral so far out of control? Much of the blame can be laid at the feet of the International Olympic Committee or FIFA, both of which rake in big dollars from their events. Broadcasting revenue makes up the bulk of the funds, but corporate sponsorships are also a significant source of largesse (all of which is distinct from public funding for the games). According to tax filings, the IOC brought in some $5 billion between 2009 and 2012 and expected to bring in close to that for the 2013 to 2016 cycle.[47] It then doles out that money to national Olympic committees, setting up a cycle of perks and back-scratching that extends into all the most powerful Olympic nations. And the IOC is notoriously opaque about its spending priorities and budgeting. "One thing that in many ways doomed Boston's bid from the start was their lack of transparency, and that's something endemic to the Olympic process," said Jonathan Cohn, one of the cofounders of No Boston 2024. "That's something that never went well in Boston to begin with."[48] And just about every critique leveled at the IOC applies to FIFA, a notorious hotbed of corruption. Former FIFA head Sepp Blatter wouldn't even travel to France for the Euro 2016 tournament because he feared an extradition attempt by US authorities, who had cracked down on allegedly corrupt soccer officials.

The myth of the Olympics boosting economic development combines with the IOC's insistence on providing a bigger and better spectacle to broadcasters and corporate sponsors each time the games comes around to create a toxic stew that ends up costing the hosts huge amounts of money. "It has to be gilded, it has to be over the top, and that drives a lot of strange behavior," Allison Stewart of the Saïd Business School told me.[49]

And it's actually the most fiscally prudent Olympics that prove how it happens.

Whenever skeptics claim that the Olympics are inevitably a financial boondoggle, "Los Angeles 1984" is the rejoinder. Those games, by most accounts, easily made a $250 million profit and were well managed from start to finish.[50] The issues that plagued subsequent games simply weren't an issue in LA. But the way the city did it puts the lie to the rest of the Olympic money myth.

In the wake of the 1976 disaster—which, remember, Montreal spent the next thirty years paying off—few cities bid to host the 1984 games. And this was already a time of hosting crisis for the IOC. Denver, Colorado, in late 1972, pulled out of hosting the 1976 winter games after voters failed to approve public funding, pushing those contests to Innsbruck, Austria, instead. "They overestimated the benefits and underestimated the costs. Colorado was generally persuaded that they didn't have an adequate grasp on the figures, and Colorado was very much liable to have to fund dramatic cost overruns," said Dick Lamm, a state representative at the time of the Denver bid who later served as the state's governor.[51] When the games were put to a public referendum at both the city and state levels in Denver and Colorado, voters rejected them by 1.5 to 1. So the IOC was already on edge about costs, and Montreal's debacle confirmed everything that Colorado residents had feared. Finding a taker for the 1984 summer games, then, was a monumental task; no one wanted to step into the breach and convince their voters that being the sequel to Montreal's mess was worth it.

In the end, only New York City and LA agreed to host in 1984; Tehran, the sole other interested city, dropped out before the final vote. Once the US Olympic Committee decided on Southern California over the Big Apple, that was it. But being the sole bidder has its perks.

Intent on not becoming another Montreal, Los Angeles did everything on the cheap. It already had most of the necessary facilities—including the Los Angeles Coliseum, used to host the 1932 games, which was again pressed into service—and much of the public infrastructure on which hosts rely was also in place. By leveraging its position as the sole bidder, the city tossed aside the IOC rule requiring the host city to cover any cost overruns in organizing the games. Peter Ueberroth, who was essentially named CEO of the LA effort, himself said, "I don't want my tax dollars wasted in Los Angeles in the same way as was done in Montreal."[52] (Ueberroth was named *Time* magazine's Person of the Year for his accomplishments organizing the LA games.)

Waiving the rule requiring the host city to bear all cost overruns was perhaps the most important part of the tale. As noted earlier, the Olympics run over budget with just about 100 percent certainty, and the IOC demands that the host city—i.e., taxpayers—cover all of the extra cost. Being host sets a ticking fiscal time bomb that inevitably explodes. And city officials who buy into the myth of Olympic development agree to it. This IOC demand was a key facet in turning the population of Boston against hosting the 2024 games. "Ultimately, that was our most effective argument," said Chris Dempsey, the No Boston 2024 cofounder. "It's hard to fundamentally trust [officials advocating for the games] when they're still pushing that blank check."[53]

But because Los Angeles was empowered as the sole bidder for the games, it got this rule waived and put on a fiscally prudent event. The IOC's monopoly power ran into another monopoly.

LA 1984, though, is the exception, not the rule. Its unique

position as the sole city willing and able to put on the games gave it leverage to make demands that other cities vying to host are usually unwilling to make, as doing so would doom their bids from the start. And requiring host cities to cover the full cost of budget overruns is merely the beginning of the IOC's list of demands.

The organization also requires hosts to provide a slew of tax breaks and exemptions to not only the organizing committee itself, but to all of its corporate sponsors as well. A similar tax-free bubble is required around World Cup host sites.[54] These exemptions give companies such as those providing the food a windfall at taxpayers' expense, simply because the IOC is in a position to require it. Brazil gave up some $530 million in tax revenue during its 2014 World Cup, for instance.[55] During the London Olympics, McDonald's and Coca-Cola even won some public relations goodwill by refusing the tax breaks that the IOC had demanded on their behalf.[56] But make no mistake: Those corporations with the foresight to sign on as sponsors of the Olympics receive a nice gift of tax-free sales in return. The games essentially become an international tax-free zone for those companies the IOC has brought into the fold.

The upshot of the IOC's insistence on big garish spectacles, new facilities, loads of tax breaks for its corporate sponsors, and foisting of cost overruns onto the hosting government causes a significant problem: Increasingly, only authoritarian countries are in the running to host. They're appealing because they don't have the sort of democratic accountability evident in Boston. "There's clearly a sense there that the IOC [is] attracted to the ability to spend money without any kind of oversight," said Robert Orttung, a professor of international affairs at George Washington University and coauthor of the book *Putin's Olympics: The Sochi Games and the*

Evolution of Twenty-First Century Russia. "The organization itself is geared in favor of these authoritarian ways."

It's no coincidence that the two most expensive Olympics in history—Beijing and Sochi—occurred in countries where the leadership didn't have to answer to the people for its spending or the blatant corruption underlying it. This notion has a foundation in Olympic history, too. Avery Brundage, who was president of the IOC from the 1950s to the early 1970s, openly admired dictators for their ability to circumvent democracy. As late as the 1950s, he was writing about the successes of Nazi Germany in the 1930s. He also played a key role in ensuring that the United States did not boycott the 1936 Olympics in Berlin, where African-American Jesse Owens famously won four gold medals under the nose of the Third Reich.[57]

The Olympics shares this penchant for avoiding the pitfalls of democracy with the World Cup. The petrostate Qatar, which bribed its way into hosting the 2022 tournament, is expected to spend $200 billion on its tournament.[58] That's not a typo—it would by far be a record amount of spending on an international sporting event, in a country of just 2 million people, nearly 90 percent of whom are temporary foreign workers. Initial plans for the tournament included ridiculous proposals to build air-conditioned stadiums—Qatar is just about entirely hot desert, after all—and when they fell through, FIFA forced the soccer world to rearrange its schedule to play the tournament in the winter, rather than its usual summer slot.

The bidding for the 2022 Winter Olympics nicely highlights what we're discussing here. Initially, several cities that would have been strong, traditional hosts for the winter games suggested they would bid. But then, one by one, just like Boston, they stepped away.

First, it was a joint bid from Davos and St. Moritz, Switzerland, which fell to public referendum, with nearly 53 percent of voters saying no thanks to hosting.[59] Then voters in Munich, Germany, did the same. "The vote is not a signal against the sport, but against the nontransparency and the greed for profit of the IOC," said Ludwig Hartmann, a local German lawmaker, at the time.[60]

Next came Stockholm, Sweden, where officials iced the bid because of cost concerns. "Although the calculations are well worked out, we estimate that revenues will likely be lower and costs higher than the investigation indicates," said Stockholm city council chairman and finance commissioner Sten Nordin. The city's ruling Moderate Party added in a statement, "Arranging a Winter Olympics would mean a big investment in new sports facilities, for example for the bobsleigh and luge. . . . There isn't any need for that kind of facility after an Olympics."[61] Kraków, Poland, followed next, where nearly 70 percent of voters in a referendum rejected the games.[62]

Finally, Oslo, Norway, bid adieu to a bid—even though a majority actually supported it in a referendum—citing the crazy demands of the IOC. One prominent newspaper columnist said the IOC's members expected "that they should be treated like the king of Saudi Arabia."[63] That left just two cities in the running: Beijing (again) and Almaty, Kazakhstan. Both are in countries where democratic accountability isn't a problem. Beijing won, which will make it the first city to host both the summer and winter games.

There's a double danger here. If the IOC and FIFA come to depend on dictatorships as the most dependable source of potential hosts, political pressure on the rest of the world to keep their athletes away from the games could increase. Even in 2014, some prominent liberal commentators called for a boycott of the Sochi Olympics due to Russia's draconian antigay laws.

In 1936, the United States also seriously considered boycotting the Berlin games. Jeremiah Mahoney, head of the Amateur Athletic Union, which at the time regulated amateur sports in America, said participating in Berlin would be akin to "giving American moral and financial support to the Nazi regime, which is opposed to all that Americans hold dearest." The IOC even considered moving the games from Berlin altogether.[64]

In the end, of course, the Berlin games went on, after the head of the US Olympic Committee personally vouched for the Germans.

Then there was the 1980 boycott of the summer games in Moscow, meant to protest the Soviet Union's 1979 invasion of Afghanistan. Anita DeFrantz, an American member of the IOC and a former Olympian, called the boycott "a pointless exercise and a shameful part of US history."[65] Even the State Department admitted as much, saying, "The Carter administration had wanted to express the extent of international displeasure with the invasion of Afghanistan and to pressure the Soviets to pull their armies out of the conflict. In actuality, the Soviet-Afghan War continued and did not end until 1989."[66] The Soviet counterboycott of the 1984 games, too, had little practical impact.

So history shows us that boycotts don't do much of anything to change the course of Olympic history. But if the games do become solely a dictator's plaything, the calls for boycotting are again going to come.

Meanwhile, the concerns voiced by residents and lawmakers in Kraków, Munich, and the rest of the cities that passed on the winter games could have come straight out of the Boston tale. In Beantown, as Boston is known, planners proposed to build a temporary stadium, which would then be removed and the surrounding area turned into an upscale neighborhood. As Jonathan Cohn said, the plan was to "build a giant stadium that they would then take down to build a new neighborhood" that would "build up a lot of capacity in upper-income housing, but nothing like schools or libraries or fire departments." Cohn said, "That definite dynamic of building things that no one asked for, and potentially knocking them down to build new things no one asked for," helped doom the bid.[67] The Boston team is now exporting its know-how, having been in touch with opposition groups in Hamburg, Budapest, and Rome on how to best argue against the spin emanating from Olympic boosters.

Before turning to some good news regarding what hosts can expect from the games—and there is some, I promise—I have one more point to make regarding the lack of tangible benefits they provide. Proponents often claim that hosting is an infomercial for a city, providing a tourism boost that outlasts the games by drawing the world's attention to a locale. The textbook example cited is Barcelona, Spain. In that instance, it seems plausible that the games did help turn the city into a tourist attraction it might not otherwise have become, since it was starting from a relatively low bar, overshadowed by other cities within its own country such as Madrid. (I visited the still-standing site of the Olympic stadium and flame in Barcelona. It's a lovely city.)

But even if some tourism dividend exists over the long term— and remember, most quantitative analyses say there isn't any—it only surfaces if the location was previously not a tourist destination. Otherwise, the substitution effect or time switching comes back into play: Olympic tourists replace existing tourists who avoid a city because of its popularity, or people who were planning to come to a city anyway move their trip around to accommodate seeing the games. Does anyone believe that places such as London,

Paris, Los Angeles, or New York needed publicity to detail their tourist attractions?

As a resident of Washington, DC, I find this nonsense to be close to home. Twice in recent years, the city has contemplated a bid for the Olympics, and showing off the city for the world was one of the reasons organizers said it should be done. "There is no bigger global spectacle, no better way to hold a coming out party, than the Olympics," said Ted Leonsis, one of the key boosters of a DC bid and the owner of the city's Washington Wizards and Washington Capitals sports franchises.[68]

But the idea that the capital of one of, if not the, most powerful nations on earth—and one that is chock-full of well-known tourist attractions already—needs a "coming out party" is absurd. DC already attracts some 19 million domestic tourists annually, as well as more than 1.5 million international tourists, the latter putting it in the top ten among US cities, ahead of Chicago and Boston.[69] Seeing shots of the Washington Monument scroll across their TV screen for two weeks isn't going to make a significant difference in the city's fortunes. (Also, the city already has severe infrastructure woes that need to be addressed without diverting funds into Olympic infrastructure.)

There are benefits to hosting, though, even if a city is not in the unique situations that both Los Angeles and Barcelona found themselves; I'm not going to be all doom and gloom. Those benefits just are of the nonmaterial kind and don't show up on a budget ledger. Economists call it the feel good effect: Hosting a major sporting event (assuming it goes well) makes the residents of a place happy. Several researchers have found that a sense of civic pride pervades a country after it hosts a sporting mega-event. "It's like a wedding," Victor Matheson says. "It won't make you rich, but it may make you happy."[70]

This is what Wolfgang Maennig, the German economist, said is perhaps the most important effect the hosts can expect to enjoy. His study of the 2006 World Cup in Germany—an event that can be treated as broadly analogous to a similar one in the United States—found that "these effects are the greatest measurable effects" of the tournament.[71] "If the World Cup makes people happy, we should invest in a World Cup," said Maennig. "But we should stop pretending that hosting a World Cup will make us rich. It's not true."[72]

Indeed, big international sporting events do not make us rich. They do, though, line the pockets of the members of the International Olympic Committee, FIFA, and the corporate sponsors who glom on to an event paid for in large part by the taxpayer. It's certainly a worse phenomenon for the developing world—where the infrastructure for hosting has to be built from the ground up—or for those living in countries where playing host is a reason to make a bleak human rights situation even bleaker. But even in those countries that can afford them on paper, the games are nearly always a budget-busting boondoggle, a terminally bad use of resources, and the IOC takes little responsibility for the large bag the taxpaying public is often left holding. As Allison Stewart, from the Saïd Business School, pointed out, what governments should be doing is "accommodating the games as an interim step, as opposed to the end in itself" in their urban planning and other development goals, because, given that such mega-events consistently cause huge fiscal problems, "as an end in itself, it doesn't make any sense."[73]

Maybe the activism of recent years will have an effect on the system. No Boston 2024 laid out a good template for how to take the fight to the IOC or FIFA and the local officials who want to use the same old Olympic playbook that doesn't consider the opportunity costs of hosting the games. As Jonathan Cohn said regarding Boston, "The more people were paying attention, the more likely they were to oppose it."[74] The end of the bidding for the summer 2024 and 2028 games—which resulted in unopposed bids won by Paris and Los Angeles, respectively, after the latter agreed to back out of the bidding for the earlier event and the IOC freaked out over so many cities passing—at least provides the opportunity for cities to prove that they can use their leverage, lower the cost of the Olympics, and still put on a good show. The same could be said for the 2026 World Cup bid by the United States, Canada, and Mexico, which would also require little in the way of new infrastructure. Hopefully they succeed. Because until the system does change—until the IOC feels sufficiently pressured into believing that its current way of doing business is no longer tenable—the Olympics and other big international sporting events will continue to be fool's gold, and hosting them a fool's errand.

5

FOOLISH GAMES: WHY LOTTERIES AND CASINOS ARE A BAD BET

THE LOTTERY IN AMERICA DATES back to well before there was an America.

A lottery was used to raise funds for the Jamestown Colony in Virginia in 1612, the first permanent settlement in what would eventually become the United States. When those states were still just a bunch of colonies, George Washington attempted to use a lottery to build a road across the Blue Ridge Mountains, while Benjamin Franklin tried to use one to build cannons that would defend Philadelphia against British forces. King George III even saw fit to ban lotteries in the colonies before American independence, on the grounds that they were sucking money away from the mother country.[1] The Constitutional Congress eventually turned to a lottery in a not very successful attempt to raise funds for the beleaguered colonial army during the Revolutionary War, as did several individual states.[2]

Following independence, states for decades used lotteries to raise money for a variety of different purposes.[3] Thomas Jefferson, who shortly before his death tried to use a lottery to raise funds to cover his ruinous personal debt, wrote of the lottery, "Money is wanting for a useful undertaking for which a direct tax would be disapproved. It is raised therefore by a lottery wherein the tax is laid on the willing only, that is to say on those who can risk the price of a ticket without injury, for the possibility of a high prize."[4]

By the turn of the twentieth century, though, thanks to payment scandals and the growing American temperance movement, lotteries had been killed off in the US. President Benjamin Harrison in 1890 decried the "widespread corruption of public and private morals which are the necessary incidents of these lottery schemes."[5] Congress got in on the act, rendering it illegal to use the mail to implement any sort of lottery-type game, at a time when the mail was one of the surest ways for such games to be run. When the Louisiana Lottery was finally shuttered in 1894—following a widespread corruption scandal that included bribery of both state and national officials—that was it for legalized lottery games in America. On the mainland United States, they wouldn't reappear until the 1960s (though Puerto Rico did implement one in the 1930s).

The first state to rejoin the lottery fray was New Hampshire, which in 1964 began a new "sweepstakes" to raise funds for its education system. "The new proceeds of the New Hampshire Sweepstakes, the first state lottery in modern history, are earmarked for public education under a bill passed last year by the legislature. It was signed by Gov. John W. King, the first Democrat to hold that office in New Hampshire in 40 years," noted *The New York Times*.[6]

The famously tax-averse state was certainly an appropriate one to push America back into the lottery business (though its lottery did not initially look a whole lot like today's lottery games with their Ping-Pong balls and televised drawings, but was instead based on the outcome of horse races; players were randomly assigned Thoroughbreds, and they won if their horse won). Getting a lottery up and running was the culmination of an effort led by state representative Larry Pickett, who spent a decade banging the drum to use a random drawing to raise funds for the Granite State.[7]

The step was hugely controversial at the time. King spent weeks mulling over whether to sign the sweepstakes bill into law and was hounded by editorial writers who were convinced that a lottery was the first step on New Hampshire's road to depravity. "Is either New Hampshire or Uncle Sam so hard up that this shabby dodge is the only way out?" asked *Reader's Digest*. "It will mean moral bankruptcy for New Hampshire."[8]

Today, though, that sort of sentiment seems almost laughably quaint. After New Hampshire, New York, and New Jersey got back into the lottery business, Massachusetts introduced the first instant-win scratch-off games in 1974.[9] As of 2017, forty-four states, the District of Columbia, Puerto Rico, and the US Virgin Islands all use lotteries to raise money for the government; the funds are dedicated to a whole host of purposes, including education, public employee pensions, state parks, and mass transit. The only six states that have thus far successfully fought the urge to implement a lottery are Alaska, Hawaii, Alabama, Utah, Nevada, and Mississippi—and the latter two have only abstained because they believe that lotteries would drain money away from their already lucrative casino businesses, so they are not exactly paragons of virtue on the issue.[10] Advertisements for lotteries are ubiquitous, appearing on the sides of buses, on billboards, and on television. States have also joined in compacts to pool larger pots of money into larger and larger prizes. For instance, Powerball is played in forty-four states, with a minimum jackpot of $40 million; again and again, it breaks records for the largest awards ever offered in a lottery game, peaking at a worldwide record of $1.6 billion in January 2016, and climbing back to $700 million again a year later.

But did those early critics in New Hampshire have it right? Perhaps.

Lotteries may look like a slam dunk for states, a way to replenish state coffers while people have a little fun watching numbers or scratching off tickets. But some moral bankruptcy, as *Reader's Digest* put it, is definitely involved. Lotteries force states to take advantage of their own people, acting as the purveyor of a game that preys on their hopes and dreams—as well as their financial desperation—to raise money without having to push unpopular taxes through the legislature. It's a cynical business, one that the state shouldn't be in.

Sharing the sentiments of Jefferson, the editor of New Hampshire's influential *Manchester Union-Leader* editorialized during the debate over the state's sweepstakes bill that a lottery was a good idea because it was, in effect, a voluntary tax. "No one has to go to the track and bet. No one has to smoke tobacco. No one has to drink. But how do those who oppose the Sweepstakes propose to raise the money? Either a sales tax or a property tax or some other kind of levy that people will have to pay, even though it will hurt them dreadfully to do so," editor William Loeb wrote.[11]

That's certainly true on its face. No one is forcing anyone into a bodega to buy lottery tickets or scratch cards. But the government is still hyping these games as a way for people to suddenly receive a ton of money and make their dreams come true. The state is dangling riches in front of people as a way to raise revenue for other things, flashing dollar signs at them to access the change in their pockets. There's no direct coercion, sure, but lotteries aren't coercion-free either, unless you think most people are able to fully ignore exhortations that they are a simple game away from becoming rich beyond their wildest dreams. Lottery games are still a tax, a payment to a government that isn't solely voluntary, with the mind games that the state is playing in order to entice people to participate. Unlike so much else in this book, the lottery isn't a case of a corporation taking advantage of taxpayers via their elected representatives, but those representatives doing it themselves. But make no mistake, the lottery is still a form of taxation that doesn't do what it is supposed to do.

This isn't a new dynamic. Adam Smith wrote in *The Wealth of Nations* that players of the British lottery were participating in "the vain hope of gaining some of the great prizes." In the modern era he might have added "particularly if they're low income." Study after study has shown that lottery tickets are disproportionately purchased by low-income, less-educated people. As far back as the eighties, a Duke University study found that the poorest third of households purchase more than half of the lottery tickets sold during a given week; newer research, if not matching that exact number, has repeatedly found that poorer Americans purchase more lottery tickets than do their richer brethren, and that higher-income people usually don't pile in until the jackpots reach exceedingly high levels, deeming it not worth their time or their money to participate before.[12] So more well-off folks don't start to play until those at the lower end of the income scale have already been thoroughly soaked.

This would perhaps be forgivable if the lottery was just a cheap form of entertainment. Researchers have also found, though, that lottery purchases go up when the economy and the unemployment rate gets worse, signaling that it is economic desperation, not entertainment, that is often the driving force behind ticket sales. According to a 2004 survey, "Rather than seeking fun and exciting entertainment, the poor appear to play because of an ill-conceived belief that participation will improve their financial well being." People in the lower reaches of the income ladder were far more likely to say that they were participating in the lottery as a way to change their economic status than because it was fun.[13] This dynamic was easily observable during the Great Recession, when twenty-two state lotteries set sales records, smack in the middle of a generational economic mess.[14]

So in times of desperation, folks turn to the lottery as a potential way out, an economic Hail Mary, a golden ticket out of the straits in which they've found themselves. Those scratch-off tickets aren't just a game, but a shot at economic salvation. And with each purchase, folks are making their current financial situation just a bit worse. As a 2008 Carnegie Mellon study put it, "Lotteries set off a vicious cycle that not only exploits low-income individuals' desires to escape poverty but also directly prevents them from improving upon their financial situations."[15]

"Some poor people see playing the lottery as their best opportunity for improving their financial situations, albeit wrongly so," said Emily Haisley, who led the Carnegie Mellon study. "The hope of getting out of poverty encourages people to continue to buy tickets, even though their chances of stumbling upon a life-changing windfall are nearly impossibly slim and buying lottery tickets in fact exacerbates the very poverty that purchasers are hoping to escape."

The whole time, the government is inflating those hopes because, as the New York Lottery slogan says, "Hey, you never know."

According to data crunched by Bloomberg News in 2012, the residents of Georgia do the most damage to their personal finances via the lottery—making them the nation's biggest "suckers," in Bloomberg's unfortunate parlance—as they spend about 1 percent of their total income on it, in a state where the per capita income is already 10 percent lower than the national average. Massachusetts, that bastion of blue state progressivism, came in second.[16] We've all heard the stories of the lottery winners who turn around and go bankrupt from lack of financial planning, the windfall giving them a short-term monetary sugar high while arguably leaving them worse off in the end, but those players who never win could be doing even more everlasting damage to their finances via trying to luck into a fortune that never materializes, egged on by a government too reluctant to use more traditional means of taxation to raise the funds it needs.

The hidden-in-plain-view downsides of the lottery don't end with the individual thanks to the gap between what the government says it is doing when it implements a lottery and what it actually ends up doing. The fiscal high experienced by individuals who win the lottery is also experienced by states that begin to oversee a lottery—lawmakers think they're instituting a new way to raise money that will fix whatever the budget woe of the moment is, but if there's any fix at all, it's usually short-term, and for some locales, it leaves everything worse off.

Consider education. In many states, the explicit purpose of the lottery is to raise funds for public schools; the unpalatable lottery and the problems it may bring are thus made palatable because, hey, it's all for the kids. In thirteen states, education is the sole area of the budget that receives lottery revenue, and in many more at least a portion of the proceeds are supposed to wind up in the classroom.[17] Funding education was the impetus behind that very first modern lottery in New Hampshire, and other states have made the same pledge. "Our people are playing the lottery," said North Carolina's governor when his state made a push to implement a sweepstakes linked to education. "We just need to decide which schools we should fund, other states' or ours."[18] Virginia even sold lottery tickets that explicitly said "Helping Virginia's Public Schools" on the back and touts the amount the games have given to public schools under a "Playing Matters" tab on its website.

However, more often than not, this turns into a shell game, with states not adding to their school budgets via the lottery, but simply swapping lottery money in for other funds that then get spent on something else. Per a pair of 1997 studies, states without lotteries were more likely to increase their education budgets than were states that had them. In the gaming states, instead, a short-term boost for the school system was then more than offset by reductions in the subsequent years.[19] In 1999, the National Gambling Impact Study Commission, which in 1996 was empowered by Congress to assess gambling in America, reported, "There is reason to doubt if earmarked lottery revenues in fact have the effect of increasing funds available for the specified purpose." The commission continued, "When expenditures on the earmarked purpose far exceed the revenues available from the lottery, as is the case with the general education budget, there is no practical way of preventing a legislature from allocating general revenues away from earmarked uses, thus blunting the purpose of the earmarking."[20]

In short, there is no way to ensure states spend lottery money on education, and it's pretty easy for them not to do so, lottery or no lottery. Case in point: four years after implementing the lottery its governor was so certain would help its schools, North Carolina cut its education funding by 12 percent. By 2016, it was spending less of its budget on education than it had before the lottery started.[21] That could have happened for lots of reasons that had nothing to do with the lottery and a lot to do with the Great Recession, but it certainly shows how lotteries are not a fiscal savior if everything else in the economy is going sideways. And it's not as if states eliminate the lotteries when they turn out not to provide the boost to schools that was promised; so taxpayers wind up not helping their kids, while simultaneously preserving the negative aspects that come with the lottery. It's a lose-lose proposition.

Plus, gambling revenue of all kinds is a boom-or-bust sort of thing, subject to the vagaries of citizens' taste for gambling, economic conditions, and competition from surrounding states, and lotteries are no exception. With more and more states piling into the lottery business, the benefits of doing so got smaller and smaller. As Citizens for Tax Justice, a tax policy organization in Washington that is almost always on the right side of things, put it, "It becomes a case of diminishing returns as neighboring states introduce new and better lotto games. Then, states either lose business to another state or hit a ceiling for how many lotto tickets a population can buy."[22] So then, in their desperation to not raise real taxes, states turn to ever more absurd forms of gimmickry to juice lottery revenue.

"The three strategies states have used to try to get more revenue out of their lotteries is change the equation on how much they can spend on advertising, privatization, and then the third one is coming up with crazy, gimmicky, stupid games," said Meg Wiehe, deputy director of the Institute on Taxation and Economic Policy, a shop in Washington that tracks mostly state-level tax policy. "A few years ago there was this trend to have themed lottery tickets, so tied to your favorite sports team. There was a *Duck Dynasty* lottery ticket, there were bacon-scented scratch-off tickets. This idea of resorting to new games to get more people to play is a way states have tried to eke a little bit more revenue out. . . . [And] the reason these are there is because lottery revenue has trailed off."

So more gimmicks, glitz, and other nonsense to squeeze ever

more money out of a population, instead of using the normal avenues of taxation to try to create or bolster more traditional revenue streams. At the end of all this, if education needs still outstrip lottery revenues, which is not an unreasonable expectation given that lotteries still only compose a tiny fraction of overall state budgets, either the education system gets slowly starved, or someone has to make the intelligent choice to find money elsewhere.

Finally, there's no guarantee that the money raised by the lottery gets shared equitably among a state's residents, which is particularly problematic considering it's the poorest ones who are usually paying a disproportionate amount to play in the first place. For instance, in 2014, *The Boston Globe* found that in Massachusetts, "189 municipalities pay more into the lottery's local aid fund than they get back as aid, including 58 where the median household income is below the state average."[23] Meanwhile, a bunch of affluent towns received far more money from the lottery fund than they paid in via tickets. The state was pulling a reverse Robin Hood, using lottery funds from its poorest residents to shift money into the hands of its richer ones.

So here's some good news and some bad news when it comes to the lottery. The good news is that younger Americans—those dreaded millennials who are popularly, and unfairly, characterized as lazy, whiny, and emotionally and economically stunted, since they had the bad luck to come of age in the middle of a national economic nightmare—aren't interested in buying tickets. In 2016, just one-third of Americans twenty to thirty-five decided to play along, and the trend line is going down.

The bad news is that rather than finding some more sustainable source of revenue that isn't dependent on gambling and seizing the opportunity a new generation is presenting to create more sustainable budget practices, states are instead freaking out and trying to figure out ways to get millennials to hop on board the lottery train, including allowing lottery games to be accessed or paid for via smartphone. States and lawmakers have become so addicted to the revenue that lotteries provide they can't allow a generation to pass the gambling addiction on by.

"I had to come around to this thinking because I myself hadn't thought about online lottery games, but I saw the way millennials are operating is really online," said the Massachusetts state treasurer during a 2017 push to create an iLottery that would allow for smartphone gaming. "This past Christmas shopping season, Cyber Monday outperformed Black Friday. We really want to be prepared to have a more modern, forward-thinking product."

And lest you think this wasn't about money: "In 2009 when lottery sales weren't as good as they are now, we heard from cities and towns asking, 'What about the lottery money?'"[24] And while this may all be framed as just a way to keep millennials playing, smartphones are also becoming more ubiquitous—and more indispensable—in lower-income communities as well. The percentage of households with an income below $30,000 that own a smartphone jumped 12 points between 2015 and 2016 alone, to 64 percent.[25] Extending the technological reach of lotteries to make them smartphone- and Web-savvy is just another way to keep on hosing the same low-income population that gets hosed today, just this time on the internet instead of in a bodega.

Moral bankruptcy, indeed.

Whether in colonial America or on a smartphone in 2017, lotteries are just another vice, one that preys on the endless capacity Americans have for believing that someday, somehow, they'll be rich. They're a form of gambling that states use to raise money—if one that is uniquely tempting to those least able to afford it—and when it comes to gambling, as the adage goes, the house always wins. But despite that advantage, sometimes the house goes under, too.

Which brings us to casinos. In much the same way that the proliferation of lottery games makes them thoroughly unreliable for states in raising money, so, too, has the explosion of casino gambling in recent years made its benefits vanish like an ace up a shady player's sleeve. Perhaps nowhere exemplifies that change better than Atlantic City.

Until the 1970s, Las Vegas was the only place in the United States where casino gambling was fully legalized. In 1977, though, Atlantic City, New Jersey, joined the party and for several decades reaped the benefits of its semi-monopoly. Being the only place east of the Rockies in which one could legally visit a casino, and having those casinos right on the famed Jersey Shore, did exactly what it was intended to do: make Atlantic City a tourist destination that brought in visitors and all the money they were willing to throw down on the boardwalk. It may not have been as glitzy as the Gilded Age Atlantic City of *Boardwalk Empire* fame, but the legal gambling gambit worked for a time.

Most good things come to an end, and for Atlantic City that ending has been especially hard, turning the city into a symbol of all that can go wrong in economic strategy. As other states in the nation got over their fear of legalizing gambling and casinos proliferated, Atlantic City fell on hard times. After losing scores of potential customers to nearby Pennsylvania and Maryland—the Keystone State's casino revenue eclipsed that of New Jersey's for the first time in 2012—Atlantic City hit rock bottom. Its casinos fell into bankruptcy, its finances fell apart, joblessness surged, and the state scrambled to come up with some sort of solution to save one of the Garden State's iconic cities from complete economic oblivion, considering just about anything that would theoretically salvage the fortunes of this once-booming city by the sea.

Thus entered Governor Chris Christie and the Revel.

Christie is better known as the governor who yells at teachers on YouTube and for the dead, hollow look he had in his eye when he became the first major politician to endorse then-candidate Donald Trump (who has a pretty lousy Atlantic City history all his own). But Christie is also extremely fond of corporate tax subsidies, doling them out like candy in New Jersey in an attempt to juice his state's jobs numbers, which consistently trailed those of its neighbors under his tenure. On his watch, the state handed out some $4 billion in corporate tax breaks, which dwarfs the total it provided in the previous two decades combined, per New Jersey Policy Perspective, an economics-focused think tank.[26] One of the biggest grants, $261 million, was to the Atlantic City Revel casino project.

The first new casino built in Atlantic City in a decade, the Revel was supposed to be the symbol of a rebirth on the boardwalk, not just a casino but a way of life, a resort that included gambling alongside spas and fine dining, a complete experience rather than just place to while away time at the poker table. In this, it's a lot like Las Vegas in recent years, which has focused more on the full entertainment experience at "resorts," rather than on just beefing up its casinos with new and better slot machines. The investment bank Morgan Stanley sank $1 billion into the Revel before abandoning construction in 2010, but the state swooped in the next year to pick up the project, believing it could be the linchpin of an Atlantic City renaissance, thereby preventing the need to directly bail out the city sometime in the future.

"The completion of Revel and its opening is a turning point for

Atlantic City and a clear sign that people once again have faith in the city's ability to come back," Christie said at the casino's grand opening in 2012.[27]

Not so much, it turned out. Despite the hoopla—and Beyoncé performing at the casino's grand opening—the Revel never turned into the luxury gambling behemoth that had been envisioned. Instead, it filed for bankruptcy twice in the next two years before finally closing in an epic bust. New Jersey's state Economic Development Authority had estimated that the casino would generate some $650 million in state tax revenue and fifty-five hundred jobs over the life of the subsidy it received. Instead, the casino never turned a profit and employed less than two thousand people full-time before it shut its doors for good.[28]

The good news for New Jersey is that, because the credits pledged to the Revel were only to offset taxes, which the flailing casino never had to pay since it didn't turn a profit, taxpayers weren't actually stuck on the wrong end of Christie's gamble—though they did spend several million dollars to train the casino's workers and for some surrounding infrastructure projects.[29] The damage could have been much worse, for benefits that were always illusory.

However, the project is symbolic of a nationwide bet on gambling as an economic development tool, a roll of the dice that more and more cities and states have made despite the ever-diminishing returns.

"[The Revel] was proven to be a bad idea when the bill actually didn't work," said Jon Whiten, vice president of New Jersey Policy Perspective. "It was a doomed project from the get-go."

Whiten added, "Boosters of the tax break program in New Jersey would say, 'Well, that's proof that our tax break programs are solid, they work, we don't give out dollars up front, blah blah blah.' And that's true to a certain extent, but at the same time, even in the process of awarding this tax break, there were some state resources that went into working on the application, vetting it, making sure that it fit the bill, and so that's all just poop blowing out into the air. It's a big waste."[30]

Other locales big and small, unlike New Jersey, did pledge public money for the construction and maintenance of casinos, enticing them with bond issues, property tax breaks, or other incentives; some even lowered the tax rate on gambling revenue for new casinos, pretty well screwing all the ones that had already been built and were paying higher taxes. For instance, several casinos received big tax breaks in 2016 when New York State gave out four new gambling licenses. Between them, these casinos will benefit from tens of millions of dollars in state and local largesse, including on property tax payments and mortgage taxes.

Local officials convinced themselves—or were convinced by the casinos' owners, more likely—that absent the tax breaks, construction would never happen. "It far outweighs, we believe and the community clearly believes, in what they might give up in real property tax or sales tax to have them located here," one official told the local paper. Some of the owners themselves claimed that they would never have been able to build without the public assistance. "It's a miracle that it's getting built at all," said Jeff Gural, who owns the Tioga Downs casino in Nichols, New York, a town in the central part of the state, not far from the Pennsylvania border.[31]

It's amazing the sort of miracles public funds can work, eh?

Across the country, from Massachusetts to Maryland to Mississippi, other states and cities went down the same road, if not incentivizing casinos directly, at least banking on gambling to bring financial benefits, creating a casino boom the likes of which modern America has never before seen.

That's the story when it comes to casinos in the United States. It's not about the tax breaks themselves, as wasteful as they often are. It's that so many states are now trying the same thing—making the same bet—that the benefits are getting spread thinner and thinner, the up-front costs yielding less and less while the downsides remain forever the same. Yet lawmakers keep making the same pitch in place after place after place, oftentimes with big consequences for important parts of the state's budget, particularly schools. States are taking a bad hand, if you will, and doubling and then tripling down on it.

As of this writing, forty states have casino gambling of some kind, way up from the just two that had it a few decades ago. Per the American Gaming Association's "State of the States" report, in 2015 the United States had 515 commercial or racetrack casinos, and another 486 casinos owned by Native American tribes. Nevada led the way in commercial casinos, followed by Colorado, Mississippi, and South Dakota. Oklahoma boasted by far the most tribal casinos, having three times the number of runner-up California.[32]

The casino explosion began in the late 1980s and early 1990s thanks to two developments: Congress's approval of casino ownership by those Native American tribes and the growth of riverboat gambling.

The first such riverboat in gambling's modern era came out of Iowa in 1991, and several other states abutting the Mississippi River and the Gulf Coast quickly followed suit, operating under the theory that since these casinos were housed in boats on water, they weren't part of the state; states embraced this legal fiction to pretend that they were still divorced from the corrupting influence that gambling would supposedly bring.

The Indian Gaming Regulatory Act in 1988, meanwhile, was

meant explicitly as a way for Native American tribes to generate economic development on reservations, a way for one of America's most neglected populations to bring in much-needed cash and jobs, while still keeping casinos in isolated areas.

So does this work? Do casinos boost incomes, job creation, or any of the other myriad things lawmakers say they will when they call for yet another expansion of state-sanctioned gambling? The unsexy answer is that it very much depends. That's why it's so important for lawmakers to understand what the odds are before they throw all their chips down on a new establishment.

Scouring the literature on casinos and economic growth is an exercise in contradiction. In many instances, job and income growth have followed the opening of a casino. In many others, they haven't, which oftentimes indicates that the casino will be shutting its doors shortly. According to a 2010 literature review by Alan Mallach of the Federal Reserve Bank of Philadelphia, "It is impossible to generalize about the economic impact of casinos."[33] Studies of casinos in Illinois and Wisconsin found bad news, whereas those of casinos in Missouri and Iowa were much more positive.

In a 2016 literature review, Douglas Walker and Russell Sobel, of the College of Charleston and the Citadel, respectively, concluded, "Overall, the more recent literature tends to support prior literature that there are likely modest gains in employment, at least in the short run, from casinos that seem to be isolated mostly to the hospitality and entertainment industries," as well as modest increases in per capita income. "However, these results are sensitive to time and jurisdiction."[34] Casinos can work if the goal is jobs and income, but they're no sure bet.

The reason for all this ambiguity is pretty clear. As Mallach explained, the local impact of a casino can be summed up by the following model: ([casino + nonlocal visitor spending] − [leakage + displacement]) × multiplier.

In plain English, the model shows that spending in the casino from people who wouldn't have otherwise been in the community, minus any money that leaks out of the local community, multiplied by whatever factors keep that money churning through the area will give you a rough outline of the casino's true economic impact.

The nonlocal part of the equation is perhaps the most critical. It's not enough to say that every dollar spent in the casino is a benefit to the local community. If someone who lives in the same area as the casino decides to spend a night at the blackjack table instead of at the movies, a local restaurant, or a sporting event, all the benefit comes out in the wash. The casino owner's gain is the restaurateur's loss. Therefore, the ability of a casino to boost the local community hinges on its ability to bring people in who would never have come to the community in the absence of a casino, new visitors who would have spent their time and money somewhere else if the casino did not exist.

This is doubly true due to the very nature of casinos: They're meant to be all-encompassing entertainment venues—you're not supposed to leave once you enter, as everything you need is provided inside, including food, drinks, music, stage shows, televisions with sports games, and so on. So a casino, more so than other entertainment options, is meant to totally beggar its neighbors. At least with a sports stadium or a retail outlet, other businesses in the vicinity might receive some bank-shot benefits. By design, casinos prevent that.

Therefore, it's no surprise that researchers have found that casinos can have an adverse substitution effect that blunts their

economic impact. One study from Missouri in the nineties estimated that fully half of the spending in a casino was just displaced
from elsewhere in the community, not new spending generated
by outside visitors. A 2007 study from Iowa put the number at
30 percent.[35] That's a pretty big effect, one that can minimize the
upside of opening the casino, at least from the wider community's
perspective.

The second half of the equation measures how much money
leaks back out of the local community via the standard leakages
discussed earlier in this book: Money flowing back to a big corporation's headquarters in another city, state, or country, for instance, does nothing to help the local area, nor do wages paid to
employees who are commuting in to work in the area and then
driving home at the end of the day to somewhere else. So the ideal
situation is for a casino to attract lots of outside visitors but lots of
local workers. That's not the easiest needle to thread.

For tribal casinos this is a slightly less complicated proposition.
Members of the tribe can be employed as the casino's workforce,
and the bulk of the customers will be from outside the area. Studies have consistently found that tribal casinos are better on the job
creation and economic development than are commercial casinos.
As Mallach explained, "Indian casinos are likely to reinvest more
of their casino profits within the tribe, in contrast to non-Indian
casinos, which, in most cases, will export their profits far from the
casino's host community."[36] Yes, tribal casinos can cause other
problems of a financial and social nature for the individuals involved, depending on how the profits are shared or the management is handled, but on purely economic grounds, they make more
sense than do many other things discussed to this point, because
of their unique ability to be run almost totally by individuals from
within the community, while drawing visitors who are almost all

from outside it, and who would not have been visiting at all were the casino not there.

Thus, the economic impact of a casino depends on a lot of variables that can't necessarily be controlled during the planning stage. But the key part of the equation is outside visitors bringing new money to the area, who, as more and more casinos sprout up, become harder and harder to find because they all have casinos to frequent that are much closer to home. And that's without thinking of the social ills that come with gambling.

I don't mean to become the morality police here, but something about the government subsidizing gambling—considering it is potentially addictive and can lead to financial ruin—is decidedly unsavory. (I find the same strangeness at work in government monopolies over liquor, such as the one in Pennsylvania.) Sure, the government finds revenue via taxing other vices, such as tobacco, marijuana, or booze, but in the case of casinos, it's oftentimes governments explicitly subsidizing the creation of a social ill, rather than just taking a cut of behavior it only regulates. After all, liquor stores aren't getting tax breaks left and right, and nobody thinks that a 7-Eleven selling packs of cigarettes is much of a jobs program.

Measuring the social ills attributable to a casino, like measuring its economic impact, is difficult stuff. Several studies have found that crime, addiction, and bankruptcy increase when a new casino opens its doors, while others have found they barely budge. At least two studies have found that the presence of casinos increases drunk driving, a perhaps unsurprising result given the prevalence of free drinks that get foisted upon the players. Overall, estimates of the cost on society per problematic gambler vary widely, from a few hundred dollars annually to tens of thousands of dollars. Any city or state getting ready to okay a new casino needs to acknowledge that not only fun and games will be coming along with it.

Also, who, exactly, does the most financial damage to themselves via a new casino, which encourages a behavior that can be addicting and destructive? On that front, the literature is clearer: Gambling takes much more of a whack out of the income of those who can least afford it.

Much like with the lottery, it's a bit odd to think of the cost of gambling as a tax, but it is, in much the same way that alcohol or cigarette taxes are: It's a payment made on a vice, a regulated activity that is frowned upon but is still a source of revenue. Gambling taxes are often set at higher rates than other taxes because, since they're essentially viewed as voluntary, there's little penalty in starting them high and hiking them further.

"Average tax rates at casinos countrywide are maybe 25 or 30 percent, and that's just off the top. The casino also pays income taxes at the federal and state level. So it's taxed at a really high rate. So even if all the money that's coming into a casino is coming out of some other form of spending, you could argue that the tax revenue is going to be higher for the politician," said Doug Walker, the College of Charleston economist. Moving spending from the movie theater to the casino may not do a whole lot for economic activity or job creation in the aggregate, but it can send more money into state coffers.

Some percentage of those taxes gets handed down to the customers, and many states also have a per head fee that must be paid by casino goers. While those with higher incomes spend more dollars each on gaming than those with lower incomes, as a percentage of income those on the lower end, particularly those with lower levels of education, get hit the hardest. The proliferation of casinos means that states or cities are banking on plenty of low-income folks coming in and blowing money on slot machines.

The changing face of casino gambling due to its proliferation is explicitly pushing more and more casino business into the lower reaches of America's socioeconomic strata. When legalized gambling was limited to Vegas and Atlantic City, for most people it was a big deal to get there, requiring an expense that the working class often couldn't afford; this glamorous activity was for those with disposable income. But now that casinos have sprung up everywhere, that's all changed.

Per the Institute for American Values (which, despite its conservative-sounding name is more middle-of-the-road, if quite scoldy), today's gamers "typically travel distances of 70 miles or less, arrive in their own cars or on buses, spend nearly all their time and money gambling at the casino, and return home to sleep in their own beds. . . . The traditional Vegas-style resort casinos catered mainly to high rollers and 'whales' partial to table games. Today's regional casinos cater overwhelmingly to middle rollers and low rollers who play slot machines."[37]

Those slot machines are a good way to waste cash in short order; their odds are much worse than are those in a hand of cards. "Payday lending, rent-to-own stores, subprime credit cards, auto title loans and tax refund anticipation loans all evolved to extract high profits from low-income groups. And the newly established state-licensed casinos have their methods, too," wrote the institute's Barbara Dafoe Whitehead in a 2014 *New York Times* op-ed.[38]

Making matters worse, the evidence that casinos bolster state finances when everything shakes out is thin to nonexistent, even with those high tax rates. A 2011 study by Doug Walker and John D. Jackson found that "for the average state, it appears that casinos have a small but negative net impact on state revenues."

Their results show a net decrease of $90 million in revenue for states with casinos; for each additional dollar bet in casinos, state revenue falls by about seven cents.[39] They wrote, "In most states' policy debates over casinos, the question has been whether the tax benefits (along with other potential economic growth effects) were worth the potential social costs imposed by pathological gamblers. Our results here indicate that the benefits side of the casino question is less of a certainty than is suggested in much of the public debate or literature."

Oops.

With so many states having now built casinos, the rate of diminishing returns is apt to grow and grow, as every new casino thins out the available business for all the others and makes sustained casino tourism that much less likely, since America only has so many gambling dollars to go around. No matter how much casinos spend on advertising or other gimmicks, willingness to gamble is finite.

"You could argue that's already been occurring," said Walker when I asked him if the casino overload would affect the ability of any one new casino to provide an economic boost to the community. "If you focus on, for example, when they first started expanding in the early nineties, it was along the Mississippi River, and those states that had the riverboats initially saw a lot of regional tourism because prior to that you'd have to go to either Atlantic City or Nevada, and so I think there were benefits of that tourism coming into those areas. That effect no longer, I would say, exists in those places. There's a lot of casinos that are just small regional properties that just serve the people nearby, which is in contrast with places like Biloxi and Atlantic City and Las Vegas, which were drawing from a much wider area." That means that more and more of the budgetary benefit of gambling comes from the pockets of a state's own citizens, rather than from drawing outside spending in. That formula blunts whatever wider effect the casino might have, as it doesn't generate much in the way of new spending.

Walker pointed out that boosters of gambling today are often not touting the tourism effects as much as they are arguing that their state or county needs to retain dollars that are disappearing to someone else's tourist attraction. The officials selling gambling as a way to help the economy aren't even talking about the creation of new business so much as fighting over the scraps of the business that's already there and trying to keep their share of diminishing dollars stable.

Take Massachusetts. "One of the biggest arguments for them legalizing was that their estimates were up to one billion dollars per year that people were spending in Connecticut casinos, so now it's more, instead of drawing in tourists, we're trying to keep our own people home and get the tax revenues instead of it going to a neighboring state," Walker said. "Whatever tax revenues were being received as a result of tourism has gone away from most markets." That line of thinking went hand in hand with the argument that, if states were going to deal with the social ills of problem gambling anyway because their residents were crossing state lines to gamble and then bringing their issues homes with them, the state might as well pick up some tax revenue along the way.

Overall, per an April 2016 report from Lucy Dadayan at the Nelson A. Rockefeller Institute of Government, casino revenue is headed down the tubes in most places where gaming has been legalized. But it's the states where casinos first opened that are particularly being hit, as players gravitate toward newer casinos that are presumably a little closer to home. New casinos beggar older ones, then get beggared themselves by even newer ones, and soon you wind up with a situation like the one in Atlantic City, where a town that once went whole hog on casinos has been picked dry by its neighbors. Since the city had bet so big on gambling and been sustained by it and little else for so long, it had nothing on which to fall back.

"For the nation as a whole, the compound annual growth rate [in casino revenue] was negative 0.2 percent between fiscal years 2008 and 2015. Moreover, the compound annual growth rate was negative 4.4 in the 'older' casino states," Dadayan wrote. "Inflation-adjusted tax and fee revenues from casinos declined by $83 million or 1.5 percent for the nation between 2008 and 2015. The 'older' casino states saw much deeper declines at 26.9 percent. Declines were reported in all 'older' casino states, indicating that casinos in those states either reached saturation or have been cannibalized by 'new' casino states."[40] There simply aren't enough gambling dollars to go around, so eventually a lot of players in the casino business have to go bust.

The moral of the story is that gambling is a huge gamble for states and cities, something that seems like a no-lose proposition that instead ends up leaving them holding a whole lot of cards and not much else. Casinos and lotteries may seem appealing to lawmakers who want to tax something that looks and smells like a vice, a voluntary payment that nobody is forced to make, rather than tackling a politically risky tax increase or some other way to raise money. But in so doing, they may actually be shooting themselves in the foot, taking a knock on the revenue side and perhaps not even creating any new employment, while hurting some of the most vulnerable of their residents. The bet needs to be considered in a much more measured fashion before cities and states start throwing more chips on the table.

6

THE STADIUM SWINDLE

IN THE MIDDLE OF THE concourse at McCarran International Airport in Las Vegas, a merch stand sold all things Golden Knights. That made sense at the time: This was October 2017, and the team was in the midst of the first home stand of the first season of Sin City's first major professional sports team. After years of what-ifs and maybes, the National Hockey League had finally brought big-time sports right to Las Vegas's famed Strip. Thus, the helmet logo of the Golden Knights, with its capital *V* in the negative space, trimmed by black and gold, was everywhere one looked. Given what a successful inaugural season the team had, winning its division in a walk and then making a run all the way to the Stanley Cup final, perhaps I should have bought some mementos and sold them off on eBay later.

But I wasn't on the prowl for Golden Knights gear on that day. In the corner of one of those airport stores where you can buy peanuts, phone chargers, and gaudy tourist T-shirts, I found what I was looking for: Raiders apparel. A few T-shirts and some mugs, with the iconic eye-patch-wearing black-and-silver player, were available. Notably, none of the stuff mentioned anything about a location. It just said "Raiders," if it said anything at all. That's because, while at the moment they were still the Oakland Raiders, plying their trade in that city's old Oakland–Alameda County Coliseum, in a few years the plan was to have them pick up and move to Vegas, the beneficiaries of the largest stadium subsidy in American history.

For years, it had been no secret that the Raiders ownership wanted out of Oakland and the aging Coliseum, which opened in 1966, making it positively ancient compared to nearly every other arena and stadium in America. The Coliseum is also the last American stadium shared by NFL and Major League Baseball teams, with the Raiders splitting time with MLB's Athletics, which makes for a suboptimal field situation for everyone involved. When Nevada put a pot of money on the table that would enable the Raiders to move, it was almost inevitable that the team would jump on it. In March 2017, by a vote of 31–1, the NFL team owners okayed the move, setting up the Raiders to follow in the Golden Knights' footsteps and come to Nevada.

And how much did Nevada taxpayers have to kick in for the shiny Las Vegas Stadium that would be the Raiders' new home? A cool $750 million.

Though the Nevada state legislature set an American record by devoting that much public money to a new professional sports stadium, big spending from the public coffers on NFL stadiums is a bet that not only Vegas has made in recent years. Per ESPN, $6.7 billion in taxpayer money has been spent on a several-decades-long stadium building spree by the NFL alone.[1] Billions upon billions more have been spent to build facilities for teams in the other major leagues, too—$17 billion between 1986 and 2012, per one Bloomberg News analysis.[2] It's rare these days to see a stadium built for any professional team—major or minor league—that doesn't include a hefty contribution from one government entity or another.

The Raiders' departure was arguably the highlight of a period of chaotic shuffling among Californian NFL franchises, the third relocation in little over a year involving the Golden State, after the St. Louis Rams moved back to Los Angeles, to be joined by their Southern California counterparts, the Chargers, formerly of San Diego. But while the other moves had more to do with the desire for owners to tap into bigger media markets, in the case of the Raiders, a huge factor—the overriding one—was that Las Vegas Stadium was receiving that hefty chunk of public change. Oakland had, for years, deliberately and defiantly refused to put public money toward a new stadium, so owner Mark Davis had been not very quietly agitating for a move. When Nevada opted to raise its hotel occupancy tax and dedicate the money toward a new stadium, that was that for Oakland.

Sports in Vegas have a complicated and interesting history. For a long time, America's major professional leagues were wary of the city's association with gambling, fearing that any team playing there would be irredeemably tainted by allegations of point-shaving or some other unsavory gambling-related activity. As far back as 1915, though, when the Chicago White Sox came to town for an exhibition game, teams have toyed with the city; other pro leagues, such as the NBA and the NHL, also hosted exhibitions in town, flirting with Vegas but never officially asking it to the dance.[3] In the meantime, a cycle of minor league teams came and went—including the Rattlers (semipro basketball), the Silver Bandits (from the International Basketball League), and the Sting (the Arena Football League)—with few leaving much of an impression. The

Las Vegas 51s, a minor league baseball team, have toiled for years at the bottom of the Pacific Coast League's attendance standings.[4] Boxing was the only sport that ever gained a toehold in the self-styled entertainment capital of the world.

With the Golden Knights and the Raiders, though, the calculus has clearly changed.

"The story of big-time sports in Las Vegas is the lack of success in professional sports and that the biggest sports franchise event or series of events ever here was the basketball team at UNLV," said University of Nevada, Las Vegas, history professor Michael Green. "I tend to think the Raiders are the only NFL team that would have come here, the Raiders being the Raiders. But what the hockey team coming here tells you is that, one, the NHL thinks it's to its benefit, but, two, Las Vegas just isn't the same city that didn't get excited about the Las Vegas Quicksilvers," a team that spent one season in the North American Soccer League back in 1977.[5]

America's taboo on gambling becoming less pronounced and the major sports league seeing fantasy sports—those ever-more-popular games in which the stats of real-world players translate into points for their digital "owners"—as a potential cash cow have driven the change that led to Vegas going from sports pariah to golden child. But perhaps more important, the city and the state changed their tune on using public money to build sports facilities, something to which they had been adamantly opposed before the Raiders received their largesse; given all the other negatives about Vegas, that it wouldn't put public money on the table seemed destined to doom it to sports irrelevancy forever.

Ponying up for the Raiders was quite the reversal, and a quick one. "I think we've hit a perfect storm where the Las Vegas market has been growing to two-million-plus now, and we're also at a point in the different major leagues where they're literally running out of cities to tap into for public subsidies. For years, we were one of the last holdouts. We did not cough up public money for quite a long time for stadiums," explained Alan Snel, who founded LV-SportsBiz.com, a website that covers the business side of Sin City's sports scene. "We're not known for these big public expenditures, so when we're raising 1.2 billion dollars over thirty years so that we can give a 750-million-dollar payment to an NFL team, that is a huge, huge deal."[6] (Officially, the Raiders stadium will be in Paradise, Nevada, an unincorporated town that abuts Las Vegas and which is actually home to most of the Strip so closely associated with that city.)

In many ways the Raiders deal epitomizes everything that is wrong with subsidizing stadiums, in a place that for a while had gotten it right. "I thought this particular deal was done extremely quickly. Typically there's a lot more public discussion," Snel said. "This was like wham, bam, thank you, ma'am, in a year. The governor called a special session, the state legislature approved the room-fee increase, and wham-o, you have a supposedly 750-million-dollar subsidy for the Raiders."[7]

I met up with Snel at the Golden Knights practice facility in Summerlin, Nevada. It's situated across the street from the Red Rock casino in a part of the state where one can see mountains every which way in the distance. The contrast between how the Golden Knights came to Vegas and the way in which it wooed the Raiders is quite striking. T-Mobile Arena, where the Golden Knights ply their trade, is one of the few new sports facilities in the United States to be privately funded. Located on the Strip behind the New York–New York and Monte Carlo casinos, it's a testament to how a dedicated ownership group and other private entities can build an arena and secure a new franchise without needing heaps of money from the state to do it. The arena was seen as a moneymaking venture and the Golden Knights' owners sensed an opportunity, so Nevada taxpayers have a new team to watch without having had to sacrifice public moneys to get it.

Unfortunately, that's not the way it usually happens, as the Raiders debacle proved shortly thereafter. The major leagues and the owners of their franchises have convinced lawmakers and fans alike that public "investment" is a necessary part of the mix in today's sporting world. Not only do the leagues and owners wield the usual promises of economic growth and job creation that will accompany a new stadium or arena, but they also have a way to go nuclear: threatening to move a team to a new locale if their demands are not met. Emotional blackmail—the thought of "their" team playing in a new city, with new colors, in front of new fans— makes taking a stand against subsidizing new stadiums even more fraught for lawmakers than it might otherwise have been. The whole thing comes together into a toxic stew for taxpayers that lets sports owners swindle the public under the guise of community building.

Let's take the first part of the owners' narrative first, as it's the easier one to deal with: Precious little evidence suggests that stadiums or professional sports franchises in a town do much of anything to boost the economy. Since the late 1980s, a host of economists have looked at whether pro sports teams, the stadiums they play in, or the special events in which they may participate— the World Series, the Super Bowl, All-Star Games, and the like— have any measurable effect on job creation, economic growth, or wages for the people who work in and around the various metro areas in which pro athletes ply their trade. Over and over, through paper after paper, data set after data set, the answer comes up the same: nope.

Dennis Coates, a professor of economics at the University of Maryland–Baltimore County, has spent years looking at the breadth and width of pro sports in the United States to find out if what the leagues and their boosters were selling regarding stadium construction had any truth to it. First in 1999 and then again in 2015 he took in all the evidence (the first time with a coauthor, Brad Humphreys) and found that cities with a major league sports team see no appreciable increase in economic activity across a host of variables. (His first paper looked at the MLB, the NFL, and the NBA, while the second added the NHL and Major League Soccer to the mix.) In many instances, the presence of a sports franchise is associated with negative income effects for a metropolitan area. The entire economic rationale that sports owners and league officials had been hanging their hat on is a load of nonsense.

"In '95 when I moved here and the [Cleveland] Browns moved here, there was all this business about job creation and income growth and all of this stuff, and I was, like, 'This is such a crock,'" Coates said about coming to Baltimore, a city that famously lost its beloved Colts in the dead of night to Indianapolis, then welcomed in the relocating Browns little more than a decade later. "There's no way that any of that could possibly be true. They play eight friggin' games. How could they create three thousand full-time jobs? That's just nonsense."[8]

But it's not just the NFL and its eight games for which estimates of economic effects are vastly overblown. Across sports, the impact that a team and whatever venue it plays in will have on its hometown is overstated. As Coates found, although proponents argue that the addition of a professional sports franchise to a community will lead to increases in income, wages, job creation, and the like, they frequently move in the opposite direction. "If the local government is looking for a policy to foster economic growth, far better candidate policies exist than those subsidizing a professional sports franchise," he wrote.[9]

This jibes with the vast, vast bulk of the academic work in this area. Economists have looked at stadiums, arenas, the events they host, and the costs they accrue, and even if individual players can move the economic needle, and the answer over and over is no, they can not. As Victor Matheson and Robert Baade, two of the country's most prominent and prolific sports economists, wrote in a 2011 survey, "Researchers who have gone back and looked at economic data for localities that have hosted mega-events, attracted new franchises, or built new sports facilities have almost invariably found little or no economic benefits from spectator sports."[10]

President Harry Truman supposedly had a joke about wanting a one-handed economist to give him advice because "all my economists say, 'On the one hand . . . on the other.'" Indeed, it's not hard to find a subject on which economists virulently disagree, even within the factions with similar political leanings. But on this one, left and right and everyone in between is united: Subsidizing sports is a sucker's game. Yet such subsidies are pervasive.

Why is it such a bad deal? For the same big reason so many other bets on entertainment are: Money is spent on something that has little economic impact when it could be spent on something else that would be much more beneficial to many more people. The economic impact of spending on sports is blunted for all the reasons you should expect, having come so far in this book.

First, money that is spent in the stadiums by the game-day crowds is not necessarily new money in the community. People don't sit around and do nothing, twiddling their thumbs, when their city doesn't have a professional sports team. On nongame days, people don't all stay home waiting for the next home match so that they can go out on the town again.

"Their most infuriating argument is, 'Well, I talked to the restaurant owners and they say how full the restaurants are on game day. With my own eyes I can see the impact this is having!'" said Coates, referring to stadium proponents. "What's infuriating about that is they don't understand that people actually eat on game day whether there's a football team in town or not."[11]

Second is that the crowding-out effect occurs. Yes, people may flock to a particular part of town to take in a game at the arena, but other savvy city dwellers know to check the schedule and avoid that same part of town when a home match is scheduled, because they don't want to deal with the traffic or noise. Some percentage of the crowd attending a game, then, is merely displacing those who would have been around the arena anyway if whoever plays there were on a road trip. (This is more applicable to downtown arenas and stadiums than the sort of fields that are out in the suburbs, set among a sea of parking spaces and little else, which is a problem in its own right for those making the case that sports will boost the local economy.)

Finally, there's every reason to think that a healthy percentage of the money made in and around an arena or stadium leaks out of the local community and back to the headquarters of the corporations providing the food, beer, and ticket processing.

But you know all that having read this much already, I hope. Sports stadiums and arenas are in the same bucket as anything else discussed in this book so far; they aren't unique and don't make big, material changes to the economic dynamics I hope you've come to recognize. So let's focus for a while on the material downside to spending on stadiums, arenas, and other things to coax sports teams to move to a city or to encourage them to stay. And let's start in Arizona.

Glendale is not your prototypical hockey town. An economist who spoke to a colleague and me who were writing about it said, "This is hockey in a nonhockey city where the average resident hasn't seen ice outside of a margarita."[12] Yet the city plowed millions of dollars into an effort to ensure that the Phoenix Coyotes, who then became the Arizona Coyotes, had an arena in which to play.

The Coyotes are perhaps the second-best example of the National Hockey League's push into the southern United States going awry. (The best would be the short-lived Atlanta Thrashers, who after a decade of futility decamped to Canada and became the second coming of the Winnipeg Jets, who had moved from Winnipeg to, you guessed it, Arizona.) Management was a mess and results on the ice were bad, matched only by the sorry state of the team's finances. In 2009, the Coyotes declared bankruptcy and were taken into league custody. Through it all, the city of Glendale made one disastrous decision after another to plow more and more money into trying to coax to life in the desert a hockey team few wanted to pay to see.

In 2003, Glendale offered up more than $100 million toward a new arena to entice the Coyotes to move out to the burbs from their home in downtown Phoenix (which was also a taxpayer-financed arena). By 2012, after the team was already a ward of the league, the city offered another $300 million to any prospective owner. Once the team had a new owner, the city paid it $15 million per season to manage its own franchise. And through it all, the Coyotes were hemorrhaging money. Estimates were that the Coyotes franchise would lose millions of dollars every single season even if the team made an unprecedented number of consecutive runs to the Stanley Cup Finals.[13] That's some bleak, bad business.

At the same time, the city faced budget gap after budget gap thanks to the lingering aftereffects of the Great Recession. It cut public jobs and even considered putting its public buildings up as collateral against the loans it received to pay for a hockey team. So the consequences stemming from the decision to subsidize sports were real. Money that could have been plowed into actual services, public safety, or even just fixing potholes instead went to ensuring that one of the least popular hockey teams in the country didn't fly the coop.

This is exactly what it means to say that the decisions cities make have opportunity costs. As one Glendale council member told me back in 2012, "I can use that fifteen million dollar [annual payment] for good things for Glendale . . . open our libraries up again . . . replace the fifty-five cops that we're short right now."[14] Yet the city kept throwing good money after bad, even when it was apparent to most observers that the smartest thing for everyone was probably to cut their losses.

Finally, in 2015, Glendale wised up and severed its agreement with the Coyotes.[15] Now the team is on essentially a year-to-year lease, threatening to move every season unless it gets a new publicly financed arena and then re-upping for a new season once said arena doesn't materialize. The city essentially called the Coyotes' bluff; the team has had every chance to leave, and it's not as if cities such as Seattle and Quebec haven't been clamoring for a franchise all their own. However, the Coyotes have instead chosen to stay, just more on the city's terms than on those of the owner or the league. But before that, those millions of dollars weren't spent on things from which the vast bulk of the city could benefit.

Situations like this happen all over the place. Cities with severe financial needs instead invest some of their precious resources in building new facilities for sports teams and their oftentimes billionaire owners. The city of Detroit, after it had gone into bankruptcy, even paid for a new arena for the Red Wings, while the city's emergency financial manager was threatening to cut pensions for public employees.[16]

Let's go back to Vegas to get the flip side of this story. In December 2014, its city council approved $56.5 million in subsidies for the building of a new Major League Soccer stadium meant to house a then-nonexistent team that the league said it may create sometime in the future. And that didn't include the cost of the land that the city would be giving away (which was worth $38 to $48 million) or the $20 million parking garage it planned to build next door.[17]

For plenty of reasons, Vegas seemed ill-suited for an MLS team: It's not a particularly big metro area and has a low median income for a city. But Vegas Mayor Carolyn Goodman put the need for a soccer stadium in nearly apocalyptic terms: "Without substantive and new reasons to visit our downtown, our city businesses will be challenged to stay open. Our casinos and hotel rooms will not be filled. Our shops, our galleries, our taverns, our restaurants will empty."[18] "With gaming all over the country, how are we going to bring people to Las Vegas?" she asked. "We have to keep doing new things."[19] Her argument had some merit, as gaming has indeed proliferated and the returns from it have diminished. However, to think that a soccer stadium was the key to changing that trend, especially with all the other entertainment options that Vegas offers, was never credible.

Thus did the battle begin, and a signature drive endorsed by some of the dissenting members of the city council quickly threw

Vegas's plan into serious doubt. In an early example of the sort of citizen power that would drive the No Boston 2024 movement, it began to look as if not only would a referendum on whether Vegas should be getting into the soccer-stadium business be on an upcoming ballot, but also that the city might lose.

"This has been the most one-sided feedback from constituents ever, saying, 'Don't do it,'" said Las Vegas Councilman Bob Beers that year.[20] Eventually, MLS pulled the plug on the deal, citing the political uncertainty in Vegas. Win one for the citizens, at least.

What does this have to do with the opportunity costs of building a stadium? I met up with Beers again nearly three years later, with the Golden Knights up and running and the state having paid dearly to bring the Raiders to town. He had lost his subsequent city council reelection campaign and had recently launched a bid to be Nevada's state treasurer. His proudest achievement from his time serving Sin City? His role in blocking the MLS stadium.

"We managed to head off the highly speculative 'If we build a stadium, they'll give us an MLS team' juggernaut, fairly successfully," he said on an exceedingly sunny day outside a Starbucks. "Instead, we built sixteen parks; most of them are in the inner city. A lot of them are one- and two-acre pocket parks that are serving individual neighborhoods.

"You can make your own social judgment as to whether society is better off having sixteen little parks or one hell of a flea market four times a year," he said, which is all that the parking lot at the stadium would have been good for had an MLS team not materialized.[21]

This is a stark example of the consequences of the choices cities make. Yes, money is fungible and can be moved around, so no one specific thing going by the wayside is usually the direct result of something else getting funded. But governing is about priorities; choosing to pay for a stadium means choosing to not use that money on something else.

"Most of what a city does is provide emergency services, fire trucks, police departments, same here. Sewer service, it's really mundane boring stuff," says Beers. "But it's routine. [Stopping the MLS stadium] was really an exceptional event, and the opportunity to spike it, as I helped do, was a rare opportunity and fortuitous timing on my part. And a pretty big public service. Sixteen parks in town today. . . . In five years' time, you have a direct thing, there it is, wouldn't have been if we'd done this. That's what the opportunity cost is."[22]

For the people of Vegas, parks are undeniably a better use of their tax money than a stadium—and just a few years later, they got a privately funded hockey arena anyway. Sports team owners have the money to build new facilities all on their own; they just don't do so because they know they can get the public to pick up part of the tab.

Where does that power come from? What is it about sports that makes lawmakers—and much of the public—throw gobs of money at the already well-off owners? After all, owners are not a particularly sympathetic bunch to the fans, generally.

Well, the same dynamic is at work in sports as in many other areas I've written about: Lawmakers want to please the donor class and their constituents and to generate good press and are perfectly happy to punt the tab to a future generation. The headlines and the handshakes make the debt and the other missed opportunities worth it; and, hey, you might get a seat in the owner's box. Nobody puts the guy who fixes potholes on the front page of the local paper. "The really cynical side of me, that's the public-choice side of me, says they know it's all hogwash but they don't care because it provides them with campaign contributions, visibility that they wouldn't get otherwise," said Dennis Coates, regarding politicians' motivation in subsidizing sports.[23]

Lawmakers also, less cynically, fear job losses, or anything that looks as if they haven't given their all to keep the economic juices flowing in the area they represent.

Beers chalks some of it up to the limits of legislating and the power of those who lobby for the industry: "I don't care if you're talking about sixty-three Nevada legislators or a hundred forty-year-old white-collar executives, not everyone is going to read all that economic analysis. So in my experience any large group of people has some who say, 'I'm mystified by economics, and so I trust that guy, and if that guy tells me this makes sense, then by golly I'm going to defend that it makes sense to the end. . . .' That's part of legislating. It doesn't matter whether it's a passage of a bond to fund a stadium subsidy or a criminal statute to limit the prison time associated with a particular offense. There's always in a group going to be people who are not interested in that part, but are interested in that part. Do some people actually believe that economic analysis? I don't, so I find it amazing that some would, but I've seen enough government discussion and argument to know that some do believe that."[24]

But something more fundamental is also at work: People love their sports teams. And their sports teams don't love them back. That means the deal making is always on the owners' terms.

As much as Americans may like to think otherwise, big-time sports in the United States is a big-time business, and everyone's favorite team is someone's profit-making venture. While we may like to think of our favorite franchise as an indelible part of the community fabric, the beating heart of a city, something that is figuratively (and often literally) tattooed onto a place's residents, the team is an asset that its owner can move. Just as business owners will leave for a more lucrative deal elsewhere when states compete against one another with tax incentives, so, too, will owners of sports teams. They're just taking with them what many people don't think of as a financial asset. Desperate to keep their teams in play, fans will overlook abuses of their money if it means avoiding the indignity of seeing their favorite players wearing new uniforms with some other city name on them next year.

"The reversion level might be that you lose your team. Your team goes away. If the reversion level was 'My seats are less comfortable,' we'd see a lot less support for stadium subsidies," says Coates. "But if the reversion level is something as horrible as the team going away, they're much more willing to support it."[25]

Moving a team is the nuclear bomb that so many sports owners have in their arsenal. And they've used it: The Colts left Baltimore, the Browns left Cleveland, the Sonics left Seattle, the Rams left first Los Angeles and then St. Louis, the Thrashers left Atlanta, the Jets left Winnipeg, the Expos left Montreal, and on and on, back to the Brooklyn Dodgers moving to California after New York's city planner refused to condemn a stretch of land and sell it to the Dodgers' owner at a below-market price. Owners have proven more than willing to take the money and run, especially now that having stadiums filled with luxury boxes and other brand-new amenities is so key to their financial planning. Having an older stadium, even if it's generally full, is assumed to be a knock on the moneymaking potential of a franchise.

Plus, we humans are not good at seeing the forest for the trees when it comes to losing what we already have. Vegas was able to defeat an MLS stadium partly because no team was already there embedded in the hearts and minds of the community, nor was there any guarantee that a team would come along. In a lot of other instances, a team that already has a home threatens to go somewhere else if its demands aren't met—and so the city pays up. Just as Americans didn't love Obamacare until Congress threatened to take it away, so, too, do residents of a place freak out about losing a team, even if it means dealing with some stuff they don't like, such as handing over their tax money for a billionaire's stadium. The billionaires are more than happy to take advantage of that dynamic, using their leverage of owning a part of the community to get what they want.

I'm making this sound evil on the part of the owners, but it isn't really. It's business. In 2017 alone, the Coyotes threatened to leave Glendale (again), and the NBA's Suns threatened to leave Phoenix, while the NHL's Senators threatened to leave Ottawa and the Flames threatened to leave Calgary, all over stadium subsidies. (Yes, two of those teams are Canadian, but since they play in American-dominated leagues, and NHL teams have a history of decamping for the States, it works basically the same.) "We have to have an NBA-quality facility. I know that. The city of Phoenix knows that. Hopefully in the next couple of years we can start construction on something," the Suns' owner said. "If we can't, we'll explore other options."[26] His comments are emblematic of how all of these "negotiations" work. The owner essentially goes, "Nice team you have here. Shame if anything were to happen to it," holding a gun to the head of the local community.

Not that the script can't be altered, of course. One of the most intriguing recent skirmishes in the stadium wars is the battle over the Columbus Crew and owner Anthony Precourt's desire to move the team to Austin, Texas. The Crew were one of Major League Soccer's founding franchises, with a home—MAPFRE Stadium— that was not only the first soccer-specific stadium to be built in America, but also the site of the biggest matches for the US men's national soccer team, thanks to a string of 2–0 wins against archri-val Mexico, the famous *dos a cero* score line that dominated that matchup for many years. Nevertheless, Precourt, who bought the team in 2013, said in the fall of 2017 that he was going to take the team to Texas if a new stadium deal couldn't be worked out with the city.

"It's become clear to us that we need a new stadium and a new business model to realize our ambitions of being a top club," he moaned, lamenting the "antiquated" stadium that was not yet twenty years old. "It's really about keeping up with our peers, hav-ing strong ambition, and getting to a world-class, state-of-the-art new soccer stadium."[27]

Precourt claimed at the beginning of the ordeal that he didn't want public funding for the new Crew stadium, yet, somehow, every proposal that surfaced involved some giveaway from the state, such as land or the extension of a "temporary" sales tax. "For all of these options, we would partner with private developers to turn the surrounding area into an entertainment district with restaurants, bars, and attractive streetscapes," Columbus officials claimed.[28] Always beware of public officials getting ready to "partner" with private concerns; it's usually not good for your wallet.

The contours looked pretty familiar for a stadium swindle, but then something interesting happened: a massive effort to save the Crew (#SavetheCrew, as the Twitter hashtag put it) without throw-ing huge money at a new stadium. Instead, local leaders tried to broker a deal to purchase the team from Precourt; Ohio's attorney general, Mike DeWine, threatened to sue, using a law passed in the wake of the Cleveland Browns' departure for Baltimore that required owners to check certain boxes before moving a franchise that had benefited from public money, which DeWine claimed the team did through parking improvements and tax-free property. "The Ohio attorney general's office has reviewed the law passed after the Browns' move. We believe the evidence will show that this law would apply to the Columbus Crew and Mapfre Stadium," DeWine said in a statement.[29] Other analysts even suggested the state use eminent domain to claim the team outright.

As of this writing, the fate of the Crew is still up in the air, though looking much better than it did before. I hope the episode is illustrative of a new trend in stadium politics, in which teams can't skip town after picking up public benefits, since these are an investment by the community that ought to be repaid in some way. Much like back in chapter three, when Greg LeRoy sued a manufacturer that threatened to leave on the grounds that it had benefited from public subsidies, so, too, should sports teams have to take into account the public moneys that support them that could have been spent on anything else.

The sunk cost for cities is going to become even more important because the current trend in stadium construction is set to hang even longer-term costs onto them. MAPFRE Stadium being considered obsolete less than two decades after it opened is part and parcel of a larger push by sports owners all over the country to renovate stadiums that, if they were people, wouldn't be old enough to drink.

Take the case of Atlanta's Turner Field, home of the MLB's Braves, which was originally built for the 1996 Atlanta Summer Olympics. The stadium was not yet twenty years old when the team began agitating for a new one, claiming that it would help loads of people who weren't on the field or in the executive suite. "We believe we're an economic driver, and we certainly don't want people to lose sight of that, and it's certainly something that helps a great deal of people beyond us just playing baseball games and trying to win that World Series," said Mike Plant, the Braves' executive vice president of business operations.[30]

Atlanta itself didn't end up kicking in money for a new Braves' stadium, but rather Cobb County, out in the suburbs. While the current average is for taxpayers to cover some three-quarters of the cost of a new baseball stadium, Cobb Country taxpayers received a relative bargain, providing $300 million, just 45 percent of the new park's total cost. "Thanks to serious, conservative leadership, Cobb County will realize a 60 percent annual return on investment from the SunTrust Park partnership," former Cobb County chairman Tim Lee wrote at the park's opening. "In fact, it will be the first private public partnership of its kind to result in a return on investment to taxpayers in the very first year."[31]

I'm sure you'll be shocked to learn that the return on investment was less than promised. As *Atlanta Journal-Constitution* reporter Meris Lutz calculated, the annual debt obligation for the stadium for county taxpayers is some $16 million per year, which the revenues don't come close to covering.[32] And that's to replace a ballpark that was barely two decades old that had hosted an Olympic games within living memory of millennials.

That's the hot new trend in stadium construction: not only getting taxpayers to pony up for stadiums, but to do so less than twenty years into the life of the old stadium. "The twenty-year time horizon is roughly the average now," Stanford sports economist Roger Noll told *USA Today*. "By the time a new one gets built, it's usually more like twenty-five years, but nobody ever stays in the same stadium for the term of their lease anymore."[33]

Here's the problem with that new math: Cities usually pay for stadiums with decades-long bond issues, meaning they raise money up front from investors and then pay them off over a long time span, usually thirty years. It doesn't take a math whiz to see that a twenty-year life span for stadiums conjoined with thirty years of payments will mean teams will start agitating for a new home when their city is still paying off the old one. When teams leave because their twenty-year-old stadium no longer cuts it, cities are stuck with an empty facility and the bill.

That's exactly what happened when the St. Louis Rams made their semitriumphant return to Los Angeles. (No one attended the games, but they made the playoffs!) Thanks to a spectacularly bad lease for the city signed in 1995, the Rams were promised a top-tier stadium, in perpetuity, by the city of St. Louis, which was inevitably a promise it couldn't keep, especially considering that the NFL's stadium boom was generating a steady stream of state-of-the-art facilities. When the Rams opted out, taxpayers in Missouri, between the debts owed at the city, county, and state levels, were on the hook still for $144 million, which won't be paid off until five years after the Rams were firmly ensconced on the West Coast. And St. Louis isn't the only city to get stuck with such a deal. As Reuters found, Seattle's Kingdome bonds were retired some fifteen years after the facility was imploded in 2000, while Philadelphia was still paying for Veterans Stadium more than a decade after it was torn down.[34]

In those latter two cases, at least, the team in question didn't move to another city, but merely a newer facility. The Rams combined insult with their injury, though, by splitting town and leaving Missouri with the check.

Of the current thirty NFL stadiums, only the Oakland Coliseum was built before the 1990s, and only two—Los Angeles's Inglewood stadium, shared by the Rams and the Chargers, and New Jersey's MetLife Stadium, shared by the Giants and the Jets—were built without public support. While it's generally a bad idea to publicly subsidize any sports facility, the case is even worse for a football stadium. In the best-case scenario, it's going to be used for twelve games in an NFL season: two preseason games, eight regular-season contests, and a couple of play-off games. Besides that, few events require the amount of seating an NFL stadium has: the odd concert, the occasional international soccer game, some college football games. The rest of the year, it lies dormant, usually surrounded by a sea of empty parking spaces that only get used on the scant few dates that the stadium is open and otherwise just get pounded by the sun and rain.

At least a baseball stadium has a guaranteed eighty-one home games every season. Shared hockey/basketball arenas have the same guaranteed eighty-something games, plus are much easier to book for concerts, wrestling events, and all sorts of other things due to their lower capacity. Those sorts of venues don't usually have big economic effects, but something such as the Staples Center in Los Angeles or the Capital One Arena in Washington—which gets used multiple times a week and is actually in the city, not out in the burbs surrounded by nothing but parking spaces—provides stadium proponents with a better story. But football stadiums? No way and no thanks.

Since the academic literature is pretty unanimous on the negative or negligible effect stadiums have on the economy, I asked Dennis Coates, the UMBC sports economist, if there's anywhere in the country, anywhere at all, wherein the proponents of stadium subsidies have a point.

"The one example I guess I would say that maybe there is some truth to is actually FedExField," he told me, referring to the home of DC's football team. "Why? Because Maryland stole it from DC, so anything that happens in Maryland you count it as benefit to Maryland as opposed to benefit to DC. In the broader context of the metropolitan area, it's a wash. But if you can steal if from the other jurisdiction—so the New Jersey Nets becoming the Brooklyn Nets, maybe? But in that metropolitan area? It's only a benefit to one side of the border."[35]

This is, again, much like those companies moving across borders back in chapter three. The "winning" state's job increases were directly offset by the "losing" state's job losses. But moving economic activity across a border doesn't create any more of it; it simply changes where that activity gets recorded. Coates brings up another important point, too: Within a metropolitan area, even the economic numbers boosters throw around amount to a rounding error.

"That's one of the things that they always bank on," Coates says. "Two hundred and fifty million dollars sounds like a hell of a lot of money, and it is. Except not in the context of a metropolitan area."[36]

In cities or states where the GDP is in the billions of dollars—if not hundreds of billions or trillions—a few hundred million is a blip on the radar. It's not life altering, though plowing the hundreds of millions of dollars spent on a stadium into, say, health care, could well be.

One interesting nugget to throw in here is that researchers at the American Enterprise Institute found that LeBron James's homecoming to Cleveland—which he famously left to ply his trade in Miami for a few seasons before returning home to help the Cavaliers finally win an NBA title—did help establishments within one mile of Cleveland's arena, without seeming to hurt establishments farther away. As Stan Veuger and Daniel Shoag wrote, "The popular YouTube video claiming that Cleveland's 'economy is based on LeBron James' was overstated but not entirely wrong."[37] However, the same effect was not found in Miami, maybe because, as an entertainment center, the latter already had a lot to offer when James came to town. "Perhaps Mr. James is particularly beloved in his native Ohio. Or maybe 'superstar amenities' are substitutes, not complements, and Miami has plenty of them even without Mr. James, generating fiercer competition and an attenuated impact of any specific superstar," they added.[38]

Even so, such hyperlocal effects in this one, kind-of-silly instance is more the exception that proves the rule. A generational superstar playing in a depressed city may have an effect within the confines of only the neighborhood in which the city's arena sits. And lest Cavaliers fans think they're getting away with a boost for free, fear not: Cuyahoga County in 2017 agreed to pay $100 million toward renovating Quicken Loans Arena, then saw James head out to Los Angeles the next year.[39] It'll take a lot of cheap beers to make that up again.

The James-inspired jump, though, does bring up one more important aspect of the stadium debate: What can higher-profile sporting events that occur less often, such as the Super Bowl, the World Series, an All-Star Game, or the Final Four, do for their host cities? If one man can bring a boost to Cleveland, in one study of one small area anyway, doesn't an event the size and scope of a major professional championship do the same?

The big leagues certainly want you to think so. They often dangle the prospect of hosting such an event as an incentive for cities and states to pony up funds for a new stadium; they almost inevitably award the next big game to whatever facility just came out of its shrink-wrap, providing cities a carrot against the stick of a team's moving. The NFL certainly played up that angle after the Minnesota Vikings' stadium in Minneapolis was tapped to host the Super Bowl in 2018—a stadium for which the public paid nearly half the cost—when within memory the league had been scaremongering that the Vikings would move to Los Angeles. "The effort that they had to bring that stadium to completion, the plans that they have for [it], and the commitment the community has demonstrated was a positive influence on several owners that I talked to," said NFL Commissioner Roger Goodell.[40] The NFL pulled the same trick in Texas, strongly suggesting a Super Bowl would come if the public chipped in to build a new stadium for the Dallas Cowboys; the game was indeed awarded to the Lone Star State in 2011.

Several states have enacted tax breaks to bring the NCAA Final Four to town (adding another level of moral messiness onto an already-sordid situation, as the NCAA and its schools make boatloads of money off the unpaid labor of "student" athletes).[41] Other leagues, which don't have a neutral-site championship match to dole out for good behavior, tend to use their All-Star Games in much the same fashion, granting it to whatever stadium is newest and shiniest, a reward for the public's generosity In covering the cost of the facility.

Cities, then, inevitably play up the economic benefits that such an event will bring, touting the hundreds of millions of dollars that visiting fans will haul into town, explicitly or implicitly justifying the cost of building the arena or stadium in question. Nary a year goes by without the production of economic impact assessments showing that major sports championships bestow tons of money upon their hosts, a veritable rain of cash that cascades into the pockets of a city's residents: $719 million supposedly came into Glendale for hosting the Super Bowl in 2015, while Houston scored more than $400 million in 2017, and San Francisco saw some $350 million in 2016.[42] The NFL was even touting a possible $800 million benefit to San Fran before that last one.[43]

Those numbers seem big and ridiculous. And they are. "*Ex post* economic analyses of the Super Bowl by scholars not financially connected with the game have typically found that the observed effects of the game on real economic variables such as employment, government revenues, taxable sales, GDP, and personal income, while generally positive, are a fraction of those claimed by the league and sports boosters," wrote sports economist Victor Matheson in a 2010 review.[44] Per an earlier assessment by Matheson and Robert A. Baade, "The economic impact of the Super Bowl is likely on average one-quarter or less the magnitude of the most recent NFL estimates."[45]

This is for all the reasons laid out in this book: the substitution effect, leakages, crowding out of folks who would have come in the absence of the Super Bowl, and that cities only have so much space to cede to tourists. But also, many economic impact assessments don't take into account the costs to a city of hosting the game, such as the heightened security, expanded transit hours, and other ancillary costs that the NFL requires hosts to shoulder. It's not that the game has no benefits, mind you; but they are vastly less than what the boosters and the league kick around. Deciding whether to spend half a billion dollars on a new football stadium in order to gain some $500 million in economic benefits thanks to a Super Bowl should be a much easier decision if that latter number is mostly an illusion. (Also, to reiterate a point made before, even if that $500 million were a real benefit, it would be a blip in most of the metro areas that actually host the Super Bowl.)

It's much the same story with the Final Four, and again we can turn to Matheson and Baade for the numbers. In a 2003 study that looked at all Final Fours, men's and women's, between 1970 and 1999, the two economists calculated that "the evidence indicates that the economic impact of the Final Four will more likely be the equivalent of a financial 'air ball' than an economic 'slam dunk.'"

They could only find two instances—the men's tournament in College Park, Maryland, in 1970 and the women's tournament in San Jose, California, in 1999—in which the local economy saw a statistically significant change in real income. For the men's tournament, the average change for a host city was a loss of income of around $44 million. As Matheson told Bloomberg News, "Since 1970, cities that have hosted the men's Final Four actually experienced [a slowdown in] economic growth. So the year that they host the Final Four, economic growth is actually lower in that city than in other years."[46]

Yes, these numbers are from a while ago, but the costs of hosting are only going up as the event gets more and more extravagant, so it's unlikely that the deal is any better now than it was at the turn of the millennium.

Ditto for the World Series. Per the same two economists, "Our detailed regression analysis reveals that over the period 1972 to 2000, cities appearing in the MLB post-season had higher than expected income growth by 0.003%. This figure is not statistically significantly different than zero, although a best guess of the economic contribution of a single post-season game is $6.8 million, roughly half that of the typical *ex ante* projection."[47]

It appears that the whole postseason, regardless of the sport, is pretty much a wash. In a 2002 paper, Dennis Coates and Brad Humphreys looked at all cities with professional sports teams and found that postseason play was not associated with any growth in real per capita income whatsoever. "Professional sports appear to have a detrimental effect on local economies, not a positive effect as proponents of subsidies for the construction of new sports facilities frequently claim," they wrote.[48]

That is why any of this matters. The huge sums of money that owners and leagues demand and that cities feel compelled to provide for a new stadium are justified by its alleged economic impacts. Those promised impacts salve the conscience of lawmakers and give the public a reason why their money needs to be spent on a stadium today. Making that money seem like an investment, rather than a straight-up outlay, is more palatable for everyone. I'd be willing to make a pretty large wager that the new Raiders stadium in Vegas will be hosting a Super Bowl before too long as a way for the league to say thanks for the $750 million the state put toward its construction.

Which brings me to my favorite study of the impact of sports on the local economy, this one also put together by Coates and Humphreys. They looked at about three decades' worth of strikes in professional sports and of basketball teams ultimately leaving their cities for new locations and found that neither has an effect on the local economy. "Work stoppages in baseball and football have never had significant impact on local economies. The departure of a franchise in any sport, particularly in basketball, has never significantly lowered real per capita personal income in a metropolitan area," they wrote.[49] Never. Ever.

Matheson, Baade, and Robert Baumann a few years later found the same thing, via looking at taxable sales in the areas affected by sports leagues going on strike.[50] When the leagues literally shut down or teams disappear, the economic effect isn't big enough to register. If that's the case, it stands to reason that the reverse is true: Teams just aren't a big enough deal to make a large economic impact.

That isn't to say that individual businesses or employees aren't affected by such things. A sports bar across the street from an arena is going to suffer when a sports league shuts down or when a team moves, and its employees may see their hours cut or their jobs disappear. I don't mean to diminish their hardship or the real economic struggle that will result from their livelihoods evaporating. I get it that those in industries connected to sports want to see teams supported by the public, for reasons that aren't all about cynical self-interest. But public policy can't be made that way; policymakers need to look at the aggregate and what's good for an entire city, state, or even nation. Spending a bunch on a sports team when the benefits are so limited to a few isn't the best use of what are always limited resources.

I know I'll be accused of hating sports for writing a lot of this; the people I talked to while researching this chapter certainly have been accused of harboring such ill feelings toward the athletic world. But that couldn't be further from the truth. I love sports—I play them, watch them, attend them. My loving wife nicely asks most weekends when the Tottenham Hotspur game is on so we're home for it, and we attend more than our fair share of D.C. United and Washington Capitals games. I was fortunate as a kid to see my home-state Devils win three Stanley Cups, and then the Caps won one in 2018. Some of my favorite childhood memories are from what was then Continental Airlines Arena, before the Devils went to a new (publicly funded) arena in Newark. When it looked for a time when I was a kid as if the Devils would move to Nashville, I was devastated.

But I understand the difference between my personal enjoyment and good policy.

Case in point, DC spent $150 million to build Audi Field for United to replace decrepit, disintegrating RFK Stadium, perhaps most famous these days for its bouncing stands and the racoons who supposedly inhabit the old press box. It's undeniably an upgrade, and I am going to enjoy attending games in the new place rather than going into a half-century old, falling-apart bowl that wasn't built for soccer. But I would have much preferred that the money spent on Audi Field had instead been plowed into alleviating DC's affordable-housing crisis or been put toward fixing its myriad public-transit problems. I'm going to benefit from the outlay on the stadium, sure, but way more people would have benefited if the money had been spent on almost literally anything else.

Here's one more thing: It would be an improvement if lawmakers stopped lying about the effects stadiums are going to have on their cities and states. I wouldn't necessarily buy it, but I can see a case being made for investing in a stadium because having a professional team in town builds community and provides a common cultural rallying point, to foster that feel-good effect that economists have found from studying the Olympics and the World Cup. Maybe taking steps to bolster that sense of togetherness is worth the money. That's a fine argument to make; it would at least be intellectually honest. Just don't tell me that the stadium is going to make us all rich, too, when every analysis that wasn't paid for by the industries involved says otherwise.

Is there a solution for the stadium swindle? Not a clear one. Owners are not going to wake up one day and decide to just forgo public subsidies when they're there for the taking. The fear of losing a team is always going to drive lawmakers and the public to make poor decisions with public moneys. The only tiny bit of good news is that, postrecession, the percentage of the cost of stadiums covered by the public isn't quite as high as it used to be. As Matheson, the sports economist, told me, "Between 1990 and 2007—the start of the Great Recession—the taxpayer was paying about two-thirds of the cost of new stadiums, with private sources covering the remaining one-third. Since 2007, the pace of new construction has slowed and the public is now covering only about one-third of the total costs. Perhaps people are getting the message and the recession forced them to make a decision about giving handouts to millionaire players and billionaire owners versus laying off teachers and firefighters."[51] However, the cost of stadiums has also risen substantially, with billion-dollar stadiums now the norm, so that the total of public dollars contributed hasn't declined.

One thing that could have helped stem the stadium swindle a bit was if the federal government had pulled back its support for such projects. In the initial version of the tax law that will be discussed in chapter eight—the one with the giant corporate tax cut—a provision would have prevented cities and states from building stadiums with bonds subsidized by the federal government; that subsidy from the feds allows cities and states to pay lower interest rates on their stadium bonds than they would otherwise.

It wouldn't have been a huge money saver at the federal level, but it would have meant higher costs for stadium projects at the state and city levels and thus perhaps discouraged the plowing of quite so much public money into them. According to economist Roger Noll, the provision could have translated into millions of dollars in higher annual costs for a city or state issuing bonds to build a stadium.[52] That ain't chump change. And getting rid of the subsidy would at least mean that taxpayers in New Jersey and Idaho would no longer be paying for stadiums in Texas or Florida, since a federal tax break is paid for by everyone.

The provision making that change was included when the House passed its version of the tax bill. However, it was not included in the Senate's version, and when the two bills were reconciled into one package, Big Sports won out, and the tax-free bonds remained ensconced in federal law.

According to *The Wall Street Journal*, President Trump himself intervened to save the stadium subsidy,[53] despite his previous big talk on the matter, and his constant use of NFL protesters and even the league itself as a PR punching bag. (I'd be willing to wager it's because one of the NFL owners got his ear, but that's just conjecture.)

Someone else, though, took much more public responsibility for the survival of the stadium subsidy: Nevada Republican Senator Dean Heller. Why? Per a statement on his website, "Heller was able to protect the tax exemption for stadium bonds, which is critical to preserving the influx of business and growth associated with the construction of the Raiders stadium in Las Vegas, NV."[54]

So it all came back to Vegas and that record-setting stadium subsidy given to the Raiders. Thanks to Sin City's big bet, we're all going to wind up paying more money to Big Sports owners for years and years to come.

7

DON'T GO SHOPPING FOR BIG RETAIL

IT WAS ADVERTISED AS THE first pyramid of consequence built in five thousand years. "It's going to be a monument like the Statue of Liberty or the Eiffel Tower, a signature for the city," said the original operator. "The difference is this will have something to do inside it."[1]

The location, though, was not alongside the Nile. It was Memphis, Tennessee, a city best known for the blues and barbecue.

Memphis is a quintessential southern town that is home to Elvis Presley's Graceland, the Blues Hall of Fame, and Sun Records, where so many of the iconic figures of the early days of rock and roll got their start. Meandering around downtown is like stepping into music history: There's the Orpheum, which was originally the Grand Opera House, in its heyday one of the most important non–New York City venues in the country. The Gibson guitar company has a factory down the street. Bronze statues of important musicians are all over, and on Beale Street, every other bar has a live band playing (even though I was there on a random Tuesday night in October).

But if you wander away from downtown for about fifteen minutes, hang a turn at the Mississippi River, and move your gaze north, you'll see something else: the Memphis Pyramid, a shiny black behemoth hugging the water amid a tangle of highways.

Opened in 1991 with the help of some $60 million in public money, the pyramid was meant to be a multipurpose entertainment venue.[2] The idea was to play off Memphis's shared name with Memphis, Egypt, providing the city with an iconic structure right on the banks of the Mississippi. Memphis had seen various plans to build pyramids come and go over the years—one of the city's original civic planners was a hard-core Egyptologist who also helped found Cairo, Illinois, hence the Tennessee city's name and the fascination with having its own mini-Giza—but none of them came to fruition until the current pyramid, originally named the Great American Pyramid, finally emerged, in all its black steel glory. Mummified pharaohs, I hear, were not included.

Sidney Shlenker, the mastermind behind the project, as well as the Houston Astrodome, was run out of town before the pyramid even opened because he failed to find the financing he had promised. But he was certainly right when he pledged that visitors would have something to do inside the pyramid that didn't involve hieroglyphics. In fact, visitors have had many, many things to do inside it over the years, as the city struggled for nearly a quarter of a century to make the pyramid into a worthwhile investment, with various dreams for its purpose meandering out of the minds of civic leaders only to prove busts shortly thereafter. The only real constant in the pyramid's existence is that it's been a money pit for taxpayers.

At its opening, the city was already expecting to lose some

$600,000 annually on the pyramid.[3] The bathrooms flooded during the venue's initial concert. Things didn't go uphill from there. (I should probably insert a joke about a mummy's curse here, I know.)

For a few years, the pyramid played host to the NBA's Memphis Grizzlies, before they moved down the street to the newly built FedExForum. For nearly a decade following the Grizzlies' move in 2004, the pyramid lay largely dormant, hosting only the odd concert.

"When I started coming to Memphis just as a visitor, the pyramid was here, and it was an active sports and entertainment venue, and then when the Forum opened and the pyramid just stopped being much of anything. For a long time it became this iconic symbol in a bad way," said Charles Hughes, a professor at Rhodes College who studies the history of the city. "There was a lot of talk that I remember about 'What's going to happen with the pyramid? Is it ever going to happen with the pyramid?'"

Finally, after several grueling years of negotiations, the pyramid became a Bass Pro Shop, the outdoor sporting company's biggest and grandest megastore. The city paid $30 million to help with the construction—with some estimates of its payments running as high as $78 million—bringing Memphis's total investment in all the various iterations of the pyramid up to around at least $100 million.[4] Some of the bonds issued to cover the costs were authorized by the 2008 stimulus bill, giving federal taxpayers a nice stake in the structure, too.

"The pyramid became a metaphor for Memphis in a sense, because on the one hand it seemed to have such promise, and after it stopped being a venue and when it looked like it was going to be a Bass Pro, people put a lot of hope into it," said Hughes. "It also symbolized a lot of Memphis's frustrations and failures. It looked like, 'Here's this huge thing right by the river that we always see when we go down there, and it's'—at that point—'just nothing.' . . . More broadly, it fit into a civic narrative of Memphis trying and working toward getting the city on the right economic track while not being there yet."

Bass Pro may seem like an odd thing to throw into a building that was meant to be a piece of a city's entertainment landscape, but the company has actually been incredibly successful in selling itself not just as a store, but as a tourist attraction, a destination retail site; something that's a complete shopping experience, with the emphasis on experience, not just a place to procure the dry goods one brings home in paper bags. The public money it receives doesn't just pay for the bricks and concrete. It buys the waterfalls and stuffed animals with which the stores are adorned, a key selling point in the company's tourism tale.

"These aren't just stores—they are natural history museums," said a Bass Pro spokesman in a 2012 article. "Every store is designed to reflect the unique natural environment of the area in which it is located."[5]

I'm not so sure about reflecting the natural environment, but the Memphis Bass Pro is quite something. After walking down the banks of the Mississippi and into what looks from the ground like an utter maze of overpasses and underpasses—and after moving beyond a giant WELCOME TO OUTDOOR PARADISE sign that greets drivers on the aptly named Bass Pro Drive—visitors are met by high ceilings, outdoorsy murals, animal dioramas, and a display case paying homage to Bill Dance, a television fishing-show host who got his start in Memphis. Not only does the pyramid house the giant store itself—complete with an interconnected waterway that is stocked with thirty-two varieties of fish, including large sturgeons, an enclosed glass area that's home to three alligators, and hundred-foot-tall mocked-up cypress trees—but also a restaurant, bar, bowling alley, waterfall, hotel, and the world's tallest freestanding elevator. Pay $10 for a ride up, and supposedly the view from the top is pretty good. (On the day I visited, the top deck was closed for a private event.) There's a duck heritage center, arcade games, as well as a store selling drinks and snacks. (Ninety-eight cents for coffee was perhaps the best bargain in the place.) The store is large and cavernous, and you can stare up into the dark apex of the pyramid from the ground floor.

Bass Pro is far from alone in attempting to play the retail-tourism game. In September 2017, it made a big move to absorb Cabela's, another sporting goods giant that, like its new corporate overlord, sells itself as a tourist destination that is worth subsidizing with public cash. When it originally went public, Cabela's sales pitch to investors explicitly noted how important subsidies were to its plans, and how much the potential failure to keep the subsidy stream flowing would alter its profit calculus.

"The failure to obtain similar economic development packages in the future could cause us to significantly alter our destination retail store strategy or format," said Cabela's initial public offering prospectus, which includes its disclosures to potential investors. "In addition, the failure to obtain similar economic development packages for stores built in the future would have an adverse impact on our cash flows and on the return on investment in these stores."[6]

In short, subsidies are key to keeping the profits coming in.

These two stores together have received, courtesy of the American public, a staggering amount. A 2012 investigation by Scott Reeder for the Franklin Center for Government and Public Integrity found that in the previous fifteen years alone, Cabela's had received $551 million in state and local assistance, while Bass Pro had received $1.3 billion.[7] Yes, that's billion, with a *b*. Don't be surprised if the numbers get even bigger now that the two have joined into one corporate monolith.

But the ability of Bass Pro and Cabela's to win subsidies is not some unique thing that only sporting goods salesmen can pull off. It's just a small part of a much larger belief in the American polity that retail is the way to drive economic development. As with so many things when it comes to tax subsidies, it's the biggest of the big that receive the bulk of the benefits.

Many of the largest big-box stores have benefited from public support: Lowe's, Home Depot, Target, Best Buy, IKEA, Walmart, and more have all received tax preferences and other goodies based on the idea that they can boost local retail, provide jobs, and anchor shopping areas in ways that smaller businesses can't. Those big retailers promise to create new employment and to give local shoppers a cost-effective way to retrieve their material needs, which is supposedly good for everyone.

When lawmakers want to go really big, they bank on entire malls as an economic driver, hoping that, say, a Macy's or a Nordstrom can anchor a larger property, creating a retail site that will not only benefit the locals but will entice shoppers from surrounding towns. When officials would rather go a bit smaller—or want an immediate economic jolt for which they can take credit—they create tax-free shopping holidays, exempting items from the sales tax for a limited time, providing a caffeine boost to an area's retail numbers.

Retail therapy, though, can't fix what truly ails an economy.

Big-box stores, as is well-known, tend to hurt smaller businesses, so job creation numbers often come out a wash, with every new job at a Walmart or a Target offsetting one at the local hardware store that had to close because it was undercut and buried by its bigger, badder competitors. Malls are threatened by both the rise of internet commerce and the growing American distaste for suburban playgrounds set off amid acres of parking lots. And all of this maneuvering on the part of officials tends to just shuffle money around, not so much creating new economic activity as moving it from place to place, store to store, taking a finite number of dollars and simply shifting when and where they are spent, without creating anything new.

An oft-cited stat is that consumer spending makes up 70 percent of the economy. That number is pretty ridiculous, capturing a lot of what most people presumably don't think of when they envision the typical American shopper hitting the mall or the grocery store, including spending on the Medicaid program and electioneering by political parties. In reality, consumer spending makes up closer to half of the economy.

But the notion that the 70 percent faux statistic represents— that retail can be an effective development tool because consumerism makes up the vast bulk of the economy—still feels correct. More people in more stores equals more jobs and more money in the community, right? This simple equation drives local officials to try to use shopping to accomplish their economic goals and to jump-start the ancillary benefits of development.

So let's start with Bass Pro and Cabela's, the big two who most explicitly push the idea that they are tourist destinations that will draw new shoppers into the community via the unique experience offered when shopping their wares.

Dipping a bit below the surface, the idea that a giant sporting goods store can serve as a tourist destination starts to break down. After all, these stores are all over the place, unlike, say, Mall of America, a unique entity with wide name recognition (more on this and other megamalls later). The United States has nearly a hundred Bass Pro stores, along with more than eighty Cabela's.

Many are within just a few hours of one another, if not closer. I have one of each within an hour of my home.

Per Greg LeRoy, the director of Good Jobs First, whom you met in chapter three, the original destination sporting goods stores did work as intended. "Those suckers really drew people from long distances because they were kind of shrines to hunters, and people would drive for hundreds of miles, buy a hotel night, eat restaurant meals," he said. "You could credibly claim that there was actually some trans-occupancy tax, and restaurant as well as the sales tax associated with the behavior."[8]

However, that effect diminishes the more the business expands. "We kept saying, okay, that's great as far as it goes, but Cabela's has a stated business plan: They're going to be in the biggest markets," LeRoy says. "Who's going to drive four hundred miles when you can drive four and get there?"[9]

It's difficult to ascertain just how much of a draw these stores are today; proponents like to claim that they're the top tourist attractions wherever they are, but it's not as if they're generally competing with the Grand Canyon or the Taj Mahal. When we're talking about Dundee, Michigan, or Buda, Texas, both of which have provided support to entice in the big sporting retailers, top tourist attraction is a low bar. Most of the time, states or cities make next to no attempt to provide concrete numbers on retail tourists.

In an admittedly crude way of measuring, a reporter for Allentown's *The Morning Call* surveyed the parking lot of a Cabela's in Pennsylvania; he was attempting to figure out how many people were traveling any distance to visit the store. He found that more than two-thirds of the license plates were from in-state drivers, in an area where, given the store's proximity to Pennsylvania's borders, retail tourists could reasonably be expected to be crossing the state line.[10]

"They go in and present this idea that they're going to be draw-ing people from a wide radius, that they're going to be effectively a tourist destination, and that people are going to cross state bound-aries, and therefore they should be subsidized," said Stacy Mitchell, codirector of the Institute for Local Self-Reliance and the au-thor of *Big-Box Swindle*. "[But] you don't have to do anything further than look at a map to see their intention has been to build those stores everywhere."[11]

That makes sense as a retail strategy, which is what these stores ultimately are. "The entire MO of modern retail chains is to build out a number of stores and then build stores between those stores until you start cannibalizing your own sales," at which point the local competition has presumably been driven into the ground, said Mitchell. Adding some dioramas and touting tourism numbers doesn't make that simple calculation any different; Bass Pro and Cabela's are clearly not content to rely on just a handful of stores to provide a one-of-a-kind experience to shoppers who make a pil-grimage to one of their few locations. They want to carpet the countryside in their shrines to guns and fishing.

The difficulty in taking on Bass Pro/Cabela's argument, though, is that everyone is fighting anecdote with anecdote, since it's in nobody's interest to track real numbers too closely: For the stores, anything that could puncture the idea that they are tourist attrac-tions would be a bad thing; and for local officials, finding out that their big gamble on retail didn't pay off would also lead to bad press and, presumably, an electoral cudgel for opponents.

Cabela's likes to throw around raw visitor numbers to claim it is a huge tourist attraction—for instance, it made a lot of noise about being the top attraction in Utah, after opening a store in Lehi in 2006—but that tells us precisely nothing about how many people were actually drawn from outside the area. As the state's

Office of Tourism noted at the time, "Visitor numbers should not be confused with tourism numbers."[12] Everyone, activists and proponents alike, is fighting with a hand tied behind his or her back.

What is known is the promises of economic development that Bass Pro and Cabela's make, and the hopes that local officials and developers have for the effect the megastores will have on their small-town economies. In many instances, those promises are unfulfilled.

In 2010, the Public Accountability Initiative, a Buffalo-based research organization that looks into big-business corruption, put together a report examining the effects of Bass Pro stores, to see if the lofty promises the company makes actually come to pass. It found that "in cities ranging from Harrisburg, PA, to Mesa, AZ, Bass Pro often falls short on its promises as an economic development anchor and major tourist destination. Bass Pro stores do draw shoppers, but economic development and revitalization often do not follow, and cities are left to deal with consequences of the sort that they were trying to avoid when they subsidized Bass Pro's entrance, such as vacancy, blight, and fiscal duress."[13]

For instance, in Mesa, Arizona, in 2005, Bass Pro received some $84 million in tax incentives and was meant to join a development that it would coanchor with Walmart. The store came in, as did Walmart, but much of the rest of the development was filled out with stores that simply relocated from the surrounding area. Estimates that more than $5 million would be added to the city's coffers annually by the development proved to be vastly optimistic, since those "new" stores were just old stores in a new place.

As *The Arizona Republic* put it in an editorial five years later that assessed the deal, "Retail is no panacea. Lobbing incentives to build shopping centers—which no matter how much we subsidize them, can only be successful if there are enough customers to support them—does nothing but make developers rich."[14] In 2007, after a few other high-profile retail subsidy attempts went sideways, Arizona largely banned the subsidization of retail outlets in the Phoenix metropolitan area.

Not every place Bass Pro has gone has been quite so unsuccessful, but in plenty of other places both it and Cabela's have failed to produce the anticipated economic boost. Despite the dioramas and the waterfalls and the lofty promises about shoppers spending all day there, it's still only a sporting goods store. Adding elements that enhance the shopping experience doesn't give people more money to spend on rods or reels. Instead, business that would have been spread out over a few other stores—the local gun shop, the tackle store, the shop that provides jeans and hats—is concentrated in one megastore.

An auxiliary point made by those who push to give big money to big sporting goods stores is that they bring jobs with them. Like so many things discussed in this book, that's a dubious claim.

For starters, if there's so much demand for sporting goods in a particular location, someone is going to fill the market void sans subsidies, so the government is almost certainly paying for something that would have happened anyway, making those new jobs costly and the spending that created them inefficient. Second, plenty of research has shown that big-box stores—Bass Pro, Cabela's, and their ilk among them—harm smaller retailers, so the jobs they create often end up being offset by job losses at other firms that can't compete with the big stores being propped up by government help. (To be fair, plenty of research makes the opposite claim, too.)

According to a study by economist Michael Hicks at Ball State University, Cabela's in the first few years in a new location does essentially nothing for job creation. Between 1998 and 2003, Hicks looked at seven new Cabela's locations and concluded, "The entrance of a large-scale specialty retail store has no persistent impact on employment in the effected or surrounding counties."[15]

Perhaps it takes longer than a few years for the effects of the store to metastasize, but Hicks believes that's not what happens. "Simply stated, the wage generated by Cabela's is insufficient to generate increases in labor force participation or economic migration that will be necessary to generate net employment impacts," he wrote. "Few workers are moving to or remaining in the affected counties because of the incomes offered by Cabela's."[16] Instead, retail workers from the area shuffle over into jobs at the store; even if that does mean a net increase in wages for that person, which is great, it doesn't mean that a new job has been created. It's just been moved from one firm to another.

"The economics of this are pretty simple," Hicks told me. "New stores don't really increase demand, so for there to be an impact, they have to attract folks from elsewhere. I love Cabela's—if they sold beer, I'd never leave—but they aren't enough of a destination attraction to materially impact a community."[17]

I wish there were more research on this matter, but as much as state and local governments don't do a lot of follow-up on whether their money is well spent on big sporting retail, neither do academics chase the question. "I'm not too surprised [by the lack of academic work in this area], since economists aren't too interested in looking at individual firms, unless they are especially novel in their line of business," Hicks told me.[18]

But there's no reason to be sure retail tourism works as intended, and plenty of reason to be skeptical. Plus, a lot of what gets spent in the stores winds up departing the local economy, making the effect even less pronounced for whatever tourism does get generated. Per Stacy Mitchell, just fifteen cents of every dollar spent in a store such as Cabela's or Bass Pro stays in the local community, mostly in employee compensation, whereas for more local businesses it'll be between thirty-five and forty cents, as they're more likely to use other local businesses to handle their needs.

Not only big sporting goods retailers have played the subsidy game, of course. Big-box stores from Target to IKEA to CVS to Home Depot and beyond have all convinced local officials that their brand of retail is a worthwhile investment of public money.

Currently, the United States has the highest amount of retail space per person in the world, at nearly twenty-four square feet. That's two dozen square feet of floor space for every last person in the country; Canada has about a third less, Australia less than half, and the United Kingdom, France, Spain, Italy, and Germany fewer than five square feet each.[19] (Other estimates place the total space in the United States both higher and lower than twenty-four square feet, but no matter what, it's a lot.) Also, a nutty amount of malls dot the American landscape: about twelve hundred. According to Cowen and Company's research analysts, between 1970 and 2015, the number of malls in the United States grew twice as fast as the population.[20]

The biggest bogeyman in this sea of retail is Walmart, which is seen either as a savior providing low-cost goods to a population that desperately needs a break or as a destroyer of local economies that undermines small businesses.

The truth is that the store is both: It does provide low-cost goods to people who could surely use the savings, and it does undercut local retailers, who don't have its economies of scale, name recognition, or overall market power.

Whether Walmart or the stores like it should be publicly subsidized is less difficult to answer: Its model doesn't lend itself to the sort of development that is worth expending public funds on.

Dating back to the early 1990s, Walmart has received at least $1 billion in public assistance to open its stores, be it tax breaks, land grants, property tax abatements, or other assorted giveaways.[21] Since no one in government tracks these sorts of things comprehensively, the total is almost certainly higher than that.

For this money, local officials are probably buying more job swapping than job creation. For every job that a Walmart or a Target creates in its store, it nullifies one down the street by driving a competitor out of business. Per a study by Joseph Persky of the University of Illinois, Chicago, and three colleagues, the opening of a Walmart in the Windy City destroyed as many jobs as it created; shops in the vicinity of the megastore had a 40 percent chance of closing within the first two years of Walmart's grand opening.[22]

Plus, the ripple effects of any jobs that are created are not as strong as if those jobs were higher wage or more specialized. By importing cheap goods from overseas, the stores aren't creating strong upstream local effects, and by creating low-pay, lousy-benefit jobs at the bottom, they aren't doing much to boost purchasing power and thus its ripple effects. Subsidizing these outlets basically means paying for the creation of not-great jobs with minimal knock-on effects to justify the overall cost.

These stores can also affect the social safety net. As has been well documented, a store such as Walmart can keep wages low enough that its employees avail themselves of Medicaid and other public programs. So taxpayers end up paying on the front end and the back end, picking up the tab to build the store and then providing support to its employees whose wages don't make for a comfortable living. (Some stores have changed that in recent years, with both Target and Walmart claiming that their minimum wages are going to be in the vicinity of $10 per hour.)

Big-box stores also undermine the fabric of the community, as they're far less likely than locally owned businesses to be engaged in whatever the issue of the moment is before the local school district or city council. "To a larger degree than other sectors, retail has an effect on the civic and social life of the community," Stacy Mitchell said. "Communities that have lots of community-owned businesses tend to have more social networks and more civic and social engagement."[23] That this dynamic exists makes sense: It's easier for those businesses to engage in the community since they don't have to run things up the chain to a far-flung headquarters for permission to get involved.

Walmart and other big-box behemoths are not part of the entertainment industry, which is the focus of this book. But all of the critiques leveled at big-box retailers don't magically disappear when a retailer portrays itself as a tourist destination. Saying that shoppers will come from all around to visit your store isn't a panacea for all the problems inherent when the public is forced to fund that store's creation. Cabela's is not Walmart and Bass Pro is not Lowe's, but the economic theory is not so markedly different that one is an outstanding investment for the community and the other is a dud. They're all just stores.

But out of either economic desperation or political expediency, local lawmakers continue to give those projects the green light. "I have some sympathy for [local officials] because they are under this pressure to show they are constantly creating growth and jobs, and if you have an empty piece of land and there's suddenly a Cabela's there, it certainly looks like you're creating jobs," said Stacy Mitchell. "There is also an incredible level of desperation across the country, so there is this feeling that something is better than nothing."[24] Just as in Memphis, desperation to not allow empty storefronts or vacant lots go to waste prods lawmakers into spending money on anyone willing to fill the void.

To add one final insult to the taxpaying public, big-box stores have in recent years been using a controversial argument to lower their property tax bills. Under what's known as the dark story theory, retailers claim that their property should not be assessed at its present value, with its inventory and decorations and paying customers, but as if it were vacant. The idea is that because the stores are customized specifically for their current tenant, the property isn't worth what it seems, as a new store would have to make all sorts of changes to fill the same space.

According to Francisco Vara-Orta at *Education Week,* judges are buying this argument to the tune of tens of millions of dollars in lost tax revenue in some states; the Texas state comptroller estimated in 2017 that, if the current trend continued, the number would be in the billions in the Lone Star State alone within five years.[25] The list of stores that have resorted to this argument is composed of the usual suspects: Walmart, Target, CVS, and Lowe's among them. In some of the small towns where these stores dominate, the legal costs of waging battle would be so high that the municipalities just give in, lowering property tax rates for the big boxes without even putting up a fight. These stores ride in, receive public money, then turn around and fight their property tax bills, threatening to tie small towns up in court and bury them under an avalanche of legal bills.

Shopper's paradise, this is certainly not.

All of this is taking place while American retail is up against the ropes; publicly supporting new, big retail sites today is making a bet on a type of economy that is quickly fading. With the rise of e-commerce, giants such as Amazon are enticing a lot of folks to shop online. According to the Census Bureau, Americans spent some $5.8 billion on e-commerce in the first quarter of 2000; in the first quarter of 2017, the total was more than $106 billion.

When the Bureau first started tracking e-commerce, it made up less than 1 percent of total retail sales; now that number is pushing 9 percent and is surely going to go even higher in the coming years.[26]

While more and more American shopping is taking place on the internet, the country is also reurbanizing, as people who had fled urban centers during the 1950s and 1960s, during the era of white flight, are coming back into denser, walkable areas. Young people, in particular, are flocking back into big cities, filling urban areas from DC to Austin to Denver with those dreaded millennials who are supposedly responsible for all of America's ills.

Those young folks are doing a lot of good by congregating in denser areas, as they are greener and more productive than the parts of the country that remain rural. The shift toward cities, however, is rendering the suburban mall, with its acres of parking lots, surrounded by nothing, particularly ill-suited to those with the most money to spend.

The rise of the mall was not only about suburbia and white flight, though. Back in the 1950s, when Americans began fleeing to the suburbs en masse, a change in tax policy contributed to the mall explosion, pushing retail out of urban enclaves as surely as people were headed the same way. Per historian Thomas Hanchett, a 1954 change in "accelerated depreciation" suddenly made commercial real estate investments much more lucrative in the short term, as investors were able to offset profits from their buildings with write-offs over a shorter time.

"Developers discovered they could now quickly earn back their initial investment and create a tax shelter for outside income as well. The tax break was biggest on newly erected business buildings, compared with alternatives such as renovation of existing structures," Hanchett wrote in a 1996 article. "Therefore, the law functioned as a powerful incentive prompting investors to funnel money into fresh commercial projects at the city's edge. As a result, beginning in the late 1950s and gathering momentum throughout the 1960s, an explosion occurred in the number and the size of shopping centers in the United States."[27] Perhaps not coincidentally, what we think of as the modern mall—an enclosed, climate-controlled complex with stores facing inward, as opposed to lining the street with separate entrances—was born in 1956, with the opening of the Southdale mall in Edina, Minnesota.[28]

Hanchett writes, "By 1970, the United States had some 13,000 shopping centers, nearly all of them erected in a period of just 15 years." The confluence of tax policy, a new vision of construction, and American distaste for urban centers caused a store boom. Malls became a quintessential part of the American landscape. And America exported the idea to the rest of the world: Currently, the five largest shopping malls on the globe are in Asia.[29]

That, though, was then. America in the twenty-first century is seeing the die-off of the mall, for the reasons outlined above. Some analysts say that about one in four malls in America is at risk of closing by 2022, while others place the number as high as half.[30] Some of the biggest store chains in the country—Sears, JC Penney, and other big department stores that typically act as anchors for larger shopping plazas—are going through an apocalypse. Since 2002, department stores have shed nearly half a million jobs.[31] The current narrative is not which store will emerge as the winner in this new era, but how soon Amazon can start delivering packages by drone, thus making the big store that has a little bit of everything decisively a thing of the past.

Still, old habits die hard, and mall owners are not yet ready to entirely surrender to the internet. Thus, states are pouring money into shopping areas precisely when every trend says they should be making plans about what to do with their large retail spaces after the American mall is finally at the end of its death throes and in its grave.

For instance, the state of Mississippi spent $24 million on the Outlets of Mississippi.[32] Tracy, California, spent $2.4 million to help Macy's move into the West Valley Mall.[33] Los Angeles dealt out a $59 million tax break for a shopping center in Woodland Hills.[34] Some $20 million was tossed at the Green Acres Mall on Long Island.[35] The alpha male of US malls—Minnesota's Mall of America—received $250 million toward its multibillion-dollar expansion in 2014.[36]

But those are all small ball compared to the mother of all American mall boondoggles: the American Dream project in New Jersey.

It's fitting that the most disastrous mall project in America is in the Garden State. After all, the tiny state has dozens of malls; they're an indelible part of the landscape and culture. Both *Mall-rats* and *Paul Blart: Mall Cop* were set in Jersey for a reason. Even in the more rural corner of the state where I grew up, several malls are within a relatively convenient drive.

The American Dream began as Xanadu, a megamall in East Rutherford, New Jersey, which is also home to the Meadowlands, the site of MetLife Stadium, where both the New York Jets and New York Giants play. (Fun fact: New Jersey is currently home to four major professional sports franchises, only one of which—the New Jersey Devils—actually uses the state in its name.) Construction on the site began in 2004, but by 2006 the project was belly-up. Not until 2011 did the current developer—Triple Five—take over construction on what Governor Chris Christie called the "ugliest damn building in New Jersey, maybe in America."[37]

That developer—which is owned by the Ghermezian family, who have done quite a bit of megamall development—has promised to turn the American Dream into a shoppers' paradise that is much more than a mall. The intended plans are to include a water park, a theme park, a ski slope, and an aquarium alongside the complex's 450 stores. Triple Five claims that such attractions will render the mall "internet proof"—"on par with Dubai" is its vision for the shopping mecca.[38]

To get there, the mall has received a hefty amount of support from the taxpayer. All told, the state and local governments have gifted it some $1 billion, and the project is also backed by more than $1 billion in municipal bonds. The numbers got so high partly out of simple desperation; with the project having been stalled for so long, New Jersey lawmakers were willing to do just about anything to kick-start the construction of what locals began to refer to as Xanadon't.[39] A decade and a half is a long time to be staring at a hole in the ground.

Triple Five was also promising that tens of thousands of jobs would be created by the mall, in a state where postrecession unemployment lingered above that in the rest of the region; it also promised $3.5 billion in tax revenue over two decades, along with billions in outside financing that will make the American Dream the envy of the tristate area. (For the record, the New Jersey Economic Development Authority has vastly lower estimates for job creation and tax revenue for the site, putting the latter more than $2 billion lower than does Triple Five.)[40]

In a state that is already smitten with tax incentives, it was a perfect storm of promises and circumstances. (As noted in chapter five, Christie seriously upped the amount of corporate incentives dished out by the Garden State, making it a dreamscape for companies looking to receive cash.)

Is there any reason to think that a gigantic mall in the Meadowlands will be worth that much?

Like so many of the projects discussed in this book, the key if and when the mall ever opens will be to draw in visitors who wouldn't have been in the area if not for their pursuit of the American Dream. There's certainly reason to be skeptical that the spectacle of the American Dream will entice enough folks to make the massive cost worthwhile, as it is situated in the mall capital of the country. Several other malls are in proximity, making it that much harder to draw in casual shoppers (who may be turned off by the hassle of visiting a Dubai in the Jersey swamp). Also, New York City, and its many attractions, shopping and otherwise, is a short hop away. Part of the boosters' calculation even seems to be that New York tourists, after multiple trips to the city, will want to spill over into New Jersey to hit the mall, having grown bored of Times Square and the Statue of Liberty.[41] That's a dubious proposition.

"In a lot of ways, the project is everything that's not working in economic development right now. It's in the middle of nowhere; it's not connected to anything that's happening organically or any other development," Jon Whiten, of New Jersey Policy Perspective, told *The Atlantic*. "The expectation that it's going to be some hugely successful destination is sort of beyond believable at this point."[42]

Indeed, the trick is going to be enticing people away from the urban centers where they congregate—be they residents or tourists—and into the American Dream, even if that means getting in a car and driving out there. "Maybe there really are tens of thousands of people who want to brave some of the worst traffic in America so they can pay to park at a high-end mall located in a swamp," wrote *The Star-Ledger*'s Paul Mulshine, the state's most curmudgeonly (and best) political columnist. "Stranger things have happened. I just can't think of when."[43]

Therein lies another problem not just with the American Dream, but with mall development writ large: parking. Since malls are self-contained entities meant to pack in loads of people, they're almost universally surrounded by acres of parking. Between 1945 and 1955 alone, when white flight and the growth of suburbia was in full force, the conglomerate Federated Department Stores increased its available parking from sixty-five thousand to 2.5 million square feet. Department stores in that era devoted more ground to parking than they did to shopping space.[44]

And parking lots are a horrible way to use land.

Economically, few things are as wasteful and inefficient as a free parking space. It's empty most of the time and earns the owner nothing, and the land on which it is built can't be home to any other more economically useful entity.[45] (The American Dream would actually be slightly bettering the situation by charging for parking, even if that does violate what most Americans seem to feel is a God-given right to plunk their car anywhere, anytime, without paying for it.) That sea of asphalt prevents many of the spillover effects one might expect from better development that's more integrated into the community; if shoppers can't walk from one thing to the next and new businesses can't open alongside whatever is drawing people in, then the overall economic effect of the thing in question is going to be blunted. This is much the same problem experienced by football stadiums, with their huge parking lots blocking whatever other development might have organically popped up around them.

So free and cheap parking can be a total buzzkill for smart

development. Because malls are offset from the community, swimming in parking, their potential for driving development is severely shortchanged. According to a McKinsey & Company report from 2014, the future of malls is more in mixed-used developments that "offer consumers an attractive, integrated community in which to live, work and shop."[46] So less suburbia and less parking, with more urbanity and more actual people living and working right in the immediate vicinity. That will be trouble for the American Dream, and for every other more traditional mall that lawmakers might want to entice into being with public money.

It's, of course, possible that the American Dream will exceed expectations and bring in hordes of visitors. Mall of America, by most accounts, does well as a tourist attraction. But that's in an area with limited other big tourism draws. Will a megamall, even with ski slopes and amusement parks and whatever else Triple Five cooks up, have the same ability to move outside visitors in when put up against everything else the greater New York City area has to offer?

If the American Dream is apt to succeed—if it's such a slam dunk that people will come from far and wide to take in some skiing, shopping, and amusement-park riding, proving all the skeptics wrongheaded and lacking in vision—why does it need so much public money? Tellingly, Triple Five is building another American Dream mall in Miami that is being privately financed, showing that public money is not the difference between the developers plowing ahead or leaving a project to rot.

According to current plans, we'll find out come 2019 whether the American Dream is truly a nightmare. While the project is an extreme example—given the years of dithering, fits and starts, and the extravagant vision its creators have for creating an entire experience out of a shopping center—every other city or state that is thinking about mall building has to grapple with the same questions. With the American consumer becoming a very different kind of consumer—one that shops online and lives and works near the stores he or she frequents—the heyday of the mall could well be behind us. Anyone in a position of power would do well to acknowledge those trends, rather than throw more money into ever-fancier malls.

But physical stores aren't the only way lawmakers attempt to boost their local economies via a shopping frenzy. The recent decades have also seen the rise of the "sales tax holiday," a period in which lawmakers exempt certain classes of good from the sales tax.

Depending on whom you ask, the sales tax in America began either in Pennsylvania in 1821, West Virginia in 1921, or maybe Kentucky or Mississippi in 1930. But no matter when it came into being, the sales tax is now almost universal at the state and local levels: Just five states—New Hampshire, Alaska, Delaware, Oregon, and Montana—don't levy one. Rates range from Colorado's 2.9 percent to California's 7.25 percent.[47]

The sales tax is generally regressive: Because it's levied at a flat rate, and low-income households end up spending more of their income than do higher-income ones, it takes a larger chunk of change from those at the bottom of the income scale than those at the top. But sales taxes remain popular because of the feeling that taxing consumption is a relatively fair and easy way to raise funds, and because sales taxes make up a significant source of revenue. In 2010, sales taxes accounted for about a third of state and local government revenue, roughly equivalent to the percentage raised by the property tax and far more than that raised by state income taxes.[48]

The ubiquity of the sales tax and that every person experiences it every time he or she buys something made it ripe for exploiting via gimmicks. Thus, America experienced the rise of the sales tax holiday.

In 2017, sixteen states implemented a sales tax holiday, with the sales tax waived for certain goods over a set time. Typically, these holidays are hooked to the back-to-school season and portrayed as giving parents a late-July or early-August break on clothing, shoes, and school supplies for their kids. But some states have also offered sales tax holidays for computers, hurricane-preparedness supplies, air conditioners, Energy Star products, or firearms.

The sales tax holiday is a relatively recent tax policy innovation. In 1980, both Ohio and Michigan granted a onetime break for the purchase of automobiles, but the real birth of the holiday was in 1997 in New York State.[49] Tired of Empire State shoppers crossing the border to purchase clothes in New Jersey, which exempts clothing from its sales tax, New York granted a one-week sales tax holiday that January. Florida implemented a sales tax holiday the next year, followed by Texas the year after that. The numbers grew steadily over the years: seven states had them in 2000, nine in 2003, and sixteen plus the District of Columbia in 2008. By the peak in 2010, nineteen states had some version of the policy.[50]

The argument in favor of these holidays goes something like this: It gives consumers, especially those with lower incomes, a desperately needed break on necessary items such as school clothes for their kids or supplies to ride out a natural disaster. Plus, it provides retailers a boost, all at a relatively minimal cost to government coffers. As a bonus, it gives brick-and-mortar stores a way to compete against internet sellers, who are not always required to collect sales tax at all (though the Supreme Court finally ruled in June 2018 that states are allowed to ensure that all internet sales within their borders be subject to sales tax).

As the head of the Retailers Association of Massachusetts wrote in a *Boston Globe* op-ed urging the state to reinstate a sales tax holiday that it had canceled, "A tax that falls disproportionately on the shoulders of lower-income families is an important part of this story. So is the effect on our shopping districts, proliferating dark store fronts, leading to fewer jobs, less commercial property tax and income tax, and—ironically—less sales tax collection."[51]

The real story of sales tax holidays, though, is that they're basically a waste of time and do little to help those at whom they're aimed.

That very first holiday in New York is an instructive place to start. According to the state's Department of Taxation and Finance, it was pretty much a dud: "Reported sales were only slightly higher in the quarter in which the exemption took place. Moreover, the sales were no higher than one would expect based on economic growth for the period."[52] The bulk of the clothing bought during the period was either going to be bought anyway or would have been bought a little later but was simply shifted to the sales tax holiday period, depriving the state of revenue but not actually generating a new purchase.

That's a common theme in academic looks at sales tax holidays: For the most part, the sales generated would have taken place anyway, but were just shifted to the holiday period. One study places the percentage of shifted purchases at as high as 90.[53] Most recently, a 2017 analysis by Federal Reserve researchers found "sales-tax holidays are associated with significant shifts in the timing of purchases by consumers."[54]

So by implementing sales tax holidays lawmakers are not generating new economic activity, but simply moving already existing activity around. But that shift comes at a pretty steep price:

According to the Institute on Taxation and Economic Policy, states cost themselves a collective $300 million in 2016 thanks to sales tax holidays.[55]

But at least for all that money, states are helping out low-income folks, who are hardest hit by the sales tax, right? After all, it stands to reason that those who are most subjected to a tax would benefit most when that tax is not levied.

Alas, that isn't the case, for much the same reason that the sales tax is so regressive: Because low-income people are living paycheck to paycheck and spending most of their income, they aren't able to shift purchases in the same way that richer households can, so they are less able to take advantage of specially timed tax breaks. Per a 2010 study by the Chicago Federal Reserve, households with incomes under $30,000 change precisely squat in their shopping habits during a sales tax holiday. In fact, "Households consisting of married couples with young children and earning over $30,000 per year are the only ones that statistically significantly increase consumption."[56]

Also, sales tax holidays may ultimately hurt the poorest residents because, to make up lost revenue, governments set the usual sales tax rate higher than it would otherwise have been. According to research by the Mercatus Center, every exemption, including holidays, that a state implements to its sales tax results in a 0.1 to 0.25 percent increase in its overall sales tax rate. That's not a lot, but for the poorest Americans, every little bit counts.[57] (Notice that I included research from both the Institute on Taxation and Economic Policy and the Mercatus Center here, which are left- and right-wing, respectively. Disapproval of sales tax holidays is one of those things that unites tax wonks, regardless of where they fall on the political spectrum.)

So if the holidays don't help the overall economy and don't help those low-income people at whom they are theoretically and rhetorically aimed, whom do they help? Well, the industries whose goods are exempted are the biggest winner. Their stuff—be it guns, backpacks, or air conditioners—receives headlines and may be preferred in the moment over other goods that aren't affected by the tax break. The government picks winners and losers, usually settling on a pretty random bucket of goods, under the guise of tax relief. Meanwhile, retailers can game the holiday, marking up prices to redirect some of the savings that would have accrued to consumers. According to one admittedly small study out of west Florida, some 20 percent of the benefit in lower prices during the Sunshine State's sales tax holiday in 2001 wound up being offset by markups.[58]

You know who loves the sales tax holiday, though? Bass Pro Shops. You can even go on its website and access a handy guide laying out which states have holidays, when they are, and what goods can be had sales-tax-free. Which brings us all the way back to Memphis.

"It's this interesting thing in Memphis now, that for Memphians, at least the Memphians that I'm around, [the pyramid is] almost like Graceland in the sense that it's not something that we're going to go to all the time. It's a marker of our civic identity, whether we think it's awesome or whether we think it's ridiculous," said Charles Hughes, the Rhodes College historian. "It's hard not to be skeptical and it's hard not to also connect this to Memphis's long and continuing, I would argue, overreliance on the tourist dollar. Oftentimes tourism is a way that we can mask or ignore deeper problems."

It's not just Bass Pro. Retail, in general, is going through a paradigm shift, and yet too many cities still throw money at it, thinking that yesterday's store can build tomorrow's economy.

"If you mention the pyramid or the Bass Pro and the city's resources committed to that in political meetings—or in rooms of people who are concerned about where the city is going in terms of education and economics and health care and all those things—I don't think you're going to get a lot of people defending it," said Hughes. "If anything, people are going to be, like, 'Ehh, what?'"

And those people are absolutely right.

8

THE MYTHOLOGY OF THE CORPORATE TAX

"I HOPE YOU CAN FIGURE it out. I'd never fool with it again. They gave me all these promises about, we'd sign a onetime, five and three-quarter percent repatriation tax, they'd put the rest of it into jobs and pay raises."[1]

That's President George W. Bush, as relayed by President Bill Clinton, talking about an experiment, a "tax repatriation holiday," that the Bush II administration undertook in 2004. The idea was to give American companies that were holding money offshore a tax break that would entice them to bring their money home and spend it domestically on new investments and job creation.

Spoiler alert: It didn't happen.

"Nobody will ever accuse George W. Bush of being a liberal. But we were having a discussion once about how to repatriate some of this corporate cash that's been overseas and how it might be directed to growing the US economy," Clinton told *Inc.* magazine. "And all it went into was management pay and stock buybacks.

And [Bush] said, 'I'm done with it.' It was really a touching conversation. He really felt personally burned by his constituents."[2]

Leaving aside the notion that big corporations were George W. Bush's constituents, an important lesson here goes to the core of the issues in this book: Showering money on corporate America is no way to help the economy. That gets the way economic growth occurs precisely backward. Everything discussed to this point stems from this fundamental misunderstanding.

America was born in a tax revolt, with patriots chucking tea into the sea because its citizens were being taxed without representation. It's not surprising, then, that our national ethos gets tied up in a lot of antitax fervor, or that taxes are popularly portrayed as a burden to be borne reluctantly. They're the only thing you can count on besides death, as the saying goes.

But what about corporate taxes?

The corporate income tax occupies a funny spot in the American tax system. For years, nobody liked the way it was structured, with a high on-paper rate mixed in with so many deductions, loopholes, and other garbage that companies paid drastically lower rates in the real world. The United States was also alone among developed countries in attempting to tax the worldwide profits of its companies, yet it only did so when, for accounting purposes anyway, they brought that money home. Reforming the corporate tax at a national level was a consistent dream of wonks and think tankers and was always talked about among the chattering class as one of those bipartisan things that everyone should have been able to get behind because no one thought the current system was ideal. Clearing out the crud, lowering the rate, and raising the same amount of money should have been an achievable goal, even in the bitterest of political climates, the thinking went.

But 2017 provided a prime example of how the conventional

wisdom in the nation's capital so often goes awry. Thanks to the unexpected presidential victory of Donald Trump and the Republicans' viselike grip on Congress, "tax reform" got put on the table as one of the big things that a Washington united under the GOP could accomplish. The original plan, according to GOP rhetoric, was to cut the corporate tax rate down to 15 percent and eliminate enough loopholes, deductions, and other provisions of the tax code that at least some of the lost revenue would be recouped. The stated reason for doing so was that a lower corporate tax rate would make America more competitive internationally, enabling companies to bring home jobs that had previously been sent to lower-tax countries, as well as allowing America's biggest corporations to pay their workers more.

The administration even explicitly promised a $4,000 raise for workers thanks to the benevolence of their corporate overlords once the full effects of the tax cut were in place. But when the monumental difficulty of the task got to the administration—when the realization that cutting deductions meant ticking off the titans of industry and slaughtering sacred cows shepherded by the sort of people who host fund-raisers and cut big checks to campaign committees—the GOP threw its noblest intentions out the window and settled for a simpler plan: just cutting the corporate tax rate down to 21 percent, which is where it landed when Trump signed the Tax Cuts and Jobs Act into law in late December, at the cost of $600 billion over a decade on a corporate tax rate reduction alone.[3] That cut, to hear conservative lawmakers and pundit types tell it, would unleash the American economy like few things done before, even if the whole "reform" part of it was a bit lacking.

Historically, though, there was little reason to think that such an outcome would actually occur. As Thomas L. Hungerford wrote for the left-leaning Economic Policy Institute in 2013, "At first glance, a link between the statutory corporate tax rate and economic growth appears to go in the 'wrong' direction—higher tax rates are consistent with higher economic growth rates! The economy grew at an annual average rate of 3.9 percent between 1950 and 1960, when the statutory corporate tax rate was over 50 percent. Between 2000 and 2010, the statutory corporate tax rate was 35 percent (over 15 percentage points lower than the rate in the 1950s), and annual economic growth averaged 1.8 percent (less than half of the growth rate in the 1950s)."[4] He looked at the effective corporate tax rate, too, and again found that as it fell, economic growth did also. Hungerford sliced and diced the data in a number of ways and found no statistically significant instance in which lower tax rates went along with higher growth.

This isn't to say that higher taxes caused higher growth. If the United States jacked the corporate tax rate up to 90 percent tomorrow, I wouldn't expect to see a big boom in the economy. But these data do suggest that the easy theory saying cutting corporate taxes equates into an automatic boost for the economy is too simple and doesn't manifest in the real world.

Lo and behold, the administration was shocked—shocked!—when a slew of corporate titans made it known that their tax cut would not be immediately shipped out as Christmas bonuses to their workers, but would, instead, go to share buybacks and dividend payments, those ways for executives to further enrich those already holding a hefty chunk of America's wealth. "The most excited group out there are big CEOs, about our tax plan," said White House Economic Adviser Gary Cohn, who was later flabbergasted at a *Wall Street Journal* event where few CEOs said yes when asked if they planned to increase domestic investment as a result of their tax cuts.[5]

Sure, a few companies did, in the hours and days after the GOP tax bill became a fait accompli, announce that they would be giving workers new bonuses as a celebration. But that was as much a part of the scammy selling of the bill as anything else; in return for a deep, permanent cut in the corporate tax rate, companies such as Bank of America, AT&T, and Comcast announced onetime bonuses of $1,000—*onetime* being the key word—and delivered at Christmastime, no less, the traditional bonus season. In Comcast's case, its PR ploy came at the same time that it announced higher cable rates for the forthcoming year.[6] Corporations received a deep reduction in taxes for what was basically the cost of a press release. According to an analysis by Bloomberg's Stephen Gandel in the months after the tax cut took effect, some 60 percent of the benefits were going to shareholders, versus just 15 percent to employees.[7] Later analyses confirmed that general dynamic.

What the invisible hand giveth, it taketh away, eh?

The moral of this story is that a mythology has been crafted around the corporate tax, one that claims American companies are uniquely burdened and buried by Washington's tax and regulatory requirements. Everything that happens with stadiums, movies, casinos, and the like can be traced back to this enduring bit of storytelling. This is the urtext of every bad deal in which cities and states find themselves. But giving companies breaks on their taxes does not and will not translate into the sort of economic benefits that boosters proclaim, a lesson that never seems to stick no matter how many times it is learned.

The corporate income tax was first imposed in 1909, after the Supreme Court struck down an earlier 1894 version as unconstitutional. In the beginning, it was a scant 1 percent, climbing as high as 52.8 percent for two years in the late sixties, before settling at 35 percent between 1993 and the GOP's big cut to 21 percent in 2017.[8]

At the state level, a corporate income tax was first levied in 1911, by Wisconsin; dozens of states jumped on board over the next few decades.[9] Today, just six states—Washington, Nevada, Ohio, Texas, South Dakota, and Wyoming—don't tax corporate income; however, the first four of those do tax gross receipts, a kind of sales tax levied on the sellers of a product, rather than the consumer, leaving South Dakota and Wyoming as the only states that exempt corporations from any tax on their sales or profits. The highest corporate income tax rate in the country is Iowa's top rate of 12 percent.[10]

Let's discuss what we're really talking about when we're talking about tax rates, because the way they're discussed in the United States can be confusing, particularly when it comes to the taxation of income or profits. For the most part, US income taxes, at the corporate or personal level, operate on marginal rates, meaning that the tax rate in question is only levied on a certain level of income. So when you hear that a tax rate is set at 33 percent, that doesn't necessarily mean that one-third of everything earned by a person or business subject to that rate is going straight to the government. The old top corporate tax rate of 35 percent didn't kick in until a business saw profits of $18 million, so that rate didn't apply until dollar 18,000,001.

To make this easy, let's imagine a world with two tax brackets of 25 percent and 50 percent, with the top rate set at incomes only above $100, and with an exemption of $20. A business that makes $200 does not have to pay $100 to the government, because the 50 percent rate is applied only to earned dollars 101 through 200. So the company owes $20 for earned dollars 21 through 100, after taking the exemption into account and applying the 25 percent rate, and then 50 for earned dollars 101 through 200, for a total tax bill of $70. That's not something quick-and-dirty descriptions or discussions of tax rates generally make clear, leading to wide-ranging misperceptions that the bracket one falls into gets applied to the entirety of one's earnings.

When you hear about personal income tax rates being as high as 90 percent in the 1950s, which they were, don't let anyone fool you into thinking that meant 90 percent of anyone's income went to the government. Ditto the estate tax, which has a huge exemption, yet is popularly portrayed as literally requiring children to sell their parents' farm to satisfy the tax man. Even if the rate is 50 percent, that doesn't mean 50 percent of anyone's inheritance goes to the government.

In this sense, progressive income taxes, which the United States uses, are exceedingly fair. Everyone pays the same rate on the same income, i.e., at 2017 personal income tax rates, every single filer paid the same 25 percent rate on dollars $37,651 to $91,150. For all those who make enough, they pay a 28 percent rate only on dollars $91,151 to $190,150. And on and on.

So what do American corporations pay? Well, pre-2017, which is all we have the data for currently, the top corporate tax rate was the aforementioned 35 percent, often referred to as "the highest in the world."

"So when it comes to the business tax, we are dead last. Can you believe that? So this cannot be allowed to continue any longer. America must lead the way, not follow from behind," President Donald Trump said during a 2017 speech aiming to boost support for a bunch of tax cuts he wanted.[11] Lots of other conservatives—and even a few liberals—made the same complaint: The United States had the globe's highest corporate tax rate, which rendered it uncompetitive. (Trump often goofed this point up—whether intentionally to mislead, because he can't keep facts straight in his brain, or because he simply doesn't know better—and said that the United States is the highest-taxed nation in the world, period, which is embarrassingly, laughably, untrue. By developed-country standards, the United States is a low-tax country.)

On paper, the United States *did* have the world's highest corporate tax rate, at 35 percent. But that number reveals little about what US companies actually paid in the real world.

The headline rate on paper is known as the statutory rate, but the more telling statistic is what's known as the effective rate, which is the rate that companies pay once the entirety of the tax code is taken into account. As noted earlier, the US corporate tax code is a wretched hive of scum and deductions, chock-full of stuff that reduces the headline rate for individual companies.

In a 2017 paper, the Congressional Budget Office, which is Congress's nonpartisan scorekeeper, took a look and found that in 2012 the effective rate that companies paid was just shy of 19 percent. That placed the United States fourth among countries the CBO surveyed—behind Australia, Japan, and the United Kingdom—and in the same ballpark as Brazil and Germany.[12] In a 2014 survey, the Congressional Research Service (CRS) also concluded that the US corporate rate was right in line with that found in other large, developed economies; the CRS looked at the fifteen largest countries in the world, placing the US effective rate at 27.2 percent in 2008, and that of companies headquartered in the other fourteen at 27.1 percent. It also sliced and diced the tax code in a variety of ways—including and excluding different incentives and other forms of taxes—but consistently found that the United States, even before the 2017 tax cut, wasn't that different from any other big, developed country.[13]

Anyone focusing on the statutory rate who claims that US companies were uniquely overburdened in the world was either ignorant of the way the system works or willfully using a misleading number to make a political case. This was even clearer when one looked at individual companies and industries. Because so much of the junk in the tax code is activity or firm specific—meaning it is meant to boost a particular product, undertaking, or sector of the economy that won favor from someone in power sometime in the past—tax rates vary widely among US companies. Typically, big retailers—the Walmarts and Targets of the world—get dinged pretty hard, while tech companies with no real product to sell, such as Facebook, pay not much at all, through a variety of tricks. Health care companies, which provide the ultimate in non-outsourceable services, are often walloped the hardest.

On the opposite end of the spectrum, some companies end up paying nothing: zip, nada, zilch, zero. According to the Institute on Taxation and Economic Policy (ITEP), which looked at several hundred companies for which it could get full records (notably, the analysis did not include some of America's heaviest hitters, such as Apple and Microsoft, because of their ability to shift profits to offshore locations), many big American companies went from 2008 to 2015 without having any federal income tax liability. During that eight-year period, companies such as General Electric, Pepco, and Xcel Energy paid a whole lot of nothing. In 2015 alone, ITEP found, "29 companies paid no federal income tax, and received $1.46 billion in tax rebates."[14]

Over those same eight years, a veritable who's who of American corporate titans managed to go at least one year without paying any federal corporate income tax: Facebook, Goldman Sachs, AT&T, Time Warner, Wells Fargo, Eli Lilly, FedEx, ExxonMobil, State Street, Yum! Brands, and Boeing all pulled that particular trick. Yes, those years encompass the recovery from the Great Recession, so business was not exactly booming all over the country, but these are some of the biggest, most successful, and most recognizable brands in the world's largest economy. That they managed to avoid all federal income tax in a given year shows that something is severely broken. Meanwhile, a quarter of the companies in the study paid nearly the full statutory corporate tax rate of 35 percent. America's corporate tax code picks a mess of winners and losers, with decades of bipartisan efforts to preference this thing or that thing resulting in some industries and companies paying full freight while others ride along scot-free.[15]

So the claim that America's 35 percent rate was dooming its business competitiveness was built on a lot of hand waving and obfuscating. But it also missed something fundamental: Big companies can't drive the economy. Only those middle- and lower-income Americans who do most of the buying can.

Companies invest and expand when they see more demand for their product and the potential for more customers, not because they simply have some cash lying around or because they received a special infusion of tax breaks. If a business sold fifteen widgets last year and anticipates selling only fifteen widgets in each of the next two years, it doesn't matter how much money you rain down on it from on high; it won't invest in new facilities, equipment, or employees until it concludes that it can expect to sell more widgets. Events on the ground change that number, not the amount of money stashed in the bank. New employees, new locations, and new equipment aren't worth it without higher sales. Without demand from customers, those new employees won't have anything to do and that new equipment will sit around idle.

So the truth that few in Washington want to say aloud is, America needs to raise a lot more money from corporations, not less.

America's reliance on corporations as a revenue source has declined precipitously in recent years, while corporate profitability has climbed ever higher. Consider a couple of quick statistics: In 1952 at its absolute height, federal corporate income tax revenue as a share of US gross domestic product, which is the fairest way to look at it in order to compare levels over time, clocked in at 5.2 percent. In 2017, that number will be about 1.6 percent. That same year—1952—the corporate income tax made up about one-third of total federal tax revenue. In 2017, it won't make up 10 percent. In that same time span, the personal income tax has remained remarkably steady, raising 7 or 8 percent in GDP and raking in about 45 percent of total revenue. So while the amount contributed on the personal side has gone basically nowhere, the amount contributed by corporations has fallen off a cliff.[16] It's not because businesses are making so much less money that their tax burden has fallen commensurately. No, in 1952, corporate profits after taxes were just above 5 percent of GDP; today, they're at nearly 9 percent. More profits, fewer taxes.

Yes, this simple story gets somewhat more complicated because many small (and some not-so-small) businesses don't pay corporate income tax at all. They are "pass-through" companies, meaning they pass their revenue down to their owners, who pay the personal income tax on their take-home pay. The use of this corporate setup has grown significantly over the last thirty years or so, so some of what was lost on the corporate side of the government's tax ledger has been transferred over to the personal side. But not enough to account for such major changes.

At the state level, the story is much the same. In 1980, the corporate income tax accounted for about 4 percent of total state revenue. By 2013, it was down to 2 percent. In certain states, the drop-off was even more dramatic: In California, the corporate income tax made up about 5.5 percent of total revenue in 1990; by 2013, it was 2.4 percent. In Connecticut, it went from 7.1 percent to 1.8 percent in the same period. In Michigan, 7.8 percent to 1.3 percent. Meanwhile, per Census Bureau data analyzed by *Governing* magazine, "Of the 43 states with income taxes, individual income tax collection growth (measured as a percentage change) outpaced corporate tax revenues in 31 states since 1990."[17]

Given how little companies are contributing today compared to what they contributed not all that long ago, they should be paying more, not less. Plus, not only are profits up, but wages as a share of the economy are way down. Productivity has increased, and companies are only getting better at squeezing more and more out of fewer and fewer workers. When leaders at every level talk about stagnant wages, the ability of corporations to sock away more and more cash is part of the problem.

Alas, the 2017 tax bill took everything in the wrong direction. It would be a heavy lift, politically, to even reverse that bill's effect, never mind returning the corporate tax back into the sort of revenue raiser that it can and should be. I wouldn't bet much on Democrats having the guts, in the short term anyway, to go about raising the corporate income tax back to where it was before the 2017 law.

One of the reasons that the corporate tax doesn't get much interest as a revenue raiser is that plenty of economists, pundits, and lawmakers don't like it, period. Since it's a tax on corporate profits, many claim that it depresses business activity and growth (more on this later). Another complaint is that, since corporations aren't people but a legal entity (according to everyone except 2012 Republican presidential nominee Mitt "corporations are people, my friend" Romney and the justices who made up the majority of the *Citizens United* Supreme Court decision), the tax just gets passed on to workers, thus lowering their wages and hurting the very people who would, in theory, benefit from someone else picking up more of the national revenue responsibilities.

Just how much of the corporate tax falls onto workers is a matter for a lot of debate. But the idea that it does hit them in a significant way is ammunition for those who argue that the tax needs to go down, not up. After all, if it's just a hidden tax on employees, cutting it does them a favor and can be portrayed as good for the working class, rather than just a giveaway for corporate titans.

A rather absurd episode from 2017 encapsulates how this all works. When the Trump administration began stumping for its tax package, which at first included a reduction in the corporate tax rate from 35 percent to 15 percent, Treasury Secretary Steven Mnuchin tried to build support by claiming that 70 percent of the corporate tax was passed on to workers. Thus, a big reduction in what corporations paid would translate into a big reduction in what workers paid, rendering workers the ultimate winners of the exchange. "More than seventy percent of the tax burden on business is passed on to workers," Mnuchin said. "This is really our version of a jobs bill."[18] He later reiterated on *Fox News Sunday*, "Most economists believe that over seventy percent of corporate taxes are paid for by the workers."[19] Don't forget that the administration was promising workers $4,000—a quite specific number!—if the corporate tax cuts came to pass.

Mnuchin's claim was echoed by corporate leaders. In an October 2017 NBC News op-ed, for instance, JPMorgan Chase CEO Jamie Dimon wrote, "Our current tax code is uncompetitive, overly complex and loaded with special interest provisions that create winners and losers. This drives down capital investment, reduces productivity and causes wages to remain stagnant. Under our current system, workers bear up to 75 percent of the corporate tax burden through lower wages."[20]

The trouble was that a 2012 analysis from the Treasury Department said otherwise: According to a paper from that department's Office of Tax Analysis, just 18 percent of the corporate tax is passed on to workers, while the rest lands on shareholders, a far cry from the upward of 70 percent that Mnuchin and his CEO friends were claiming.[21] The Treasury Department solved the discrepancy in the good old-fashioned way: by removing the offending analysis from its website and throwing it down the memory hole, as *The Wall Street Journal* reported in an excellent catch.[22]

Yes, since the paper dated from the previous administration, one could make the argument, as Mnuchin did, that it was not reflective of current thinking. But the economists who work on that sort of paper aren't political appointees, they're career number crunchers. What that paper found is in line with what other governmental analyses, such as those produced by the Joint Committee on Taxation and the Congressional Budget Office, have come up with as well: that less than a quarter of the corporate tax ultimately comes out of the pockets of a firm's employees. Even then, some of those employees will be already well-off managers or executives—not exactly the downtrodden plant workers to whom most politicians try to pander when they run around the country selling trickle-down tax cuts.

When Mnuchin claims that "most economists" think otherwise, he's incorrect. But his rhetoric might make for good politics, which is probably why he doubled and tripled down on it in an attempt to get a corporate rate reduction through. Indeed, implementing pro-corporate policies while claiming they are pro-worker is a time-honored Washington tradition; it's easier than making the case on the merits, since corporations aren't the most sympathetic of political actors.

So what do Americans think of all this corporate tax talk? As much as they love their job creation and economic growth, they really, really don't like the notion that companies are taking advantage of the tax system to pay less than their fair share. Per Gallup's polling, which goes back to 2004, two-thirds or more of Americans consistently say that corporations are paying too little in taxes.[23] Only about one-fifth, and often fewer, say that the amount corporations are paying is about right. And other polls back that up: Per a 2017 ABC News/Washington Post effort that coincided with the Trump administration's ultimately successful push for corporate rate cuts, 65 percent of Americans feel corporations pay too little.[24] In a 2015 Pew Research Center poll, 64 percent said the same.[25]

To get a sense for what these numbers mean as something more than figures on a page, I met up with Vanessa Williamson, a fellow in governance studies at the Brookings Institution and the author of *Read My Lips: Why Americans Are Proud to Pay Taxes*, who specializes in studying Americans' attitudes toward the tax system. She got into the topic via a Tea Party Tax Day event, and the way conservatives portray the duties of being a taxpayer.

"I started noticing that conservatives often define themselves as taxpayers," she said. "It's a shorthand for being an upstanding community person."

Her research has found that, far from hating to pay taxes as the conventional wisdom would have it, Americans see taxpaying as a civic responsibility. It's the shirking of that responsibility—perceived or actual—that they despise. And they often think that corporations aren't paying their share of the overall tax bill.

"An open-ended question I sometimes ask is 'What are you glad that tax money goes to and what are you upset that tax money goes to?' And you can measure that on two dimensions: how often something's mentioned and how positive those mentions are," Williamson says. "So roads and schools get mentioned a lot and almost always positively. Foreign aid is actually relatively rarely mentioned, but no one ever brings it up except to complain about it. Corporate tax aid, like bailouts, corporate subsidies, all that stuff, is never, ever mentioned in a positive way. It's somewhat partisan: Democrats are more likely to mention it than Republicans, but no one mentions it, not Republicans, no one, in a positive light.

"If you let people talk about corporations and taxation, there are a couple of stories you tend to hear a lot," she continued. "One is about a specific company, a name-brand company, that they know doesn't pay taxes because they read an article." For instance, "'I heard that GE paid zero dollars last year, or something.' It's not always one hundred percent accurate," she said. "But it usually is a company that is in the news for these things."[26]

All that said, you can find polls showing that Americans think the corporate tax rate should be cut. Look closely, though, and those sorts of answers will often be to leading questions, meant to craft a veneer of support for distasteful public policy. For instance, in September 2017, just as the ABC News/Washington Post poll was showing that nearly two-thirds of Americans think corporations pay too little in taxes, a poll from the right-leaning American Action Network found that nearly 60 percent would support cutting the corporate tax. The trick is, the latter poll prompted respondents with the qualifier that lowering the corporate tax rate "would help level the playing field in international competition."[27] Of course everyone is in favor of that! Who wants to be internationally uncompetitive? Depending on how the question is asked, you can get poll respondents to go just about any which way on the corporate tax.

"People don't have very much information about taxes in general and corporate taxes in particular. On any particular reform you can push-poll really easily, for instance, because they don't have a lot of information to actually work with, so the information you provide, you can shape attitudes really strongly," Williamson said. "You can definitely write poll questions like 'This will provide everyone with a puppy,' and if it's on an obscure-enough policy, of course people are going to be, like, 'Well, I do think we should all have puppies.' . . . It's not a judgment on people, this stuff's hard, they don't know a lot about it, they're busy. It's not every American's job to do what the Tax Policy Center does." (That's a respected DC-based think tank.)

But from my reading, and that of the people who know what they're doing on taxes and polling, Americans think corporations are paying too little in taxes (which is true) and that it's darn unpatriotic for them to duck, dodge, and avoid paying up.

So why is it so hard to raise the corporate income tax? Why is real corporate tax reform such a heavy lift? The place to look isn't 2017 at all, when the Republican Congress took the easy way out by lowering taxes without much reform, but 2014, when someone tried to take the task much more seriously.

The Obama administration was then looking to deal with a Republican-controlled House, and supposedly corporate tax reform was one of those things upon which the administration and the rabidly antitax Tea Partyers who had ridden into town in the last couple of elections could agree. To his credit, the House Ways and Means Committee chairman, Dave Camp of Michigan, actually tried to craft a plan that could garner genuine bipartisan support. It wasn't ideal, but it was a good-faith effort to write something that roughly split the difference between Obama's desires and those of the GOP caucus, slaughtering sacred cows for each. It included lower on-paper rates in exchange for clearing out some of the underbrush and making corporate taxes more consistent across the board. If a deal was ever to be struck between a Republican Congress and a Democratic president, it would have to look something like what Camp cooked up. By trading lower rates for clearing out the crud, it wouldn't have lost revenue but would have made things fairer, with fewer industry- or activity-specific provisions that benefit a few companies while providing no such help to everyone else.

But the House never even voted on it. When the Speaker of the House, John Boehner, who was not a Tea Party zealot by any stretch of the imagination but instead liked to fashion himself one of the last bipartisan deal-cutters on Capitol Hill, was asked to describe the details, he replied, "Blah, blah, blah, blah." The most plausible plan for actually achieving what everyone said was an achievable goal was yada-yada'd by the guy who led the same party as the guy who wrote the bill.[28]

Proving how short everyone's memory is in Washington, after the 2014 elections, when Republicans added a Senate majority to their House one, again the talk among Obama and the GOP was that corporate tax reform was on the agenda. It still didn't happen.

It's no surprise that Camp's plan was suffocated in its cradle or that no momentum ever built behind a corporate tax reform effort throughout the Obama administration or the administrations that preceded it. The trouble is, while lowering the corporate tax rate and cleaning out loopholes to pay for it sounds appealing, the "blah,

blah" makes it decidedly less so for lawmakers and companies alike. A corporate tax deal produces some winners, but also, inevitably, a whole lot of losers. Every "loophole" exists for a reason and has a constituency that uses it and wants to protect it. To whoever benefits, a loophole isn't a loophole; it's a vital job-creation program. Since this is the corporate tax code we're talking about, those corporations can put a lot of time and money into safeguarding their particular handouts.

The 2017 tax bill makes this problem worse, not better, as companies now see that waiting until there is united GOP control of the government can give them everything they've wanted on the cutting side of the tax debate without much of the pain of the reform side. The Republican Congress and Trump administration have done the easy part of corporate tax reform—lowering the rate, to the tune of more than half a trillion in lost revenue over ten years—without doing the hard part. Making up the difference will be left to some future Congress, whose task will be all the more difficult without a carrot to offer companies along with the stick of fewer deductions and loopholes.

Perhaps nothing exemplifies just how bad the 2017 tax bill was, though, than the item noted at the beginning of this chapter, the one that burned President Bush so badly: repatriating offshore funds.

Per Vanessa Williamson, the tax-attitude expert, one thing in particular earns corporations a special level of ire in the American psyche: offshoring. "The version of corporate tax avoidance that people are familiar with is offshoring. And I think one reason that story resonates with people is it's a symbolic way of thinking about a deeper truth. People see taxpaying as part of being a responsible American, so they like to describe people they don't really love as

Americans as nontaxpayers, but it also applies to corporations. Offshoring is a very concrete way in which you're not doing your part for the country, so people find that metaphor really potent."

She added, "Of course, [offshoring is] a real thing that costs a great deal of money. But it's something that I think resonates for multiple reasons. There are a lot of tax avoidance schemes that cost America a lot of money that aren't as familiar, but the idea of holding your profits offshore or of keeping your jobs and your tax money overseas, that's really quite clear as an idea."

It's also quite clear that we're talking about a lot of money here. According to the Institute on Taxation and Economic Policy, the Fortune 500 have some $2.6 trillion offshore, which is in line with other estimates.[29] That's a pretty big pot of dough that did not, for a long time, get taxed until those companies characterized it as having been brought back to the States. (Overall, according to economist Gabriel Zucman, some $7.6 trillion in global wealth is stored in tax havens, about 8 percent of total worldwide wealth, and some 80 percent of it is totally off the books and out of the reach of tax authorities.)[30]

That trillions of dollars are "offshore" leaves the impression that underneath the European or Caribbean offices of major American companies are vast vaults filled with money. But Jeff Bezos and Mark Zuckerberg aren't swimming around in pools of gold coins in Brussels or Dublin, Scrooge McDuck–style. *Offshore* simply means that the profits in question are, for accounting purposes, booked as being held by a foreign subsidiary, giving companies the option to defer paying taxes on them. As the Center for American Progress's Kitty Richards and John Craig wrote, "It is true that for accounting purposes, multinational corporations keep these dollars off of their U.S. books. But in the real world, the money is often deposited in U.S. banks, circulating in the U.S. economy, and available for a wide variety of domestic investments. For nearly all practical purposes, that money is already here, being put to work in the U.S. economy."[31]

It's totally understandable that Americans see this as an abdication of responsibility. In 2004, the Bush administration set out to do something about it, allowing companies to bring back their offshore moneys at a tax rate of 5.25 percent, far below the normal 35 percent top rate at the time.

The tax cut—known as the Homeland Investment Act, which was packaged with the larger American Jobs Creation Act—was supposed to create half a million jobs and boost domestic investment by corporations by several percentage points. It did have a seductive logic to it; under the rules at the time, companies would probably never repatriate that money, lest they get dinged by the top corporate tax rate; leaving it offshore indefinitely was a sensible option. But at 5 percent, corporate titans would jump to bring the money home and inevitably plow their unexpected savings into new and better stuff for themselves and their employees, right?

Nope.

Instead, per a study by three economists, including one who was in the Bush administration and worked on the proposal, some 92 percent of the money companies brought back went to enriching executives and buying back their own company's shares. Many companies that took advantage of the tax break actually reduced jobs in the subsequent years.[32]

"Repatriations did not lead to an increase in domestic investment, employment or R&D—even for the firms that lobbied for the tax holiday stating these intentions and for firms that appeared to be financially constrained. Instead, a $1 increase in repatriations was associated with an increase of almost $1 in payouts to shareholders," the study found.[33] That study's authors aren't the only ones to come to that conclusion. As the Congressional Research Service summed up in 2009, "A number of researchers have studied the impact of the reduction in the tax on repatriated earnings that came out of the American Jobs Creation Act. . . . In short, the studies generally conclude that the reduction in the tax rate on repatriated earnings led to a sharp increase in the level of repatriated earnings, but that the repatriations did not increase domestic investment or employment. They further conclude that much of the repatriations were returned to shareholders through stock repurchases."[34]

So much for that. No wonder Bush felt burned by his corporate buddies.

The tax break did do one thing, though: encourage more money to be pushed into the offshore accounting column. Companies saw that they had received a steep tax discount on their offshore money and figured that another would come along someday, so they pushed more money away in anticipation of that future break. There's no sense paying 35 percent today, or 20 percent, or 15 percent, or even 12 percent, if you feel fairly confident that you could pay 5 percent tomorrow.

The Joint Committee on Taxation, in evaluating a 2014 repatriation plan, called this the idea's "moral hazard problem."[35] As Northwestern School of Law professor Thomas Brennan wrote, "Legislation permitting such a reprieve sends a signal to those subject to certain rules that the legislature is willing to grant occasional suspensions of the rules. This signal operates to condition those subject to the rules to anticipate the opportunities of future holidays and arrange their affairs accordingly, and this long-term effect needs to be taken into account when considering the policy implications of a proposed holiday. The fact that such conditioning can occur is certainly not new, and it dates at least back to

Pavlov and his dogs."[36] Congress intended for the break to be a onetime thing, never to occur again, but clearly, corporate America didn't believe that legislators could stick to their guns.[37]

And corporate America was right: Republicans in the 2017 tax bill included a new, low rate for repatriation. It's not exactly the same thing, as they do require that offshore money be "deemed" to have been brought home, rather than leaving the choice up to the individual companies, but the result will be the same: untaxed money flowing to the United States and straight into shareholders' pockets, doing nothing for the workers or for the taxpaying public that gave up revenue.

Along with the 2017 tax bill's switch from what's known as a worldwide system—one in which an American company's profits from anywhere are taxed—to what's known as a territorial system—in which non-US profits never face the US corporate tax, even when earned by US companies—the bill as a whole is a giant incentive to move money out of the United States and into low- or no-tax jurisdictions (or at least make it look as if that's where the money is, for tax purposes). A broken corporate tax was smashed further into smithereens in the name of making America great again.

So why does any of this matter? Well, it's no secret that America has some pretty severe budget problems coming down the pike. To maintain programs that are vital parts of American life and to rebuild infrastructure that has been allowed to decay and crumble—and to tackle the problem of climate change, which has been allowed to fester for far too long thanks to one political party's antiscience nonsense—federal and state revenue is going to have to go up. For too long, America has been content with taxes far below the level of the rest of the developed world; no one's saying we need to become Denmark overnight, but neither can we continue to be below Zimbabwe and Kazakhstan in the taxes we ask citizens and companies to contribute to the national cause. Some problems can't be solved by apps and entrepreneurs, but only by the federal government, and the necessary money has to come from somewhere. That taxes aren't higher is simply a political choice, not an economic one.

Unfortunately, the average American generally finds it difficult to draw a line between tax cuts and any corresponding spending cuts or underinvestment on stuff that might affect them. "It's hard to make that connection because people naturally think there's a great deal of government waste," said Vanessa Williamson. "And when people are thinking of government waste, they're not just thinking of inefficiency, though that's on the list. They're often thinking of entire programs they don't like. . . . So connecting taxes to spending is mediated by this waste question." It took a complete catastrophe in Kansas, for instance, for that state to finally reverse a set of ruinous tax cuts, including big cuts on business income, that decimated its education system without boosting the economy, and even then it was a close-run thing; in the interim, the state reelected the governor who had spearheaded the whole effort. Making clear that every dollar that goes into a corporate coffer winds up being one dollar less that gets spent on roads, bridges, or hospitals takes that sort of episode, wherein a state stares into the abyss and has the abyss stare back; otherwise people think that the money they sent to the tax man probably went to someone less deserving, so it might as well go to a business.

It doesn't help that one of America's political parties has been gripped by an antitax fervor for decades that subsumes pretty much any and all other considerations. Once upon a time, at least a healthy portion of the Republican Party believed in fiscal responsibility at the federal level, and not just cutting taxes willy-nilly, especially for those at the top of the income scale. But today, lower taxes, especially for the rich, is the one overarching drive the party seems to have. It whines and yelps about federal finances when it's out of power—as it did all through the Obama administration, even though economic conditions at the top warranted big increases in federal spending—yet when it comes into power, the GOP can't wait to slash taxes, regardless of the costs or the efficacy of the last round of cuts it initiated.

I know that sounds flip, but it's true, and there's no countermanding ideology on the other side of the political aisle. If there were, Democrats wouldn't have gone out of their way to fully pay for something such as Obamacare, which they did. Republican zealotry on taxes is simply unmatched by a corresponding Democratic obsession, thus tilting the two-party system in such a way that tax policy becomes basically impossible to deal with in an intelligent way. That attitude trickles down to all levels of government, so even local school boards become obsessed with tax rates and tax cuts, to the detriment of the actual services they need to provide.

But at the state level, too, there's reason to be skeptical that corporate tax cuts do much good. According to the preponderance of the academic evidence—and this question has been studied quite a bit—reducing corporate taxes at the state level either does nothing or has an effect so small as to be barely worth it.[38] Two states in recent years have gone so far as to wipe out large swathes of their business tax—Ohio eliminated its own completely in 2005, replacing it with a gross receipts tax, and Kansas exempted most small businesses from taxes in 2012—and neither saw an effect worth writing home about. Since states have balanced-budget requirements, all of those drops in revenue need to be paired with corresponding tax increases elsewhere or cuts in services. Even more so than at the federal level, reducing corporate taxes has a corresponding direct effect on what the state can otherwise do for its citizens.

The corporate tax cut myth has such a grip on America for one final reason: Politicians love to vote for tax cuts. Even when what they're doing is simply approving new spending, they yearn to craft that spending as a tax cut, just so they can say, "Hey, this is a tax cut!"

Consider the funny case of tax expenditures. Per the Congressional Budget Act of 1974, tax expenditures are "revenue losses attributable to provisions of the Federal tax laws which allow a special exclusion, exemption, or deduction from gross income or which provide a special credit, a preferential rate of tax, or a deferral of tax liability." They're called expenditures because they look and act very much like spending programs; the government wants to accomplish a particular goal or outcome with a particular group of people and, instead of just appropriating money for it, tries to engineer the outcome through the tax code. The largest such expenditure is the exclusion for health benefits; the government wants to encourage businesses to provide health insurance to employees, so it gives them a tax break. Other big ones are the mortgage interest deduction and the deduction for charitable contributions.[39]

The political benefit of using the tax code to accomplish these things—rather than the government's spending power—is twofold: First, it allows lawmakers to say that they gave someone (anyone!) a tax cut, even if the same thing could have been accomplished just by, say, cutting checks for a percentage of health care costs (or, heaven forfend, the government just covering health insurance directly). Second, it makes it easy to characterize any change in the policy as a tax increase.

Consider: If the government sent a check to all homeowners for a percentage of their mortgage costs each year, not doing so in the future would be ending a spending program, and many people would cheer because they believe such programs always benefit people other than themselves. But getting rid of a tax break that covers a percentage of annual mortgage costs would be raising taxes. Plus, spending programs need to be reauthorized by Congress annually (except for the "mandatory" programs, such as Social Security or Medicare). Tax breaks do not. They live on until someone affirmatively gets rid of them.

While the vast bulk of the $1.3 trillion or so in annual tax expenditures goes to individuals, some are targeted for corporations. According to the Government Accountability Office, the federal government loses about $181 billion annually on corporate tax expenditures. Of that, nearly $60 billion is corporation specific.[40] (The rest comes from expenditures available to both companies and individuals.)

That's real money, and that's the point of discussing the mythology of the corporate tax and what allowing that tax to rot has wrought in the real world. I'm not bashing companies for taking advantage of the laws as they're written to pay lower taxes; no person or corporation has an obligation to pay a dime more than is required by the tax code. Taxes aren't charity. The problem is the system itself, and the lawmakers who have bought into the mythology that companies and antitax advocates sell, despite all of the evidence showing that the story they tell about how companies react to tax changes isn't true.

The myth of the corporate tax has had huge consequences in the real world, where it has trickled down to state and local governments, leading them to make all the bad investments outlined in the preceding chapters. Every cent that gets spent in the hopeless chase for jobs via reducing corporate taxes is one less cent that can be spent on something that would be far more effective, efficient, and presumably more in line with what voters say they want. As Supreme Court Justice Oliver Wendell Holmes wrote, "Taxes are what we pay for civilized society." America's corporations need to pay up.

EPILOGUE

Look, I know that the industries I say need to get off the public dole provide plenty of people a paycheck, and that those people could possibly be hurt if the public dollars stopped flowing. Without subsidies, a lot of the hubs for, say, movies or retail that have cropped up would likely not be self-sustaining, and the people who work in those jobs would be in a bad place. I get that no one wants his or her job to vanish, or to see their uncle, aunt, sister, neighbor, or whomever wind up looking for work because of something that happens in a statehouse or because pointy-headed econ wonks say the money would be better spent somewhere else. I understand why those folks—even though there are far fewer of them than the advocates of subsidy schemes would have you believe—have a genuine interest in maintaining the status quo. If everything I've advocated in this book happened tomorrow, an unfortunate by-product is that some people, somewhere, would see their jobs disappear. Almost no policy choice has zero ramifications on anybody. Even if it's far fewer jobs than those pushing these tax breaks claim, the number of losses couldn't possibly be zero. Nothing is ever that easy.

But you can't make economic policy via anecdote; you have to look at the aggregate and, on the whole, subsidizing the entertainment industry—or many other actions that America's corporate titans undertake—via the tax code, even if it does help some individuals here and there, is a waste of money that could be used for the greater good. Those dollars that benefit a few via projects that could easily be funded by the private sector entirely, or that prop up otherwise economically nonsensical movie shoots, malls, or casinos, could go a whole lot further if they were spent on schools, on the health care system, on infrastructure, on job retraining, or to create industries that actually are vital to the national interest, be it via investments in some new technology or an alternative-energy product. Government is always about prioritizing; there are never enough dollars for even the core functions that Americans depend on every day, such as roads or food inspections. Throwing money down the various rat holes described in this book is unforgivable, given the consequences of underfunding other areas. Not paying for a particular government program can be life-and-death; not paying for a stadium won't be.

Does that mean every stadium, arena, mall, or retail tourist attraction is inevitably doomed to failure? Not necessarily (though I'd argue that the operating assumption should be that such things are a waste of money until proven otherwise). The illusory benefits often prove irresistible to lawmakers; thus they're going to make every case seem to be a slam dunk. So keep in mind these few rules if your city or state proposes to invest in these sorts of projects, to evaluate whether they might be a good idea.

The first and perhaps most important thing to look at is whether the final product can attract visitors who would not have come to town in that thing's absence, and without displacing other local spending. That's a high bar to surmount. The odd casino or store might possibly clear it; envisioning sporting venues that could do the same is basically impossible. Those places are always going to displace other spending in local shops and restaurants, since they're almost inevitably in urban areas that aren't lacking in entertainment options. A sports arena or stadium is almost certain to just shuffle money around the economy, without creating much of anything new.

The second factor to look at is where the employees filling jobs in the new thing will come from. In a perfect world, the visitors to the new place would be mostly from out of town, while the employees would all be from the local community, thereby limiting the number of people who take their wages and spend them somewhere else. That's a hard needle to thread. That doesn't just go for employees, but to the beneficiaries of the profits, too: Keeping to a minimum the amount of money that leaks out to other areas will boost the economic effectiveness of any new facilities, but since they almost always include big national or multinational corporations as owners, that is again a tall order.

So that's the rule: Lots of outside visitors who wouldn't have come anyway, plus lots of local employees, plus no big corporate partners from somewhere else siphoning off the profits. You can see why the odds of success are pretty low.

Assessing a project in this way leaves aside the questions of opportunity cost and the market itself: What goes unfunded when an arena gets built? Why can't the owners of a megamall afford to build it themselves? If a Bass Pro Shop is such a tourist attraction that people will flock to it in droves, why does it need the state's help to get off the ground? Presumably, all those visitors will make the investment worthwhile for a private company in the long run, no? A principle is at work here regarding the free market and what the government should be doing to prop it up that goes beyond dollars, cents, and figures on a spreadsheet: Whom does the government work for, and what should be its goals in facilitating and regulating commerce?

That final question points to why the debate around using tax breaks to help America's entertainment titans so often takes a turn for the absurd. In almost every case, the ultimate beneficiary is going to be some corporation, a wealthy owner, a CEO, shareholders, or whoever else is invested in the success of the company in question. Ancillary effects on the community are very much a secondary concern. But because the company is asking for public support, its boosters make it seem as if the community benefit is the first order of business, the reason that a new facility should be built. That's never the case, so the discussion is out of whack as soon as it begins. If the starting premise is that private businesses need to be subsidized—and not doing so dooms a place economically—things are already stacked against the public receiving smart investments for its tax money. The narrative that results in taxpayers losing out is already baked into the cake.

I wish there were a better playbook for a local community to fight back against being sold out to the entertainment industry. But because the fact that cities and states can be played off against one another makes things exceedingly difficult. Just look at the campaign Amazon waged for its second headquarters; Greg LeRoy put it best when he said that lawmakers were acting like trained seals, jumping when Amazon CEO Jeff Bezos said jump. Few blinked when states said they were prepared to throw billions at the company or were willing to exempt it from taxation—or even to let it decide where tax revenue for its area of town would be spent, totally abdicating the concept of collective governance to a private company. The whole thing was a discouragingly predictable example of why everything I've laid out in this book is the way it is.

Perhaps things must get as bad as they clearly were for the Olympics before a mass movement can start to push back against the corporate story line. The games had become such a mess, and the rotting venues in so many cities such an obvious symbol of something having gone awry, that Boston was able to organize and fight back, other cities gave the International Olympic Committee the slip, and Los Angeles and Paris were able to dictate better terms for 2024 and 2028 because the IOC feared having nowhere else to turn. But several cities had to have a horrendous experience before that groundswell began, leading to real crises, and even then there's no telling how long it'll last. Come 2032, we may well have forgotten the lessons of Athens, Rio, and Pyeongchang. Perhaps a deal as big as the one Amazon is hunting for will have to blow up in the face of an American city before we realize just how far down the wrong road we've all been driven.

It should be easiest for citizens to stand in the way of more localized efforts to give away tax dollars, such as subsidies for malls or retail tourism destinations. But in those instances the jobs argument is often the most effective. A down-on-its-luck town jumps at the chance to have a few dozen jobs in a Bass Pro, even at an exorbitant cost or if it means sacrificing the local tackle shop. So smaller projects actually prove the toughest to derail. Thanks to economic desperation, a few million dollars that could go a long way in a smaller place winds up paying a huge portion of the cost for a handful of jobs.

To me, the best way to defeat these projects is long before they're even a suggestion, or a glimmer in the eye of the corporate spokesperson who is going to write a glowing press release about all the supposed benefits—by electing lawmakers who won't indulge in these economic fantasies. It took a brand-new city council in Anaheim to finally stand up to Disney, while antistadium lawmakers in Las Vegas stopped an MLS stadium. Having the right people in the right place could be the difference between billions of dollars going to billionaires or a city joining the ranks of those that have said thanks but no thanks to the entertainment juggernaut.

It's easy to see why corporate America wins so often. Its story is embedded in the way we all talk about the economy, in the way reporters write their stories, and in the way lawmakers give their stump speeches. So much of what's in the public sphere is geared, intentionally and unintentionally, toward the perspective of those who want to throw more and more of the public's money into private concerns. Trying to say otherwise—to explain that there's another way, and that subsidizing the entertainment industry or other corporate behemoths isn't some inexorable march that all American cities and states must undertake if they want to stay economically viable—can feel like screaming into the void or trying to reason with people on a random internet comment thread. The sheer amount of nonsense coming the other way can be overwhelming.

It can be done, though. I wish some magic bullet or mystical bit of speechifying could guarantee success. But there's just engaging in politics, at every level, making sure the voice of the community gets heard over the din of the mad rush to throw money at America's biggest companies. When people disengage, when they assume that getting involved is pointless because the cause is hopeless, that's when the insiders, lobbyists, and their paymasters win.

I don't mean to sound all hopey, changey, as some would put it, at the end here. Nothing about what I've laid out in this book is fair or easy to fix, and the rich and connected are still going to notch a lot of victories, even if the opposition to the sort of deals I've described intensifies significantly.

But public policy changes can also happen incredibly fast. With the right people in the right places being pushed to adopt the right ideas under the right circumstances, anything can happen. After all, nobody likes a boondoggle.

ACKNOWLEDGMENTS

Writing this thing has been quite the ride, and I definitely couldn't have done it alone. I will be eternally grateful to everyone listed here, and to all of the people who contributed something to the cause but whom I failed to thank. Any and all goof-ups are entirely my fault.

For starters, thanks to everybody who took the time to meet with me when this volume was just an idea in my head. Thanks to Helaine Olen for her advice on finding an agent. Many, many thanks to Ulrich Boser for his help at the beginning of the proposal process and throughout the drafting of this book. It's been invaluable.

Thanks to my opinion team comrades—Emily Arrowood, Hayley Hoefer, Rachel Brody, Bree Hocking, and most especially Robert Schlesinger—for all the support and encouragement. And thanks to Andy Soergel for making sure my chapter on federal corporate taxes was where it needed it be.

Thanks to all the editors with whom I've worked over the years at the publications I've been fortunate enough to publish in. Special thanks to Faiz Shakir and Amanda Terkel for giving me my first journalism job and letting me do some of the initial writing that turned into all the material here. And thanks to Travis Waldron for being my econ partner in crime and for cowriting that piece in *The Atlantic*. May it live on in internet glory forever.

Thanks to everyone who took the time to speak with me about the events and issues covered in these pages: Allison Stewart, Alan Snel, Charles Hughes, Robert Tannenwald, Jack Gerbes, Lee Shapira, Mike Davis, Tiffany Zappulla, Kathy Szeliga, Jonathan Cohn, Michael Hicks, Chris Dempsey, Doug Walker, Jon Whiten, Lauren Heller, Wolfgang Maennig, Meg Wiehe, Mike Green, Robert Nelson, Heywood Sanders, Stacy Mitchell, and Vanessa Williamson. Special thanks to Bob Beers, who has been a source of excellent stories for many years now, and I hope for many more.

Thanks to Greg LeRoy for not only being an encyclopedia of information regarding subsidies, but for being the quickest responder to email I have ever had the pleasure of working with. And thanks, too, to all the other folks at Good Jobs First, whose tireless efforts to maintain a subsidy database made my job a whole lot easier.

Thanks to all the sports economists who have put together so much work in this space over the years and who provided my gateway into these issues. Without their efforts, there'd be very little to write about. Thanks especially to Victor Matheson for spending so much time talking with and writing for me, at several publications now. Special thanks to Dennis Coates, who has been my go-to guy on sports stadium issues for as long as I've been covering them, and who is a great person to just sit and chat with, too.

Thanks to Stephen Power and Samantha Zukergood at Thomas Dunne Books. Stephen saw the potential in these stories immediately, while Samantha has been an excellent guide to the nuts and bolts of the publishing process. I couldn't hope for a better crew with which to work.

Thanks to my agent, Rob Kirkpatrick, for believing in this project from the very beginning. It very simply wouldn't have happened without his efforts, or those of the rest of the Stuart Agency crew. COYS, mate.

Thanks to all the friends who encouraged me to take this project on and have read my articles and listened to my rants about stadiums and the Olympics in the meantime.

Thanks to my Mom and Dad for teaching me to love reading as a little kid, buying me every book I wanted, sending me to the best schools, and being supportive of my notion that typing stuff on the internet was a viable career path. Thanks to the rest of the Garofalo and Maron families for all of their encouragement over the years, too.

Finally, and most importantly, thanks to my wonderful wife, Dina, who is the best partner for whom anyone could ask. She was the first reader of most of this tome, and put up with all of my early mornings during the proposal and drafting process. There's simply no way to measure the joy she has brought into my life. Love you, darling. I hope this suffices as chapter 13.

NOTES

1. The Blockbuster Scam: How Hollywood Is Ripping You Off

1. John Wagner, "Benefits of Maryland's Tax Credits for Films Are Questioned," *Washington Post*, November 15, 2014.
2. "MRC Letter to Gov. Martin O'Malley."
3. Jenna Johnson and John Wagner, "Kevin Spacey Whips Votes for Maryland Film Tax Credits," *Washington Post*, March 22, 2014.
4. Jenna Johnson, "'House of Cards' Threatens to Leave If Maryland Comes Up Short on Tax Credits," *Washington Post*, February 20, 2014.
5. Author interview, October 28, 2016.
6. Dominic Patten, "Deal Reached to Film 'House of Cards' Season 3 in Maryland After All," *Deadline*, April 25, 2014.
7. Elaine S. Povich, "Some States Yell 'Cut!' on Film Tax Credits," Pew Charitable Trusts, May 18, 2015.
8. Bill Gale, "Is R.I. Becoming a Center for Film Production?," *Backstage*, March 6, 2006.
9. "Evaluation of the Maryland Film Production Activity Tax Credit," Department of Legislative Services, September 2015.
10. Robert Tannenwald, "State Film Subsidies: Not Much Bang for Too Many Bucks," Center on Budget and Policy Priorities, December 9, 2010.
11. Pat Garofalo, "And the Loser Is . . . Taxpayers," *U.S. News & World Report*, February 20, 2015.

12. Author interview, December 15, 2016.

13. Tannenwald, "State Film Subsidies."

14. Gordon Russell, "Giving Away Louisiana: Film Tax Incentives," *Advocate,* December 2, 2014.

15. Tim Mathis, "Louisiana Film Tax Credits: Costly Giveaways to Hollywood," Louisiana Budget Project, August 2012.

16. Russell, "Giving Away Louisiana."

17. Greg Albrecht, "Film and Video Tax Incentives: Estimated Economic and Fiscal Impacts," State of Louisiana Legislative Fiscal Office, March 2005.

18. "Evaluation of the Maryland Film Production Activity Tax Credit."

19. Richard Verrier, "Gov. Brown OKs Tripling State Film Tax-Credit Funding to $330 Million," *Los Angeles Times,* August 27, 2014.

20. Michael Thom, "Fade to Black? Exploring Policy Enactment and Termination Through the Rise and Fall of State Tax Incentives for the Motion Picture Industry," *American Politics Research,* 2016.

21. Ibid.

22. "A Report on the Massachusetts Film Industry Tax Incentives," Commonwealth of Massachusetts Department of Revenue, July 2009.

23. Steven R. Miller and Abdul Abdulkadri, "The Economic Impact of Michigan's Motion Picture Production Industry and the Michigan Motion Picture Production Credit," Center for Economic Analysis, Michigan State University, February 6, 2009.

24. Author interview, October 28, 2016.

25. Ibid.

26. Gerry Smith, "Hollywood Is Running Out of Tombstones," *Bloomberg Businessweek,* April 7, 2016.

27. Ibid.

28. Jessica Stearns, "A Look Past *Gone Girl* Excitement Reveals a Raw Deal for Missourians," Show-Me Institute, January 2, 2015.

29. Russell, "Giving Away Louisiana."

30. Steve LeBlanc, "Mass. Tax Credits Used to Cover Movie Stars' Wages," Associated Press, January 12, 2011.

31. Pat Garofalo, "Batman v. Superman v. Taxpayers," *U.S. News & World Report,* March 24, 2016.

32. Jack Newsham, "Cost of Film Tax Credit: $108,000 per Mass. Job," *Boston Globe,* September 19, 2014.

33. William Luther, "Movie Production Incentives: Blockbuster Support for Lackluster Policy," Tax Foundation, January 2010.

34. Jessica Stearns, "*Gone Girl,* Gone Jobs," Show-Me Institute, November 7, 2014.

35. "How Atlanta Became the Hollywood of the South," Associated Press, August 31, 2015.

36. "Evaluation of the Maryland Film Production Activity Tax Credit."

37. Author interview, November 3, 2016.

38. Richard Verrier and Saba Hamedy, "Gov. Brown Signs Bill That Triples Tax Credits for Films," *Los Angeles Times*, September 18, 2014.

39. Sharon Bernstein, "California Triples Tax Breaks for Film Production," Reuters, September 18, 2014.

40. Kevin Litten, "Bobby Jindal Declines to Veto Controversial Film Tax Credit Bill," *Times-Picayune*, June 19, 2015.

41. Margaret Newkirk, "'Duck Dynasty' Keeps Tax Break as Bobby Jindal Cuts Louisiana Colleges," *Bloomberg Politics*, May 4, 2015.

42. Gordon Russell, "Amid Louisiana Film Downturn, 'Deepwater Horizon' Sets New Mark for State Subsidies," *Advocate*, September 29, 2016.

43. John Tozzi, "How to Sell Your Tax Credit," *Bloomberg Business*, April 11, 2013.

44. Tannenwald, "State Film Subsidies."

45. "Unilateral Disarmament," *Economist*, June 9, 2011.

46. Phillip Tutt, "*Star Wars* Movie Gives This Global Finance Chief a Credit," CNBC, December 18, 2015.

47. "British Film Industry Tax Breaks Approved by EU," BBC, August 21, 2015.

48. Ibid.

49. Christian Sylt, "Rags to Riches: Disney Earns £170m in Tax Breaks as UK Film Industry Grows," *Guardian*, October 1, 2014.

50. Leo Barraclough, "U.K. Pays Out $2.24 Billion in Film Tax Relief in Nine Years," *Variety*, December 18, 2015.

51. Stuart Kemp, "U.K. Tax Credit Vital to Film Industry Health: Study," *Hollywood Reporter*, September 17, 2012.

52. Pat Garofalo, "The Jedi Tax Trick," *U.S. News & World Report*, December 30, 2015.

53. Hannah Shaw-Williams, "How the British Film Industry Became a Hollywood Backlot," *Screen Rant*, July 4, 2015.

54. Sylt, "Rags to Riches."

55. Jordan Bateman, "It's Time to Wean B.C. Film Off Taxpayer-Funded Subsidies," *Huffington Post*, January 18, 2016.

56. Ibid.

57. "Tax Incentives for Film and TV Production Around the World," Reuters, October 18, 2015.

58. Richard Verrier, "'Veep' and 'American Horror Story' Among Shows Relocating to California," *Los Angeles Times*, June 2, 2015.

59. Russell, "Giving Away Louisiana."

60. Author interview, October 28, 2016.

61. Email from Jonathan Glickman, published by WikiLeaks, November 13, 2014.

62. David Zin, "Film Incentives in Michigan," Senate Fiscal Agency, September 2010.

63. Jon Sanders, "Iron Man? No, the Real Hero Is the Super Multiplier," *Carolina Journal*, May 14, 2013.

64. Tannenwald, "State Film Subsidies."

65. Author interview, October 28, 2016.

66. "Tax Credits for Movie Makers? Two Thumbs Down," Citizens for Tax Justice, May 21, 2012.

67. Ted Sherman, "No Sequel: Christie Vetoes Film Production Tax Credits," New Jersey Advance Media, January 12, 2016.

68. Ted Sherman, "N.J. Remains a Hollywood Backlot, Despite End to Tax Credits," New Jersey Advance Media, August 9, 2015.

69. Toby Eckert, "Some States Nix Film Tax Credits, but Cost Is Up," *Politico*, August 13, 2015.

70. Congressional Research Service, December 9, 2011.

71. Author interview, October 28, 2016.

72. Author interview, December 20, 2016.

73. Author interview, December 19, 2016.

74. Author interview, October 28, 2016.

2. Have a Good Night's Sleep on Us

1. Jonathan O'Connell, "Trump Deal Could Be First of Several in Downtown Area," *Washington Post*, February 12, 2012.

2. Petula Dvorak, "Donald Trump Will Fit Right In on Pennsylvania Avenue," *Washington Post*, February 9, 2012.

3. Jonathan O'Connell, "More Big Names Enter Competition for D.C. Old Post Office," *Washington Post*, November 13, 2011.

4. National Park Service, accessed March 8, 2017.

5. James Lankford, "Federal Fumbles: 100 Ways the Government Dropped the Ball," November 2015.

6. Charles V. Bagli, "A Trump Empire Built on Inside Connections and $885 Million in Tax Breaks," *New York Times*, September 17, 2016.

7. Kris Hudson, "Subsidized Hotels: Boon or Boondoggle?," *Wall Street Journal*, December 25, 2012.

8. Robert R. Nelson, Jan A. deRoos, and Russell Lloyd, "The Impact of Publicly Subsidized Hotels in the United States on Competing Proper-

ties," *The Center for Real Estate and Finance Working Paper Series, 2014–004,* August 6, 2014.

9. Author interview, March 22, 2017.

10. Ingrid W. Reed, "The Life and Death of UDAG: An Assessment Based on Eight Projects in Five New Jersey Cities," *Publius,* January 1, 1989.

11. Joseph Pimentel, "Wincome Group, Disney to Get $550 Million from Tax Revenues for Building Luxury Hotels," *Orange County Register,* July 14, 2016.

12. Author interview, March 14, 2017.

13. Pimentel, "Wincome Group, Disney to Get $550 Million."

14. Author interview, March 14, 2017.

15. Pimentel, "Wincome Group, Disney to Get $550 Million."

16. "Does Disney's New Luxury Hotel Really Need a Public Subsidy?," *Los Angeles Times,* July 16, 2016.

17. Good Jobs First, Subsidy Tracker data, accessed March 16, 2017.

18. Michael Hiltzik, "The Mayor of a Disney Company Town Pushes Back, in Vain, Against a Tax Handout to Disneyland," *Los Angeles Times,* July 13, 2016.

19. Jill Replogle, "Anaheim's New City Council Sets About Reversing Disney-Friendly Past," *Southern California Public Radio,* December 21, 2016.

20. Author interview, March 14, 2017.

21. David Zahniser, "L.A. Should Be More Selective with Hotel Tax Breaks, Some Say," *Los Angeles Times,* April 18, 2014.

22. *Forbes* valuation.

23. Author interview, March 22, 2017.

24. Bianca Barragan, "AEG, Miffed over Convention Center Hotel, Won't Expand LA Live Marriott." *Curbed Los Angeles,* June 24, 2016.

25. "Fenty Signs Bill for 1,160-Room Convention HQ Hotel," Office of the Deputy Mayor for Planning and Economic Development, August 13, 2009.

26. Steven Pearlstein, "Debunking the Conventional Wisdom About Conventions," *Washington Post,* June 27, 2014.

27. Luke Broadwater, "City-Owned Hilton Baltimore Hotel Reports $5.2M Loss in 2015," *Baltimore Sun,* May 31, 2016.

28. Luke Broadwater, "City-Owned Hilton Lost $5.6M Last Year," *Baltimore Sun,* April 8, 2015.

29. Mark Reutter, "Financial Losses at City-Owned Hilton Hotel Pile Up," *Baltimore Brew,* June 7, 2017.

30. Kevin Shea, "Trenton's Only Hotel Reopens After Passing Reinspection," New Jersey Advance Media, June 8, 2017.

31. Heywood Sanders, *Convention Center Follies: Politics, Power, and Public Investment in American Cities* (Philadelphia: University of Pennsylvania Press, 2014), 13.
32. Ibid.
33. Author interview, March 22, 2017.
34. Sanders, *Convention Center Follies*, 43.
35. Pearlstein, "Debunking the Conventional Wisdom."
36. Rachel Solomon, "DNC Officials Announce Opening of Philadelphia Office Ahead of Convention," CBS Philly, October 15, 2015.
37. Brianna Ehley, "GOP Convention Could Give Tampa a $153M Boost," *Fiscal Times*, August 22, 2012; and Robert Simonson, "Republican Convention Hits Broadway Right in the Box Office," *Playbill*, September 3, 2004.
38. Dennis Coates and Craig A. Depken, "Mega-Events: Is the Texas-Baylor Game to Waco What the Super Bowl Is to Houston?," Working Paper Series No. 06–06, International Association of Sports Economists; North American Association of Sports Economists, January 2006.
39. Lauren Heller, Victor Matheson, and E. Frank Stephenson, "Unconventional Wisdom: Estimating the Economic Impact of the Democratic and Republican National Political Conventions," Working Paper 17-01, College of the Holy Cross, Department of Economics Faculty Research Series, August 2017.
40. Author interview, April 11, 2017.

3. "Alexa, Can I Have a Job, Please?"

1. Mike Rosenberg and Ángel González, "Thanks to Amazon, Seattle Is Now America's Biggest Company Town," *Seattle Times*, August 23, 2017.
2. Irina Ivanova, "Amazon's HQ2 Opens Bidding War Among Cities," CBS, September 20, 2017.
3. "Arizona Group Sending Giant Cactus as Welcome Gift to Amazon," Associated Press, September 14, 2017.
4. Amazon HQ2 Request for Proposals.
5. Ibid.
6. Ray Hagar, "Reid: Reno Shouldn't Start Counting Tesla Jobs Just Yet," *Reno Gazette-Journal*, August 18, 2014.
7. Pat Garofalo, "Tesla Is Playing You (and Me and Everyone)," *U.S. News & World Report*, August 21, 2014.
8. Colin Lecher, "Inside Nevada's $1.3 Billion Gamble on Tesla," *Verge*, February 8, 2016.

9. Pat Garofalo, "Boeing's Corporate Tax Blackmail," *U.S. News & World Report*, November 13, 2013.
10. Timothy J. Bartik, "A New Panel Database on Business Incentives for Economic Development Offered by State and Local Governments in the United States," W. E. Upjohn Institute for Employment Research, 2017.
11. Kenneth P. Thomas, "Who Provides the Most Investment Incentives: EU vs. US" in *Investment Incentives and the Global Competition for Capital* (New York: Palgrave Macmillan, 2011), 96–108.
12. Louise Story, "As Companies Seek Tax Deals, Governments Pay High Price," *New York Times*, December 1, 2012.
13. Bartik, "New Panel Database."
14. Ibid.
15. Arlette Saenz, "Rick Perry in California to Lure Businesses to Texas," ABC, February 11, 2013.
16. Ibid.
17. Scott Cohn, "Trump's Carrier Deal Is Not Living Up to the Hype—Jobs Still Going to Mexico," CNBC, June 22, 2017.
18. Max Ehrenfreund, "A Company Trump Attacked Will Receive State Tax Breaks to Keep Jobs in the U.S.," *Washington Post*, November 30, 2016.
19. Greg LeRoy, Kasia Tarczynska, Leigh McIlvaine, Thomas Cafcas, and Philip Mattera, "The Job-Creation Shell Game," Good Jobs First, January 2013.
20. "Why Did the Job Cross the Road?," *Planet Money*, National Public Radio, May 4, 2016.
21. "The New Border War," *Economist*, March 22, 2014.
22. "Why Did the Job Cross the Road?"
23. Richard Florida, "The Uselessness of Economic Development Incentives," CityLab, December 7, 2012.
24. Bartik, "New Panel Database."
25. Timothy J. Bartik and George A. Erickcek, "Simulating the Effects of Michigan's MEGA Tax Credit Program on Job Creation and Fiscal Benefits," W. E. Upjohn Institute for Employment Research, 2012.
26. Todd M. Gabe and David S. Kraybill, "The Effect of State Economic Development Incentives on Employment Growth of Establishments," *Journal of Regional Science*, 42, no. 4 (2002): 703–30.
27. Ibid.
28. Lauren McGaughy, "Toyota Says $40 Million Incentive Not a Deciding Factor in Move," *Houston Chronicle*, April 30, 2014.
29. Jerry Hirsh and Tim Logan, "Was Toyota Driven out of California? Not So Fast," *Los Angeles Times*, May 1, 2014.
30. Senate Finance Committee hearing, January 17, 2001.

31. Philip Mattera and Kasia Tarczynska, with Greg LeRoy, "Megadeals: The Largest Economic Development Subsidy Packages Ever Awarded by State and Local Governments in the United States," Good Jobs First, June 2013.
32. Author interview, September 28, 2017.
33. Nathan M. Jensen, Edmund Malesky, Mariana Medina, and Ugur Ozdemir, "Pass the Bucks: Credit, Blame, and the Global Competition for Investment," *International Studies Quarterly* 58, no. 3 (2014): 433–47.
34. Nathan M. Jensen, "Business Location Incentives Are Ineffective—So Why Do They Persist in American States and Localities?," Scholars Strategy Network, September 2016.
35. Heather Long, "Where Are All the Startups? U.S. Entrepreneurship near 40-Year Low," *CNN Money*, September 8, 2016; and J. D. Harrison, "The Decline of American Entrepreneurship—in Five Charts," *Washington Post*, February 12, 2015.
36. Author interview, September 28, 2017.
37. Ibid.
38. "Charter of the Sum," Acts of the Seventeenth General Assembly of the State of New Jersey, accessed October 2, 2017.
39. Booker T. Coleman Jr., "Location Incentives and the Negative Commerce Clause: A Farewell to Arms?," *Marquette Law Review* 89, no. 3 (Spring 2006): article 5.
40. Michael D. LaFaive, "A Brief History of State Economic Development," Mackinac Center for Public Policy, October 6, 2005.
41. Connie Lester, "Economic Development in the 1930s: Balance Agriculture with Industry," Mississippi History Now, the Mississippi Historical Society, May 2004.
42. Greg LeRoy, *The Great American Jobs Scam* (Oakland, CA: Berrett-Koehler Publishers, 2005).
43. William M. Adler, *Mollie's Job: A Story of Life and Work on the Global Assembly Line* (New York: Simon & Schuster, 2001).
44. Pat Garofalo, "Rick Perry's Hot (Sauce) Mess," *U.S. News & World Report*, May 13, 2014.
45. Richard Verrier, "Iowa Film Tax Credit Program Racked by Scandal," *Los Angeles Times*, January 19, 2011.
46. Katherine Sayre, "Louisiana's Movie Tax Credits Attracted Corruption Along with Film Industry," *Times-Picayune*, March 11, 2014.
47. Bob Dreyfuss and Barbara Dreyfuss, "The Saga of Christie, Samson and the American Dream Megamall," *Nation*, July 1, 2014.
48. Alison Felix and James R. Hines Jr., "Who Offers Tax-Based Business

Development Incentives?," Federal Reserve Bank of Kansas City, Economic Research Department, November 2011.

49. Arthur J. Rolnick and Melvin L. Burstein, "Congress Should End the Economic War Among the States," Federal Reserve Bank of Minneapolis, January 1, 1995.

50. Arthur J. Rolnick, "Congress Should End the Economic War Among the States Testimony," Domestic Policy Subcommittee on Oversight and Government Reform, October 10, 2007.

51. Alina Selyukh, "'A Major Distraction': Is a Megadeal Like Amazon's HQ2 Always Worth It?," National Public Radio, October 18, 2017.

4. Don't Go for Gold: It's a Waste to Host the Olympics or the World Cup

1. Steve Annear, "Walsh Says Olympics Opposition Coming from '10 People' on Twitter," *Boston Globe,* July 27, 2015.

2. Author interview, April 25, 2017.

3. "Thank You," No Boston Olympics.

4. "Factbox: How the Olympic Games Are Funded," Reuters, March 8, 2012.

5. "Bridging the Gap." Olympic Games Study Commission.

6. Jules Boykoff, *Power Games: A Political History of the Olympics* (New York: Verso, 2016).

7. Olympic Games Study Commission

8. John R. Short, "Globalization, Cities and the Summer Olympics," *City,* November 26, 2008.

9. Jeffrey G. Owen, "Estimating the Cost and Benefit of Hosting Olympic Games: What Can Beijing Expect from Its 2008 Games?," *Industrial Geographer* 3, no. 1 (2005): 1–18.

10. "Olympic Games: Federal Government Provides Significant Funding and Support," Government Accountability Office, September 2000.

11. Ibid.

12. "Olympic Games: Costs to Plan and Stage the Games in the United States," Government Accountability Office, November 2001.

13. Ibid.

14. John Pletz, "Chicago 2016's Final Tally: $70.6M Spent on Olympics Effort," *Crain's Chicago Business,* May 17, 2010.

15. Scott Malone, "Boston 2024 Olympics Could See $5 Billion Economic Boost: Study," Reuters, March 18, 2015.

16. "Tokyo Summer Olympics to Provide Major Boost to Economy . . . Maybe," *Capitalist Review,* December 29, 2015.

17. Owen, "Estimating the Cost and Benefit."

18. Victor A. Matheson, "Mega-Events: The Effect of the World's Biggest Sporting Events on Local, Regional, and National Economies," College of the Holy Cross, Department of Economics Faculty Research Series, Paper No. 06–10, October 2006.
19. Dennis Coates and Brad R. Humphreys, "Do Economists Reach a Conclusion on Subsidies for Sports Franchises, Stadiums, and Mega-Events?," International Association of Sports Economists Working Paper Series, Paper No. 08–18, September 2008.
20. Matheson, "Mega-Events."
21. "Olympic Report," European Tour Operators Association, 2006.
22. Owen, "Estimating the Cost and Benefit."
23. Wolfgang Maennig, "One Year Later: A Re-appraisal of the Economics of the 2006 Soccer World Cup," IASE/NAASE Working Paper Series, Paper No. 07–25, July 2007.
24. *New York Times*, July 26, 1896.
25. Andrew Zimbalist and Fred Dews, "The Economic Consequences of Hosting the Olympics and the World Cup," Brookings Institution, July 24, 2015.
26. Author interview, April 26, 2017.
27. Owen, "Estimating the Cost and Benefit."
28. Samantha Edds, "Economic Impacts of the Olympic Games Through State Comparison," April 2012.
29. Robert A. Baade and Victor Matheson, "Bidding for the Olympics: Fool's Gold?"
30. Binyamin Appelbaum, "Does Hosting the Olympics Actually Pay Off?," *New York Times*, August 5, 2014.
31. Bent Flyvbjerg, Allison Stewart, and Alexander Budzier, "The Oxford Olympics Study 2016: Cost and Cost Overrun at the Games," Saïd Business School, Research Papers, July 2016.
32. Bent Flyvbjerg and Allison Stewart, "Olympic Proportions: Cost and Cost Overrun at the Olympics, 1960–2012," Saïd Business School Working Papers, University of Oxford, January 21, 2014.
33. Paula Newton, "Olympics Worth the Price Tag? The Montreal Legacy," CNN, July 19, 2012.
34. "Quebec's Big Owe Stadium Debt Is Over," CBC News, December 19, 2006.
35. Flyvbjerg and Stewart, "Olympic Proportions."
36. Nick Malkoutzis, "How the 2004 Olympics Triggered Greece's Decline," *Bloomberg Businessweek*, August 2, 2012.
37. Mark Arsenault, "Atlanta Games' Venues Left Some Lessons for Boston," *Boston Globe*, August 3, 2014.

38. Pat Garofalo, "The Diplomacy Olympics," *U.S. News & World Report*, February 8, 2018.

39. Rupert Neate, "South Africa Recoups Just a Tenth of the £3Bn Cost of Staging World Cup 2010," *Telegraph*, December 10, 2010.

40. Florian Hagn and Wolfgang Maennig, "Labour Market Effects of the 2006 Soccer World Cup in Germany," Hamburg Contemporary Economic Discussions, No. 8, 2007.

41. Robert A. Baade and Victor A. Matheson, "The Quest for the Cup: Assessing the Economic Impact of the World Cup," *Regional Studies* 38 (2004).

42. James Young, "South Africa, Brazil World Cup Stadia Largely Remain National Burdens," *Sports Illustrated*, February 2, 2015.

43. Lourdes Garcia-Navarro, "Brazil's World Cup Legacy Includes $550M Stadium-Turned-Parking Lot," *All Things Considered*, National Public Radio, May 11, 2015.

44. Pat Garofalo, "The Cost of a Good Time," *U.S. News & World Report*, June 11, 2014.

45. Ibid.

46. Simon Romero, "Protests Widen as Brazilians Chide Leaders," *New York Times*, June 18, 2013.

47. Tripp Mickle, "TV Rights Push IOC Revenue to Record," *Sports Business Daily*, August 26, 2013.

48. Author interview, July 29, 2016

49. Author interview, April 27, 2017.

50. Alissa Walker, "How L.A.'s 1984 Summer Olympics Became the Most Successful Games Ever," *Gizmodo*, February 6, 2014.

51. Jack Moore, "When Denver Rejected the Olympics in Favour of the Environment and Economics," *Guardian*, April 7, 2015.

52. Jules Boykoff, *Celebration Capitalism and the Olympic Games* (New York: Routledge, 2014).

53. Author interview, April 25, 2017.

54. "Football's FIFA and the African Tax-Free Bubble," Tax Justice Network, May 11, 2010.

55. Olivia MacDonald, "FIFA's World Cup of Tax Breaks," *Tax Justice Blog*, June 26, 2014.

56. "Olympic Tax Breaks Turned Down by Corporations Looking to Build Public Goodwill," Century Group.

57. Boykoff, *Celebration Capitalism*.

58. Dashiell Bennett and Joe Weisenthal, "Here's How Big of a Deal the World Cup Is to Qatar," *Bloomberg Businessweek*, May 28, 2015.

59. "St. Moritz and Davos Winter Games Bid Rejected by Public," Reuters, March 3, 2013.

60. "Voters Deliver Resounding No to Munich 2022 Winter Olympics Bid," *DW.com,* November 11, 2013.

61. "Stockholm Pulls Plug on 2022 Games Bid," Reuters, January 17, 2014.

62. Monika Scislowska, "Kraków Withdraws 2022 Winter Olympics Bid After Majority of Residents Vote Against It," Associated Press, May 26, 2014.

63. "Oslo 2022 Bid Hurt by IOC Demands, Arrogance," Associated Press, October 5, 2014.

64. Pat Garofalo, "Russia's Coming Out Party," *U.S. News & World Report,* February 7, 2014.

65. Ronald Smothers, "Bitterness Lingering over Carter's Boycott," *New York Times,* July 19, 1996.

66. "The Olympic Boycott, 1980," US Department of State Archive, accessed September 25, 2017.

67. Author interview, July 29, 2016.

68. Jonathan O'Connell and Mike DeBonis, "Ted Leonsis and Other Organizers of D.C.'s 2024 Olympics Bid Make Their Pitch," *Washington Post,* September 16, 2014.

69. Perry Stein, "D.C. Breaks Tourist Record in 2015 with Visitors Spending $7.1 Billion," *Washington Post,* May 3, 2016; and Samantha Shankman, "20 Most Popular U.S. Cities Among International Travelers in 2013," *Skift,* June 18, 2014.

70. Appelbaum, "Does Hosting the Olympics Actually Pay Off?"

71. Maennig, "One Year Later."

72. Garofalo, "Russia's Coming Out Party."

73. Author interview, June 29, 2016.

74. Author interview, July 29, 2016.

5. Foolish Games: Why Lotteries and Casinos Are a Bad Bet

1. Kevin Flynn, *American Sweepstakes: How One Small State Bucked the Church, the Feds, and the Mob to Usher in the Lottery Age* (Lebanon, NH: ForeEdge, 2015), 18.

2. National Gambling Impact Study Commission.

3. Sarah Laskow, "Colonial America Was Built on Lottery Revenue," *Atlas Obscura,* April 21, 2017.

4. "Thomas Jefferson's Thoughts on Lotteries, ca. 20 January 1826," University of Virginia Press, accessed July 11, 2017.

5. Ibid.

6. "New Hampshire Set for Lottery," *New York Times,* June 21, 1964.

7. "History," NHLottery.com, accessed July 12, 2017.

8. "Anniversary Timely for NH's 1st-in-Nation Lottery," Associated Press, March 16, 2009.

9. Melissa Schettini Kearney, "The Economic Winners and Losers of Legalized Gambling," Brookings Institution, February 2005.

10. Brad Tuttle, "Why You Can't Buy Powerball Tickets in Some Seriously Gambling-Friendly States," *Money*, January 12, 2016.

11. Flynn, *American Sweepstakes*, 46.

12. Elizabeth Winslow McAuliffe, "The State-Sponsored Lottery: A Failure of Policy and Ethics," Public Integrity, Fall 2006.

13. Garrick Blalock, David R. Just, and Daniel H. Simon, "Hitting the Jackpot or Hitting the Skids: Entertainment, Poverty, and the Demand for State Lotteries," *American Journal of Economics and Sociology* 66 no. 3 (July 2007): 545-70.

14. Katie Zezima, "Sweet Dreams in Hard Times Add to Lottery Sales," *New York Times*, September 12, 2008.

15. "Why Play a Losing Game? Carnegie Mellon Study Uncovers Why Low-Income People Buy Lottery Tickets," Carnegie Mellon University, July 24, 2008.

16. Khadeeja Safdar, "Lottery: Georgia Lotto Players Gambled Away the Largest Percentage of Their Incomes," *Huffington Post*, March 15, 2012.

17. Niraj Chokshi, "The States That Rely on Powerball and Lotteries the Most," *Washington Post*, January 13, 2016.

18. Ron Stodghill and Ron Nixon, "For Schools, Lottery Payoffs Fall Short of Promises," *New York Times*, October 7, 2007.

19. Pat Garofalo, "Mega Failure: Why Lotteries Are a Bad Bet for State Budgets," ThinkProgress, March 30, 2012.

20. National Gambling Impact Study Commission Final Report, August 3, 1999.

21. David Goldman, "Does Powerball Really Fund Education?," *CNN Money*, January 14, 2016.

22. "Lotto Fever, Fiscal Madness," Citizens for Tax Justice, March 30, 2012.

23. Catherine Cloutier, "Lottery Often Gives Aid to Affluent, Takes from Poor," *Boston Globe*, June 5, 2014.

24. Gerry Tuoti, "Online Lottery Proponents Renew Their Push," *Herald News*, January 12, 2017.

25. Aaron Smith, "Record Shares of Americans Now Own Smartphones, Have Home Broadband," Pew Research Center, January 12, 2017.

NOTES

26. Jon Whiten, "New Jersey's Surge in Business Tax Subsidies Reaches New Heights," New Jersey Policy Perspective, June 11, 2014.
27. Paul Kane, "Chris Christie Loses a Big Atlantic City Bet, Posing Another Challenge for 2016 Run," *Washington Post*, September 5, 2014.
28. Whiten, "New Jersey's Surge in Business Tax Subsidies."
29. Adam Michel, Tyler Dennis, and Joseph Henchman, "The New Jersey Casino That Tax Credits Could Not Save," Tax Foundation, June 25, 2014.
30. Author interview, June 16, 2017.
31. Joseph Spector, "House Wins Big with Casino Tax Breaks," *Democrat & Chronicle*, November 27, 2016.
32. "State of the States," American Gaming Association, 2016.
33. Alan Mallach, "Economic and Social Impact of Introducing Casino Gambling: A Review and Assessment of the Literature," Federal Reserve Bank of Philadelphia, March 2010.
34. Douglas M. Walker and Russell S. Sobel, "Social and Economic Impacts of Gambling," *Current Addiction Reports* 3, no. 3 (September 2016): 293–98.
35. Mallach, "Economic and Social Impact."
36. Ibid.
37. "Why Casinos Matter: Thirty-One Evidence-Based Propositions from the Health and Social Sciences," Institute for American Values, 2013.
38. Barbara Dafoe Whitehead, "Gaming the Poor," *New York Times*, June 21, 2014.
39. Douglas M. Walker and John D. Jackson, "The Effect of Legalized Gambling on State Government Revenue," *Contemporary Economic Policy* 29, no. 1 (January 2011): 101–14.
40. Lucy Dadayan, "State Revenues from Gambling: Short-Term Relief, Long-Term Disappointment," Nelson A. Rockefeller Institute of Government, April 2016.

6. The Stadium Swindle

1. Kevin Seifert, "With $6.7 Billion in Public Money, NFL Closes Stadium Era," ESPN, March 28, 2017.
2. Aaron Kuriloff and Darrell Preston, "In Stadium Building Spree, U.S. Taxpayers Lose $4 Billion," Bloomberg News, September 5, 2012.
3. Nevada State Museum.
4. MiLB.com.
5. Author interview, October 16, 2017.
6. Ibid.
7. Ibid.

8. Author interview, October 5, 2017.
9. Dennis Coates, "Growth Effects of Sports Franchises, Stadiums, and Arenas: 15 Years Later," Mercatus Working Paper, September 2015.
10. Victor Matheson and Robert A. Baade, "Financing Professional Sports Facilities," Paper No. 11-02, College of the Holy Cross, Department of Economics Faculty Research Series, January 2011.
11. Author interview, October 5, 2017.
12. Travis Waldron and Pat Garofalo, "If You Build It, They Might Not Come: The Risky Economics of Sports Stadiums," *Atlantic*, September 7, 2012.
13. Ibid.
14. Ibid.
15. Travis Waldron, "Glendale's Latest Arena Woes Are a Cautionary Tale for Other Cities," *Huffington Post*, June 11, 2015.
16. Pat Garofalo, "Let Them Eat Pucks," *U.S. News & World Report*, July 25, 2013.
17. Pat Garofalo, "Sin City's Major League Gamble," *U.S. News & World Report*, January 16, 2015.
18. Ibid.
19. Conor Shine, "Major League Soccer Passes on Las Vegas; Stadium Deal Dead," *Las Vegas Sun*, February 12, 2015.
20. Garofalo, "Sin City's Major League Gamble."
21. Author interview, October 16, 2017.
22. Ibid.
23. Author interview, October 5, 2017.
24. Author interview, October 16, 2017.
25. Author interview, October 5, 2017.
26. Scott Bordow, "Phoenix Suns' Robert Sarver Says Coyotes-Suns Shared Site 'Highly Unlikely,'" *AZCentral*, July 19, 2017.
27. Jeff Carlisle, "Exclusive: 'Dramatic Change' Needed to Keep Crew SC in Columbus—Precourt," ESPN, October 17, 2017.
28. Rick Rouan, "Columbus Offered Crew SC Two City Parks as Stadium Sites," *Columbus Dispatch*, November 29, 2017.
29. Andrew Erickson and Megan Henry, "DeWine Ready to Sue to Keep the Crew," *Columbus Dispatch*, December 7, 2017.
30. Claire Simms, "Atlanta Braves Start Season, Stadium Talks," Georgia Public Broadcasting, April 1, 2013.
31. Meris Lutz, "Braves Stadium Hardly a Home Run for Cobb Taxpayers," *Atlanta Journal-Constitution*, December 26, 2017.
32. Ibid.

33. Jorge L. Ortiz and Ray Glier, "As Turner Field Shuts Down, MLB Ponders: Is 20 Years New Stadium Life Span?," *USA Today*, September 28, 2016.

34. Robin Respaut, "With NFL Rams Gone, St. Louis Still Stuck with Stadium Debt," Reuters, February 3, 2016.

35. Author interview, October 5, 2017.

36. Ibid.

37. Daniel Shoag and Stan Veuger, "Where LeBron Takes His Talent, There the Jobs Will Be Also," American Enterprise Institute, May 10, 2017.

38. Daniel Shoag and Stan Veuger, "Taking My Talents to South Beach (and Back)," American Enterprise Institute, updated July 2017.

39. Nick Castele, "Cuyahoga County, Cavaliers Move Ahead with Quicken Loans Arena Deal in 2018," Ideastream, December 26, 2017.

40. Tim Nelson, "Minnesota Wins Super Bowl 2018 Bid," *MPR News*, May 20, 2014.

41. Pat Garofalo, "An Air Ball for Taxpayers," *U.S. News & World Report*, April 4, 2015.

42. Bryant McInerney, "Super Bowl Benefits Host City, but by How Much?," CNBC, January 31, 2016; Kenneth McGill and Jon Gray, "The Economic Impact of Super Bowl LI on Greater Houston," Rockport Analytics, May 2017; and Warren Strugatch, "Super Bowl 50 Produces $350M Economic Impact," *Chief Executive*, February 8, 2016.

43. McInerney, "Super Bowl Benefits Host City."

44. Victor A. Matheson, "Economics of the Super Bowl," Working Papers 1001, International Association of Sports Economists; North American Association of Sports Economists, 2010.

45. Victor Matheson and Robert A. Baade, "Padding Required: Assessing the Economic Impact of the Super Bowl," Paper 04-03, College of the Holy Cross, Department of Economics Faculty Research Series, September 2004.

46. Victor Matheson and Robert A. Baade, "An Economic Slam Dunk or March Madness? Assessing the Economic Impact of the NCAA Basketball Tournament," College of the Holy Cross, Department of Economics Faculty Research Series, September 2003.

47. Victor Matheson and Robert A. Baade, "A Fall Classic? Assessing the Economic Impact of the World Series," Paper No. 05-01, College of the Holy Cross, Department of Economics Faculty Research Series, February 2005.

48. Dennis Coates and Brad R. Humphreys, "The Economic Impact of Postseason Play in Professional Sports," *Journal of Sports Economics*, August 2002.

49. Dennis Coates and Brad R. Humphreys, "The Economic Consequences

of Professional Sports Strikes and Lockouts," *Southern Economic Journal* 67, no. 3 (2001): 737–47.

50. Robert A. Baade, Robert Baumann and Victor Matheson, "The Economic Consequences of Professional Sports Strikes and Lockouts: Revisited," Paper 06-04, College of the Holy Cross, Department of Economics Faculty Research Series, April 2006.

51. Author interview, January 22, 2018.

52. Travis Waldron, "With Obama Budget, Your Federal Tax Dollars Won't Pay for Sports Stadiums," ThinkProgress, February 4, 2015.

53. Richard Rubin and Siobhan Hughes, "GOP Is Poised to Pass Sweeping Tax Overhaul," *Wall Street Journal,* December 15, 2017.

54. "Heller Applauds U.S. Senate's Passage of Tax Cuts for Nevada's Middle-Class Families," HellerSenate.gov, December 20, 2017.

7. Don't Go Shopping for Big Retail

1. Peter Applebome, "Era of the Great Pyramid Is Dawning in Memphis," *New York Times,* July 23, 1989.

2. Woody Baird, "Memphis Will Celebrate," Associated Press, September 15, 1989.

3. Woody Baird, "Big Pyramid, Little Wonder," Associated Press, November 9, 1991.

4. Chris Butler, "Inverted Pyramid: Bass Pro Shops Resort Cost Memphis Taxpayers $78 Million, Says One Estimate," Watchdog.org, May 13, 2015.

5. Scott Reeder, "Why Have So Many Cities and Towns Given Away So Much Money to Bass Pro Shops and Cabela's?," CityLab, August 13, 2012.

6. Cabela's Initial Public Offering prospectus, Securities and Exchange Commission, 2004, accessed September 12, 2017.

7. Reeder, "Why Have So Many Cities and Towns?"

8. Author interview, September 28, 2017.

9. Ibid.

10. Sam Kennedy, "Have Cabela's Tax Breaks Paid Off?," *The Morning Call,* October 17, 2004.

11. Author interview, October 3, 2017.

12. Mike Gorrell, "Cabela's Store Among Utah's Top Tourist Attractions," *Salt Lake Tribune,* September 10, 2006.

13. Andrew Stecker and Kevin Connor, "Fishing for Taxpayer Cash," Public Accountability Initiative, June 2010.

14. "Mesa Riverview Teaches Lessons as Economy Rebounds," *Arizona Republic,* May 11, 2010.

15. Michael J. Hicks, "A Quasi-Experimental Test of Large Retail Store Impacts on Regional Labor Markets: The Case of Cabela's Retail Outlets," *Journal of Regional Analysis and Policy* 37, no. 2 (2007): 116–22.

16. Ibid.

17. Author interview, September 25, 2017.

18. Ibid.

19. Marc Bain, "America's Vast Swaths of Retail Space Have Become a Burden in the Age of E-commerce," *Quartz*, July 19, 2017.

20. Derek Thompson, "What in the World Is Causing the Retail Meltdown of 2017?," *Atlantic*, April 10, 2017.

21. See Wal-Mart Subsidy Watch for a full accounting.

22. Joseph Persky, David Merriman, Julie Davis, and Ron Baiman, "The Impact of an Urban WalMart Store on Area Businesses," *Economic Development Quarterly* 26, no. 4 (September 3, 2012): 321–33.

23. Author interview, October 3, 2017.

24. Ibid.

25. Francisco Vara-Orta, "Tax Breaks for Big-Box Stores Can Drain Money from Schools," *Education Week*, August 2, 2017.

26. US Census Bureau, "Monthly & Annual Retail Trade," accessed September 25, 2017.

27. Thomas W. Hanchett, "U.S. Tax Policy and the Shopping-Center Boom of the 1950s and 1960s," *American Historical Review* 101, no. 4 (October 1996): 1082–110.

28. Natasha Geiling, "The Death and Rebirth of the American Mall," *Smithsonian*, November 25, 2014.

29. Roberto Fantoni, Fernanda Hoefel, and Marina Mazzarolo, "The Future of the Shopping Mall," McKinsey & Company, November 2014.

30. Hayley Peterson, "America's Shopping Malls Are Dying a Slow, Ugly Death," *Business Insider*, January 31, 2014.

31. Josh Sanburn, "Why the Death of Malls Is About More Than Shopping," *Time*, July 20, 2017.

32. R. L. Nave, "Pearl Mall: Symbol of Misplaced Priorities?," *Jackson Free Press*, November 14, 2013.

33. Jonnelle Marte, "10 Things Shopping Malls Won't Tell You," *Marketwatch*, June 26, 2011.

34. "L.A., Where Tax Breaks Come Easy—for Some," *Los Angeles Times*, April 22, 2014.

35. Stefanie Dazio, "Tax Breaks for Green Acres Mall Unfair, Say State Lawmakers," *Newsday*, October 10, 2016.

36. Janet Moore, "Mall of America Nets Up to $250 million in Tax Breaks," *Star-Tribune*, May 22, 2013.

37. Spencer Peterson, "A Look at the 'Ugliest Damn Building' in Jersey, 'Maybe America,'" *Curbed*, January 29, 2014.

38. Susan Berfield, Ilya Marritz, and John Reitmeyer, "How Not to Build a Supermall: $5 Billion, 5 Governors, 3 Developers, and 15 Years," *Bloomberg Businessweek*, December 15, 2016.

39. Ibid.

40. John Reitmeyer, "Developer Secures Key Financing for Long-Stalled American Dream Mall," *NJSpotlight*, May 23, 2017.

41. Amanda Kolson Hurley, "Does America Still Want the American Dream?," *Atlantic*, October 9, 2015.

42. Ibid.

43. Paul Mulshine, "Xanadu Two? Malls Are Dying All over America but Tax Dollars Will Go to American Dream," *Star-Ledger*, August 14, 2016.

44. Louis Hyman, *Borrow: The American Way of Debt* (New York: Vintage Books, 2012), 110.

45. Pat Garofalo, "How Free Parking Is Screwing Up Our Cities," *U.S. News & World Report*, April 11, 2014.

46. Fantoni, Hoefel, and Mazzarolo, "The Future of the Shopping Mall."

47. Sales Tax Institute.

48. Liz Malm and Ellen Kant, "The Sources of State and Local Tax Revenues," Tax Foundation, January 28, 2013.

49. Joseph Bishop-Henchman and Scott Drenkard, "Sales Tax Holidays: Politically Expedient but Poor Tax Policy, 2017," Tax Foundation, July 25, 2017.

50. Ibid.

51. Jon Hurst, "Save the Sales Tax Holiday," *Boston Globe*, July 3, 2017.

52. "The Temporary Clothing Exemption: Analysis of the Effects of the Exemption on Clothing Sales in New York State," New York State Department of Taxation and Finance, November 1997.

53. Adam J. Cole, "Sales Tax Holidays: Timing Behavior and Tax Incidence," University of Michigan, 2009.

54. Aditya Aladangady, Shifrah Aron-Dine, Wendy Dunn, Laura Feiveson, Paul Lengermann, and Claudia Sahm, "The Effect of Sales-Tax Holidays on Consumer Spending," FEDS Notes, March 24, 2017.

55. "Sales Tax Holidays: An Ineffective Alternative to Real Sales Tax Reform," Institute on Taxation and Economic Policy, July 2016.

56. Nathan Marwell and Leslie McGranahan, "The Effect of Sales Tax Holidays on Household Consumption Patterns," Federal Reserve Bank of Chicago, August 2010.

57. Thomas Stratmann, Andreea Militaru, and Rachel Reese, "Sales Taxes and Exemptions," Mercatus on Policy, August 2014.

58. Richard K. Harper, Richard R. Hawkins, Gregory S. Martin, and Richard Sjolander, "Price Effects Around a Sales Tax Holiday: An Exploratory Study," *Public Budgeting and Finance* 23, no. 4 (December 2003): 108–13.

8. The Mythology of the Corporate Tax

1. James Ledbetter, "Bill Clinton on How Entrepreneurs Can Transform the Country," *Inc.*, September 2015.
2. Ibid.
3. "Cost Estimate for the Conference Agreement on H.R. 1, a Bill to Provide for Reconciliation Pursuant to Titles II and V of the Concurrent Resolution on the Budget for Fiscal Year 2018," Congressional Budget Office, December 15, 2017.
4. Thomas L. Hungerford, "Corporate Tax Rates and Economic Growth Since 1947," Economic Policy Institute, June 4, 2013.
5. John Harwood, "Gary Cohn: A Year Ago, I Was Advising Companies to Move out of the US," CNBC, November 9, 2017; and Toluse Olorunnipa, "Trump's Tax Promises Undercut by CEO Plans to Help Investors," *Bloomberg Politics,* November 29, 2017.
6. Michael Farrell, "Cable, Satellite Rates to Rise in 2018," *B&C,* December 21, 2017.
7. Stephen Gandel, "Five Charts That Show How Companies Are Spending Their Tax Savings," Bloomberg, March 5, 2018.
8. "Historical Corporate Top Tax Rate and Bracket: 1909–2014," Tax Policy Center.
9. Liz Emanuel and Richard Borean, "When Did Your State Adopt Its Corporate Income Tax?," Tax Foundation, June 19, 2014.
10. Morgan Scarboro, "State Corporate Income Tax Rates and Brackets for 2017," Tax Foundation, February 27, 2017.
11. "Remarks by President Trump on Tax Reform," Springfield, MO, August 30, 2017.
12. "International Comparisons of Corporate Income Tax Rates," Congressional Budget Office, March 2017.
13. Jane G. Gravelle, "International Corporate Tax Rate Comparisons and Policy Implications," Congressional Research Service, January 6, 2014.
14. "The 35 Percent Corporate Tax Myth," Institute on Taxation and Economic Policy, March 9, 2017.
15. Ibid.
16. Office of Management and Budget historical tables, accessed October 10, 2017.

17. Mike Maciag, "How States' Dependence on Corporate Taxes Has Declined," *Governing*, January 6, 2016.

18. Rachael Levy, "Mnuchin Tells Wall Street: 'You Should All Thank Me for Your Bank Stocks Doing Better,'" *Business Insider*, May 1, 2017.

19. *Fox News Sunday*, September 3, 2017.

20. Jamie Dimon, "The Real Beneficiary of Corporate Tax Reform? American Workers," NBC News, October 11, 2017.

21. Julie Ann Cronin, Emily Y. Lin, Laura Power, and Michael Cooper, "Distributing the Corporate Income Tax: Revised U.S. Treasury Methodology," Office of Tax Analysis, Technical Paper 5, May 2012.

22. Richard Rubin, "Treasury Removes Paper at Odds with Mnuchin's Take on Corporate-Tax Cut's Winners," *Wall Street Journal*, September 28, 2017.

23. Gallup "Taxes" data, accessed October 11, 2017.

24. ABC News/Washington Post poll, September 26, 2017.

25. "Federal Tax System Seen in Need of Overhaul," Pew Research Center, March 19, 2015.

26. Author interview, October 10, 2017.

27. Joseph Lawler, "Most Support a Corporate Tax Cut If It Boosts US Competitiveness. Poll," *Washington Examiner*, September 26, 2017.

28. Pat Garofalo, "Bursting the Corporate Tax Reform Bubble," *U.S. News & World Report*, November 6, 2014.

29. "Fortune 500 Companies Hold a Record $2.6 Trillion Offshore," Institute on Taxation and Economic Policy, March 28, 2017.

30. Gabriel Zucman, *The Hidden Wealth of Nations: The Scourge of Tax Havens* (Chicago: University of Chicago Press, 2015), 35.

31. Kitty Richards and John Craig, "Offshore Corporate Profits: The Only Thing 'Trapped' Is Tax Revenue," Center for American Progress, January 9, 2014.

32. Pat Garofalo, "Flashback: Corporations Used 2004 Tax Holiday to Repatriate Billions, Then Laid Off Thousands of Workers," ThinkProgress, May 14, 2011.

33. Dhammika Dharmapala, C. Fritz Foley, and Kristin J. Forbes, "Watch What I Do, Not What I Say: The Unintended Consequences of the Homeland Investment Act," National Bureau of Economic Research, Working Paper 15023, June 2009.

34. Donald J. Marples and Jane G. Gravelle, "Tax Cuts on Repatriation Earnings as Economic Stimulus: An Economic Analysis," Congressional Research Service, January 30, 2009.

35. Joint Committee on Taxation, letter to Senator Orrin Hatch, June 6, 2014.

36. Thomas J. Brennan, "What Happens After a Holiday?: Long-Term Effects of the Repatriation Provision of the AJCA," *Northwestern Journal of Law & Social Policy* 5, no. 1 (Spring 2010).

37. Marples and Gravelle, "Tax Cuts on Repatriation Earnings as Economic Stimulus."

38. "State and Local Business Taxes Are Not Significant Determinants of Growth," Grading the States.

39. Tax Policy Center briefing book on tax expenditures, accessed October 12, 2017.

40. "Corporate Tax Expenditures: Information on Estimated Revenue Losses and Related Federal Spending Programs," Government Accountability Office, March 2013.

INDEX